Whitetown, U.S.A.

WHITE-TOWN, U.S.A.

by Peter Binzen

VINTAGE BOOKS

A Division of Random House • New York

To Virginia

ACKNOWLEDGMENTS

Several institutions and many people helped me with this research and writing project and I'm indebted to all of them. I want first to thank the Carnegie Corporation for the grant which allowed me to study working-class white neighborhoods and schools in big cities for a year. Peter J. Caws encouraged me to pursue the study. Carnegie's Margaret Mahoney was most helpful in arranging the grant and most understanding when my original plan to teach for a full year was changed for reasons that are explained within these covers. My paper, the *Philadelphia Bulletin,* gave me a leave of absence to engage in the research, and the editor of its book division, B. A. Bergman, was a never-failing source of encouragement.

The Philadelphia Board of Education and the boards in seven other cities—Boston, New York, Cleveland, Detroit, Chicago, Los Angeles, San Francisco—were completely cooperative in permitting this outsider to poke around within their bureaucracies. I especially want to thank Mark Shedd, Philadelphia's superintendent, and Richardson Dilworth, board president, as well as Dick Hanusey, superintendent of the district where I spent most of my time, and the principals there who cooperated so fully. If I appear in this book to have bitten some of the hands that helped me I hope they will understand.

Murray Friedman not only offered much useful counsel but also, at one critical juncture, office space. In the Whitetowns themselves I got all kinds of help from a lot of fine people like Dick Torpey, Nancy Kandle, Kay Gruenbaum, Henry Kreiss, Anna Stecyna, Betty Quintaralle, Bob Lendzinski, Nick Paonessa, among many others literally too numerous to mention. They may not agree with what I have written but they assisted a stranger, and I appreciated it. Bill Claflin's insights were especially penetrating. Over many suppers John and Ruth Shenk shared what they had learned about people and places in their section of Philadelphia. On the homefront, my long-suffering wife was always optimistic even in those periods when I felt there was very little to be optimistic about. Finally, I am enormously indebted to Jason Epstein for editorial help in planning and writing this book. His advice and guidance were invaluable.

P.B.

CONTENTS

Whitetown, U.S.A.

The Whitetowners

The Whitetowner's row house is fourteen feet wide.

Five rooms on two floors with a postage-stamp yard out back. One of hundreds of small properties in a vast, dreary industrial landscape—clogged streets, drafty factories, fouled air, a noisy elevated line. Hardly a tree. And the few tiny parks are littered with broken bottles.

The Whitetowner was born and raised in this section and his parents still live near by. They don't think of moving out. Neither does he.

The Whitetowner is a steady worker and a family man. He quit school in tenth grade to get a job. His wife, also a native of the area, dropped out to marry him two months before her graduation. She was a better student than he was. She manages the family finances. Their house and car are paid for.

It is evening. The Whitetowner's wife is in the front room with their three children watching a bang-bang TV show. Her hair is in pink plastic curlers. The television set is a big new color model. The house is neat and better furnished than its plain gray exterior would lead one to expect. On the wall behind the TV is a proud affirmation in needle point: A MAN'S HOME IS HIS CASTLE. On the kitchen wall is the prayerful GOD BLESS OUR HOME. In both rooms are religious ornaments and bouquets of plastic flowers.

The Whitetowner sits in the kitchen answering the questions of an outsider who is trying to find out what makes Whitetown tick. The questions bear on things that concern the Whitetowner deeply. Despite his lack of formal education, he expresses himself forcefully. Asked if he favors Bible reading in public schools, he says Yes and adds, "The Bible is the beginning of knowledge. A *must* for all!" He supports physical punishment of pupils but explains, "I also believe fairness should be shown and two sides of a story told."

He doubts that his children will go to college. He doesn't really want them to. "It would be a waste of money," he says, "with all this riot nonsense." He thinks the United States would be improved "if people with *guts* were in high places." He complains that his city's schools are too lax on discipline, too political, and too lenient toward student demonstrations.

Proudly, he describes his community:

> Whitetown people are, and have been as long as I can remember, people who like to pay their own way. To be sure, there are a lot of "renters" moving in, but they aren't the result of Whitetown. They come from God only knows where. Whitetown may look run-down to an outsider, but the politicians are to blame for its condition. Compared to other sections, it is a decent place to raise children and to live. If outsiders would stop condemning Whitetown and her people, her future would become brighter. We have a minority that drink too much, but ninety per cent are social drinkers.

Asked to comment on Whitetown's reputation as a "provincial, backward section with strong prejudices," the Whitetowner swings both fists:

Who gave it the reputation you stated? And, anyway, just what is wrong with being provincial, backward (if that means opposing someone else's ideas), and having strong prejudices? Rich people have children that commit suicide, drive like maniacs, and are unruly. Rich people live on high parties and are social climbers, the mental hospitals are full of them. Why aren't the Negroes living in the suburbs? The suburbs are full of Whitetown people that are loaded down with high mortgages.

We are honest hard-working people with children we love dearly. If the Negro moves into Whitetown it will only be to push this issue of integration—and the people here are sick of having it shoved down our throats. We are sick of reading in the paper where looters, arsonists, and murderers are allowed to do whatever they damn well please. We don't want them, they would ruin our community and our property values would drop.

And, then, in a parting shot, the Whitetowner asks:

Why the sudden interest in our community? Could it be to help these poor lazy slobs get rent-free houses? Whitetown *does* have a future. When you *eggheads* run out of surveys to take and the dust begins to settle, we will be able to enjoy the life we have always known and feel contented with.

I don't know this Whitetowner's age or even his occupation. He might be a truck driver or a policeman, a turret-lathe operator or a white-collar office worker. All I know for sure is that he is white, he makes between five and ten thousand dollars a year, he owns his house, and he speaks his mind. (The comments are his; I've changed the name of his community.) I'm also certain that he speaks for a vast army of white American workingmen in Boston's Charlestown, New York's Belmont, and Philadelphia's Kensington; in Chicago's Southwest Side, Cleveland's West Side, and San

Francisco's Eureka Valley. Law and order is their watchword and, for many, George Wallace was their candidate for President in 1968.

Not long ago this white workingman was almost a folk hero in our national life. He was the honest, respectable, law-abiding citizen, the backbone of the community. More than likely, he was the son or grandson of immigrants, and the melting pot was his kettle. Whether of Irish, Italian, German, Polish, Russian, or Ukrainian extraction, he was a hundred per cent American and proud of it. From Belleau Wood to Anzio and the Choisin Reservoir he fought for his country. He supported his church (usually Roman Catholic), backed his local political leaders (usually Democrats), and provided the votes for most of the progressive domestic and internationalist legislation enacted in Congress.

All this has now changed. Today the white workingman always seems to be *against* things. He's *against* open housing, *against* school bussing, *against* hippies, Yippies, and draft dodgers. He's *against* letting Negroes into unions, and China into the United Nations. He's even *against* his own church when it gets embroiled in civil-rights causes.

In the drama of a nation striving for interracial justice, for true equality in education, housing, and employment, Whitetowners often emerge as deep-dyed racists. While some are silent protesters, others have made spectacles of themselves. In recent years Whitetowners have rioted half a dozen times. Their strong feelings are potentially as explosive as the force that detonated Watts, Hough, Detroit, and Newark.

Who are these people? What are their origins? What makes them act as they do? Robert C. Wood, former Undersecretary of the United States Department of Housing and Urban Development, describes* the Whitetowner as the

* In a speech at Lincoln, Mass., on Dec. 8, 1967.

"working American—the average white ethnic male . . . the ordinary employee in factory and office, blue collar and white," who lives in the "gray area" fringe of central cities and constitutes the majority of the nation's work force.

The *New York Times* labels him the "$8,000-a-year shoe clerk." During the 1968 Presidential election campaign, Richard M. Nixon called him "the forgotten American" and George C. Wallace identified him as "the little man." The American Jewish Committee speaks of him as "the reacting American," writer Elizabeth Hardwick considers him "the cheerless American," *Newsweek* magazine describes him as "the troubled American," and social scientist David Riesman rates him "the man in the middle." More recently he's been identified as part of that amorphous mass known as the "silent majority."

By whatever name, the people we are talking about are drawn mainly from the ethnic groups that differ from the basic white Protestant Anglo-Saxon settlers in religion, language, and culture. Many of these "ethnics" are among the thirty-four million foreign-stock Americans—that is, immigrants themselves or having at least one immigrant parent. Most are descendants of Eastern and Southern European peasants. Many others are Irish. Of course, not all white Anglo-Saxon Protestants have made their fortunes and moved to the suburbs. Especially in the South but also in Northern cities sizable numbers of Protestants, often fundamentalist or evangelical, are struggling to keep their heads above water. Conversely, a great many immigrants and immigrants' children have enjoyed success beyond their dreams and wouldn't deign to set foot in Whitetown. More often than not, however, the Whitetowns of America are populated by the ethnics and by first- and second-generation (and often third-generation) immigrants.

Whitetowns come in all ages, shapes, and sizes. Chicago's Scottsdale is new. It sprang up after World War II on former prairie in Chicago's extreme southwest corner, ten miles from the Loop. In neat single houses with pink flamingos on front lawns and two cars in many garages live fourteen thousand militant Caucasians, who are, says Scottsdale's school principal, "united in their determination to keep their community segregated." Many Scottsdalers are municipal employees required by ordinance to live within the city limits. For them Scottsdale, which extends to the city boundary, is the end of the line. They've run as far as they can. There appears to be no real poverty in Scottsdale, but many men hold two jobs to make ends meet, and average income there was last estimated at just over eight thousand dollars.

Boston's Charlestown is old. Its working-class whites cluster in drab surroundings at the foot of Bunker Hill, which dominates the area. The Boston Navy Yard is near by and many Charlestonians work there. It was in grimy, faded Charlestown that John F. Kennedy began his political career in 1948, and it was to Charlestown that he returned to start every subsequent campaign. Charlestown has poverty and it has Negroes—a few living in public housing. Now it is engaged in a mighty renewal effort, with help from Washington and with the knowledge that along with new schools, new housing, a beautiful community college, will come meaningful racial integration.

New York's Belmont, in the Fordham section of the Bronx, is a small city of twenty-five thousand people, ninety-five per cent of them first- and second-generation Italians. Theirs is a classic ethnic enclave holding out against pressure from Negroes moving north from Manhattan. Curiously, some of the proudest and bitterest Belmonters are those who have moved to suburban Whitetowns but return regularly to Belmont's markets and its church and desperately want always to be able to do so. Every year brings another three hundred families to Belmont from Italy. Belmont's Our Lady of Mount Carmel Roman Catholic Church is an Italian national parish with six million dollars invested in the neighborhood. As Father Mario Zicarelli says with a smile, "While I take care of all Italians, whatever their color, maybe I have to be interested in my community."

In Cleveland's Near West Side, in Chicago's Uptown, and in sections of Detroit are examples of festering Anglo-Saxon poverty. Here live Appalachian white migrants from the hills of Tennessee, Kentucky, and West Virginia. These are truly forgotten people, just as miscast for city life as the most backward plantation Negroes. And often more miserable because they cannot blame their pigmentation for holding them back. Tough, mean sections of burned-out pride, homesickness, and contention as bitter as that in the hillbilly ballad:

> *Fight like dogs,*
> *If you ain't no kin,*
> *If you kill one another,*
> *It ain't no sin.*

Philadelphia's Kensington is a nineteenth-century mill area, a Dickensian factory town. Here you find working-class whites in their fourteen-foot-wide row houses. Here you also find middle-class workers with boats and summer places at the Jersey shore, still living in Kensington because it is home and they are proud of it. There are many pensioners just scraping by. And elderly widows. And, increasingly, poor white families moving in from mixed sections downtown. To the established homeowners of Kensington these newcoming renters are white trash. The clash between these two groups is almost as bitter and traumatic as the racial collision.

Poverty, we should note, doesn't draw the color line in America's big cities. The 1960 United States census counted almost twice as many poor white families in metropolitan areas as poor nonwhite families. Poverty was then considered to be three thousand dollars a year for a family of four. By this definition, there were 10.7 million impoverished white families in urban America and 5.6 million impoverished nonwhite families. The 1960 census did not reach all the nonwhites, its figures were not very reliable and they are now out of date. Furthermore, since whites in the general population outnumber nonwhites by about ten to one while white poor outnumber nonwhite poor by less than two to one, the poverty problem is obviously greater among nonwhites. But the message of the 1960 census still holds: In American urban areas, life is desperately difficult for great numbers of whites and blacks alike.*

What Whitetowners of different classes, sections, backgrounds, occupations, religions, national origins, and even political parties—for they cut across party lines—share is their alienation from the American "mainstream." This alienation is reflected in distrust of most politicians, in contempt for white rich and black poor, in a bristling defensiveness and a yearning for the recent past when life was

* The very existence of poor whites sometimes seems to be intentionally obscured. A case in point is the March 1968 Report of the National Advisory Commission on Civil Disorders, the Kerner Report. It used 1960 census data to show that in the Milwaukee Standard Metropolitan Statistical Area the proportion of poor nonwhites was three times that of poor whites. That is, 26.1 per cent of the nonwhite families had incomes under three thousand dollars a year compared with only 8.8 per cent of the white families. A valid point. The report failed to note, however, that in actual numbers the poverty problem in Milwaukee was largely a poor-white problem: 30,026 poor whites to 4,191 poor nonwhites.

simpler and loyalties less complex, when children were reared by the Bible and the beltstrap, when the schools stuck to the three R's, and when patriotism meant "My country right or wrong."

Despite wealth and political success, Vice-President Spiro T. Agnew, whose father was born in Greece, is an authentic Whitetown voice. When, in defending the Nixon Administration's Vietnam policy late in 1969, Agnew attacked war critics as "an effete corps of impudent snobs," he spoke for the truckers, policemen, and factory workers of American Whitetowns. When he mentioned the intellectuals' "disdain to mingle with the masses who work for a living" and said it was time for "the preponderant majority, the responsible citizens of this country," to stop dignifying the acts of "arrogant, reckless elements" within American society, he was telling the Whitetowners what they wanted to hear.

In the 1968 Presidential election, many Whitetowners voted not for Nixon but for George Wallace. They helped the Alabama segregationist pile up nine million votes. Theirs was a protest against what's been going on in this country. "The central problem [in America]," Joseph Kraft, the syndicated columnist, wrote in the summer of 1968, when the Whitetowners' wrath first became evident, "is not the visible problem of disaffected Negroes and young people. The central problem is that the lower-middle-class whites who comprise the great body of the electorate have lost confidence in the upper-middle-class whites who have been running the country for the past decade." This dilemma was clearly exemplified at the time in New York City as white schoolteachers, policemen, and parents revolted against the leadership of Mayor John V. Lindsay. As the *New York Times* noted, these people felt Lindsay was "too interested in the stylish rich and the striving poor." "Lindsay," said the director of a New York civic organization, "just doesn't seem to understand the life of a mailman or a cop. They feel he is buying racial peace by giving away to Harlem what the middle class needs." Lindsay owed his subsequent re-election in 1969 to the fact that two conservative candidates, Democrat Mario A. Procaccino and Republican John J. Marchi, split the Whitetown vote. He also worked hard in the months before the election to win back the Whitetowners. But the *Times,* in a post-election analysis, found that the city's nonwhite poor and the rich were keys to the Mayor's victory.

Whitetown's problem is basically economic. Twenty years ago, seventy-five hundred dollars sounded like easy street. For a family man today it is not enough for real comfort. The havelittles in Whitetown find themselves just one notch above subsistence. Their tax burden is heavy, their neighborhood services poor, their national image tarnished, and their political influence slight. As they stew and fret about their place on the lower rungs of the economic ladder, they see the black man moving up. They worry about job security and about the value of their houses should Whitetown—God forbid—ever be integrated. And so they react bitterly, viscerally, to Black Power, black militancy, the thrust of Negroes in politics, jobs, housing, and education.

This racial crisis poisons our body politic today and preoccupies our politicians and people. The fact is, however, that Whitetown's basic problem transcends the color line. It is rooted in the past, in the class structure of American life, and in the effect that ethnicity, national origins, and religion have had on the ability or inability of individual white Americans to "make it" in America. Many of the Whitetowners haven't made it because the cards have been stacked against them. For many, alienation, underrepresentation, voicelessness, and violence have been historical conditions of life.

"We shall not understand the contemporary United States," wrote Frederick Jackson Turner in 1893, "without studying immigration historically." This is still true. The United States is, of course, a nation of immigrants. But some classes of immigrants have almost always been on top while others remain on the bottom. Changes occur only gradually over a period of not years but generations.

For a long time we deluded ourselves into thinking that such was not the case. We were persuaded that America was one giant mixing bowl where all men became equal. "Here individuals of all nations are melted into a new race of men," wrote St. John de Crèvecœur in 1782. And much later, in 1908, Israel Zangwill exulted, "America is God's Crucible, the great Melting Pot where all races of Europe are merging and reforming. . . . Germans and Frenchmen, Irishmen and Englishmen, Jews and Russians—into the Crucible with you all! God is making the Americans."

In the century and a quarter between Crèvecœur and Zangwill, more than thirty-five million men, women, and children came to the United States. It was the greatest migration in human history. This incredible uprooting reached into every nook and cranny of Europe. More than four and a half million emigrated from Ireland, over four million from Great Britain, six million from what became Germany, eight million from the old Austrian and Russian empires— Poles and Jews, Hungarians, Bohemians, Slovaks, Ukrainians, Ruthenians; three million from the Balkans and Asia Minor—Greeks and Macedonians, Croatians and Albanians, Syrians and Armenians.

There were many exceptions, of course, but millions of these immigrants, Oscar Handlin concluded from an exhaustive examination of their letters, were simple peasants.

With a heritage of centuries of life on the land in close-knit villages, they were conservative. Their traditions and religious faiths were deeply implanted. In the Old World, these people "knew their place." They were ignorant of democratic processes and American politics.

Even those who quickly learned how one makes one's way in the United States found formidable obstacles massed against them. More than half of the immigrants up to 1860 were Roman Catholics, and millions of Catholics followed in the period up to 1920. But the United States was largely white Anglo-Saxon Protestant turf. Anti-Romanism was the oldest and most deeply entrenched of American prejudices. Discrimination against non-WASPs was almost as pervasive, though certainly not as brutal or relentless, as the repression of Negroes. It was no accident that of the thirty-three American Presidents from George Washington to Dwight D. Eisenhower, twenty-eight were of British stock and thirty were Protestants. John F. Kennedy, who broke the string in 1960, was distinctly Protestant in his education and style, and his religious faith seemed closely attuned to the liberalism and humanitarianism of the "Protestant Pope," John XXIII. Before he could be elected, Kennedy was virtually forced to promise not to side with his coreligionists (in the parochial-school-aid battle). He simply was not perceived as an Irish Catholic in the same way that, for example, Alfred E. Smith was, in his losing race for the Presidency in 1928.

It was no accident, either, that of the scores of Cabinet officers appointed by Presidents between 1789 and 1933, only four were Catholics. Despite the very heavy emigration from Italy, the first Italian-American was not elected governor of a state until 1936 and the first Italian-American United States Senator was not seated until 1950. (In both cases the state was Rhode Island and the successful politician, John Pastore.)

The WASPs who ran the country in the eighteenth and nineteenth centuries welcomed non-WASP immigrants for two reasons. First, America's growing economic machine needed unskilled manpower to dig canals, lay railroad beds, mine coal and iron, work as domestics, and fill the many low-echelon service jobs in burgeoning cities. Second, it was universally accepted that authentic Anglo-Saxons could be produced whatever the mixture of nationality groups. That is, the WASPs thought the immigrants would quickly shed their ethnic identities, forsake their "foreign" cultures and churches, and become "just like us." And so there would be one vast nation of Americans all reflecting the ways of thinking and doing of the majority group. The melting-pot assimilation concept took hold and the WASPs didn't feel threatened.

For the most part, the immigrants came here and did what they were supposed to do. In 1850, 48 per cent of Boston's Irish were manual laborers and 15.3 per cent were domestic servants—almost two-thirds thus at the very bottom of the economic pyramid. As late as 1900, a study found that for every hundred dollars earned by a native-born worker, the Italian-born immigrant earned eighty-four dollars, the Hungarian sixty-eight, and other Europeans fifty-four. For good jobs the word continued to go out: "Irish need not apply."

Just as Negroes are blamed for most of the urban crime and social unrest today, so were the immigrants a century ago. They were often ill-fed, ill-housed, illiterate—and rebellious. Handlin found that 57 per cent of the convicts in Boston's House of Correction in 1862 were Irish and 75 per cent of the 12,914 persons arrested in Boston two years later were Irish.

From 1830 to 1870, the Irish caused riots in nearly every major city. Because so many Irish-Americans named Patrick, or Paddy, were carted off to jail, the vehicles that transported them came to be known as paddy wagons. The name has stuck, even though many of today's riders in police vans in the cities are black.

Needless to say, the natives viewed the immigrants' life style with extreme distaste. They blamed the newcomers for the rise in pauperism, crime, drunkenness, and political corruption. In a burst of invective in 1839, Philip Hone, who had formerly been Mayor of New York, charged that his city was "infected by gangs of hardened wretches, born in the haunts of infamy, brought up in taverns . . . [who] patrol the streets, making night hideous." Never one to mince words, Hone identified the Irish as "the most ignorant and consequently the most obstinate white men in the world."

His speech was relatively mild compared to the anti-immigrant tirades of Southerners. In the same year that Hone was accusing the Irish of ruining New York, the Louisiana Native American Association outdid him. "When we see hordes . . . of beings in human form," it cried, "but destitute of any intellectual aspirations—the outcast and offal of society, the pauper, the vagrant and the convict—transported in myriads to our shores, reeking with the accumulated crimes of the whole civilized and savage world and inducted by our laws into equal rights, immunities and privileges with the noble, native inhabitants of the United States, we can no longer contemplate it with supine indifference."

The press was also guilty of incredible excesses. Fortunately for them, many of the immigrants could not read, for they would have seen themselves often maligned in the newspapers. Roman Catholics were abused on every hand. In 1833 the Second Provincial Council of American Bishops issued a pastoral letter accusing the press of being "unkind and unjust" to Catholics.

"Not only do they assail us and our institution in a style

of vituperation and offense, misrepresent our tenets, vilify our practices, repeat the hundred-times' refuted calumnies of the days of angry and bitter contention in other lands," cried the bishops, "but they have even denounced you and us as enemies to the liberties of the Republic."

Still, the onslaught against foreign visitors continued.

"Madam Castellan's concert in Philadelphia on Saturday night was a complete failure," reported a Philadelphia paper in November 1843. "We are glad to perceive that the petty parsimony of these foreign adventurers is met by a corresponding want of patronage." The Boston *American Traveller and Farmer's Advocate* reprinted the Philadelphia story and added: "Madam Ciuti and some fiddler who performed here on Saturday night did not come off much better. It is astonishing how our citizens will continue to be humbugged and taxed by these beggars from other shores. . . . Away with your Castellans and Ciutis and give us a concert from our own brigade band or one of our city musical organizations."

The fact was, of course, that the immigrants did bring grave social problems to the cities. But often they became the scapegoat for every urban woe and shortcoming. Certainly, a breakdown in city government similar to what we are witnessing today occurred when immigration tides ran high. Already in 1888 James Bryce, in *The American Commonwealth,* was saying that "the government of cities is the one conspicuous failure of the United States." He noted that blame was being heaped on the immigrants and wrote: "Nevertheless the immigrants are not so largely responsible for the faults of American politics as a stranger might be led, by the language of many Americans, to suppose. There is a disposition in the United States to use them, and especially the Irish, much as the cat is used in the kitchen, to account for broken plates and food which disappears. The cities have, no doubt, suffered from the immigrants . . . But New York was not an Eden before the Irish came."

Whatever headaches the immigrants gave urban authorities were more than offset by their contributions to America's economy and to its expanding military strength. During the years of heaviest immigration, from 1890 to 1910, United States coal production tripled and steel output multiplied seven times. The foreign-born, Samuel Lubell wrote in *The Future of American Politics,* accounted for 60 per cent of the nation's packing-house workers, 57 per cent of the iron- and steelworkers, 61 per cent of the miners, and 70 per cent of the textile and clothing workers. For their labor, the immigrants received low pay and discriminatory treatment. Nowhere was this more evident than in the one-industry coal and steel towns. The separation of foreign-born laborers and WASP managers in these towns was as complete, says Lubell, as that between serfs and lords on a feudal manor.

In fighting for their country, the ethnic Americans have compiled a record that is unexcelled in the annals of United States military history. With the waging of unpopular wars in Korea and Vietnam, their flag-waving patriotism has gone out of style and their exploits on the battlefield have been largely forgotten. Yet they helped make the United States a world power. Of course, it is often the ethnic Americans who are the most militantly anti-Communist, the most chauvinistic, the most willing to support higher and higher arms spending, and most inclined to see the world as dividing between the forces of good (us) and the forces of evil (the other guys). But their fighting spirit is unmistakable.

The Irish especially have felt a compulsion to prove their patriotism in battle. In the Civil War, they formed a major portion of the Union Army, not so much because of their devotion to abolition—their antidraft riots in 1863 shook New York—but because they lacked the financial means to avoid conscription as so many WASPs avoided it. The famed Irish Brigade distinguished itself in combat in the Civil War just as New York's "Fighting Sixty-ninth" Regiment was to do in World War I.

Throughout the Civil War years, immigrants flocked to America. In the first four months of 1863 alone, 38,720 landed in New York. The *Philadelphia Inquirer* printed these figures and editorialized:

> Such a phenomenon as is here presented, of vast numbers of immigrants seeking a country afflicted by Rebellion, can scarcely be paralleled in the world's history. It speaks with telling emphasis of the confidence of the European masses in the future of our country, and of the stability of the Government whose blessings they have come to enjoy.

Of the first hundred thousand United States Army volunteers in 1917, no fewer than forty thousand were said to be Polish-Americans. Although the Poles were only four per cent of the population, they accounted for twelve per cent of the United States war dead in World War I. And, according to Army and Navy records, about twenty per cent of the American armed forces on the eve of Pearl Harbor consisted of men of Polish extraction.

It appears that even now disproportionate numbers of Whitetowners are in uniform. A *Philadelphia Bulletin* study in September 1966 found both induction and enlistment rates in Philadelphia higher among whites than nonwhites. The differences were statistically significant. And most of these white servicemen came from working-class sections where the college-going rate—and draft-deferment rate—is low. What's more, the Whitetowners are proud of their rec-

ord. Drive through an ethnic neighborhood in Philadelphia
or Chicago or Cleveland or Detroit and you will see entire
blocks welcoming servicemen home with flags and bunting.
In the old sections of every big city there is this kind of
spirit; in the suburbs, where properties are bigger and loyalties less intense, you rarely find it no matter how hard you
look.

For the last forty-five years immigration has been negli-
gible, and we have tended to forget how the country—and
the Congress—treated the immigrants. What happened in
the early years of this century may help to explain, however,
what's happening in Whitetown today.

Through most of the nineteenth century immigration was
unrestricted. There were no national "quotas" and no limit
on the number of people admitted to these shores each year.
Until roughly 1890 the immigrants came largely from the
British Isles, Germany, and Scandinavia. Besides the much-
maligned Irish, these included many urban Jews and middle-
class Protestants who adjusted quickly to American life and
were assimilated. But then came the great wave of Italian
and Polish peasants, Jews fleeing persecution in Russia,
and other "undesirables" from Eastern Europe. The figures
tell their story:

IMMIGRATION

Country of Origin	1871–1880	1881–1890	1891–1900	1901–1910	1911–1920
Italy	55,000	300,000	651,000	2,045,000	1,100,000
Russia (including many Poles and Jews)	39,000	213,000	505,000	1,500,000	1,000,000
Austria–Hungary (many Poles, Slavs)	72,000	350,000	600,000	2,150,000	Unavailable

Among the "right people," the cultural reaction to this tremendous influx of poor foreigners was harsh. It amounted to a WASP backlash. Concerns grew lest the nation be overrun by Catholics, Jews, and radicals and the purity of the race imperiled. Indeed, Henry Steele Commager sees the 1890s as the watershed separating rural, idealistic, confident America and urban, pragmatic, insecure America. By 1900, one-third of all American farmers were tenants. Ignatius Donnelly's preamble to the 1892 Populist platform had warned: "We meet in the midst of a nation brought to the verge of moral, political and material ruin . . . business prostrated, homes covered with mortgages, labor impoverished, and the land concentrating in the hands of capitalists. The [native-born] urban workmen are denied the right to organize for self-protection. Imported, pauperized labor beats down their wages."

In this climate, the Ku Klux Klan gained wide support in the North and Middle West. To separate the "old" immigrants from the "new," such Protestant patriotic societies as the Daughters of the American Revolution and the Sons of the American Revolution were organized and flourished. To control the newcomers' drinking habits, the Anti-Saloon League was founded in 1893. Together with the older Women's Christian Temperance Union, it successfully led the fight for a nation-wide ban on the sale of alcoholic beverages. And later, in Oregon, an attempt to close all Catholic schools reached the Supreme Court, where it was thwarted in a historic decision.

The migration of Southern Negroes to Northern cities during and after World War I lessened the need for cheap foreign labor. With the nation in no mood to accept more immigrants anyway, Congress in 1921 and 1924 drastically reduced immigration and overhauled the entire system.

Previously, the criterion for admission to this country had

been personal merit regardless of nationality. Now the criterion was pegged solely to race and ethnic origin. For the first time a quota system was instituted. And each national group's quota was based on its ethnic representation in the United States back in 1890, before the heaviest tide of Italian and Eastern European immigration.

Congress knew what it was doing. By turning back the calendar, it guaranteed that seventy-nine per cent of all future immigrants would come from "safe" countries—Great Britain, Germany, the Netherlands, Scandinavia—plus Ireland. For the unwanted Italians and Poles immigration fell to almost nothing. Asians, being considered unassimilable, were excluded altogether. This blatantly racist policy remained in force, with only minor changes, until October 3, 1965, when President Lyndon B. Johnson signed a more liberal law returning to the criterion of individual merit regardless of nationality. Since then immigration from Southern and Eastern Europe has markedly increased, thus adding to the number of Whitetowners.

Although the last period of heavy immigration is long past, it is important to note that even today half of the Roman Catholic adults in this country are immigrants themselves or the children of immigrants. "We are," Father Andrew M. Greeley, priest-sociologist at the University of Chicago, has written, "but a generation or two away from the peasant farms of Europe."

Many Catholics in the Whitetowns of America have had difficulty throwing off the shackles of their peasant heritage. "It seems that Catholics creep forward rather than stride forward in American society," wrote John J. Kane in *The American Catholic Sociological Review*, "and the position of American Catholics in the mid-twentieth century is better, but not so much better than it was a century ago."

What all this means is that just as Negroes today find it

hard to advance in American society so, historically, did large numbers of immigrants and so do many still.

"Today, whites tend to exaggerate how well and quickly they escaped from poverty," reported President Johnson's National Advisory Commission on Civil Disorders, headed by former Governor Otto Kerner of Illinois.

> The fact is, among the southern and eastern immigrants who came to America in the last great wave of immigration, those who came already urbanized were the first to escape from poverty. The others who came to America from rural backgrounds, as Negroes did, are only now, after three generations, in the final stages of escaping from poverty. . . . Because of favorable economic and political conditions, these ethnic groups were able to escape from lower-class status to working-class and lower-middle-class status, but it has taken them three generations.

I have no intention of suggesting that the immigrants' existence was totally bleak or in any way comparable to the oppression visited upon black people. There is simply no comparison, and those who attempt to draw comparisons have not read Negro—or American—history. America wasn't the land of milk and honey for all newcomers, as the history books suggested, but it did offer unparalleled opportunities. Rags-to-riches didn't happen often, but it happened. While countless immigrants found life terribly hard, the achievements of others have been remarkable.

It is true that all kinds of stunts were used to entice immigrants here. Steamship brokers recruited throughout Europe, U.S. railroads vigorously colonized for foreign workers, and some states sent agents abroad scouting for laborers. Yet all who came to America came voluntarily. And the greatest inducement to come was provided by those already here. The expectations of the immigrants crowding into the big cities seventy-five years ago were not as high as are those of the urban migrants—the Negroes—in today's affluence. Expecting less, the immigrants made do with less and were pleased with less. And in their letters home many no doubt embellished their own limited successes.

"A letter to those who feared to take the risk of emigration," wrote Joseph A. Wyrtrwal, in *America's Polish Heritage,* "would put the entire Polish village in a state of tingling excitement. Every word was received like a jewel. The clear, detailed sentences were first read and reread by the simple, credulous people to whom they were originally addressed, then widely circulated among relatives and friends, and often through the whole village."

Coming from autocratic Europe, with its rigid class structure, the immigrants found American society, with all its defects, much more open and democratic. For the "huddled masses yearning to breathe free," this *was* the land of opportunity. Their letters were full of poignant references to their new rights and responsibilities. "Schools here are free for everyone." "Any man may speak what is on his mind without the least fear." "If a man will work, he need never go hungry." "Here it is not asked, What or who was your father, but the question is, What are you?" "Learning flows free . . . I saw before me free schools, free colleges, where I could learn and keep on learning."

What's more—and this is of key importance—the political structure in American cities took the special needs of immigrants into consideration. The immigrants needed jobs, loans, and often food, coal, rent money, help in dealing with police and the city bureaucracy. In those days, there were few places to turn for help. There were no social workers or welfare agencies, no United Fund, no aid-to-dependent-children programs, no Social Security, no unemployment compensation.

Into the breach stepped the political machines. Reaching down into the wards and the precincts, the bosses took the immigrants by the hand and, in exchange for votes—lots of votes, often more than one vote per man—they helped them survive in the cities. All blessings flowed not from Washington but from the political clubhouse. At wakes and weddings, confirmations and *bar mitzvah*s, your friendly neighborhood committeeman or precinct captain could be counted on. And if a man needed a pushcart license, the party would see that he got one.

So immigration and machine politics fitted hand in glove. "The classic urban machine and the century of immigration which ended in the 1920's," wrote Elmer E. Cornwell, Jr., in the *Annals of the American Academy of Political and Social Science,* "were intimately intertwined phenomena. . . . The machine would probably not have been possible, and certainly would not have been so prominent a feature of the American political landscape, without the immigrant."

As the Kerner Commission stated in its 1968 report, the political bosses traded economic advantages for political support: "Ward-level grievance machinery, as well as personal representation, enabled the immigrant to make his voice heard and his power felt."

In other words, the kind of local control over political decision-making that minority groups now are seeking in big cities actually existed to a marked degree for the immigrants. If they didn't actually control their own destinies, the men who did were down the street. And starting with Alfred E. Smith's bid for the Presidency in 1928, the immigrants found a national voice within the Democratic Party.

With the decline of immigration, a new urban political structure began to take shape. The style that Richard Hofstadter, in *The Age of Reform,* described as stressing "strong personal loyalties above allegiance to abstract codes of law or morals" was gradually discarded. This was the city boss, immigrant Catholic style. In its place came the middle-class Protestant reformer style of city government, emphasizing honesty, efficiency—and a cold impersonality.

"The introduction of a merit system and a professionalized civil service," said the Kerner Commission, "has made management of the cities more businesslike, but it has also tended to depersonalize and isolate government."

City Hall thus became less susceptible to corruption, but swept out with the scandals were the close ties between the people and the political machines. As City Hall reformers installed computers and began accounting for every paper clip, they lost touch with the "little people" in Whitetown and Blacktown.

The Kerner Commission pointed out the damaging effect of this change on urban Negroes. They suffered, it said, a "profound sense of isolation and alienation from the processes and programs of government." The same can be said of the foreign-stock Whitetowners. And, as we have seen, there are more low-income whites than low-income non-whites in every major American city.

Just as city politics changed to the disadvantage of the ethnic Americans so did national politics. In the administrations of John F. Kennedy and Lyndon B. Johnson, the great Democratic coalition begun by Smith and forged masterfully by Franklin D. Roosevelt in the thirties began to fly apart. Always a totally implausible amalgam—blacks and whites, workers and intellectuals, Northern liberals and Southern segregationists—nobody really knew how it lasted as long as it did. But when the coalition weakened in the 1960s it was the Whitetowners who walked out. They turned to Wallace or Richard M. Nixon. They turned to the right, to "law and order" and conservatism.

To them, it appeared that upper-middle-class whites were shaping policies to benefit poor blacks. There didn't seem to be anything in it for them. And they had a point.

"This—majority—group of Americans . . . has to be asking whether the government is playing favorites, or greasing squeaky wheels, or whatever," observed Daniel P. Moynihan, then director of the Harvard-MIT Joint Center for Urban Studies and now President Nixon's Special Assistant for Urban Affairs, in an article in *The Public Interest* early in 1968. "We have established a Job Corps for the dropout and a Peace Corps for the college graduate, but the plain fellow with a high school diploma, and his parents, have little to show from either the New Frontier or the Great Society."

Taking the same position, columnist Joseph Kraft, in June 1968, argued that low-income whites had been "conned" into support of liberal economic and social welfare policies without really approving of them. What the nation must do, said Kraft, is "re-engage the sympathies of the low-income whites . . . for humane purposes."

Politics is not alone, however, in isolating and alienating the Whitetowners. In this period of sexual permissiveness, God-is-dead theology, student revolts, and war protests, their old-fashioned patriotism, religious fundamentalism, and family togetherness have gone out of style. True, the sex revolution, for example, troubles American parents across the board. But in Whitetown, where the authoritarianism has been more rigid and the attachment to old rules of conduct stronger, the blow has fallen harder.

Whitetown was not ready for the technological revolution, either, having traditionally valued brawn over brains. Its youth have gone to vocational schools and then into the mills and blue-collar jobs. But in today's world-wide competition for what Alfred North Whitehead termed "trained intelligence," working-class skills have lost their importance. Only six per cent of the "working Americans" described by Robert Wood, formerly of the Department of Housing and Urban Development, continued their education beyond high school, while forty-three per cent stopped at eighth grade. Income and education being inextricably linked in American economics, few high-school dropouts will ever make it. Many Whitetowners are thus lost in the shuffle.

For all of these reasons, Whitetown—to outsiders, at least —appears to be on the skids. Its housing is deteriorating. It is losing population. It has few responsible spokesmen at the local level and no leadership. In the black ghettos of big cities where renewal and redevelopment have been carried out extensively, if often controversially, there is a vitality, a sense of change, even improvement, that is lacking in Whitetown.

Rarely do you see new houses, new businesses or industries in Whitetown. Often, though, you see new expressways slicing through its heart. In many cities freeways crisscross the old ethnic neighborhoods en route to the expensive housing, fancy shopping centers, and modern industrial parks of shiny suburbia. Not only do these freeways destroy the unity of America's Whitetowns but they also hasten the exodus of Whitetowners, thus undermining what little stability these old ethnic neighborhoods have left. The Federal government rarely spends a nickel to help Whitetown, but it has put billions into expressways.

In light of these facts and in historical perspective, it should be no surprise that the working-class white is angry and frustrated, that out of economic fear and a sense of his own powerlessness he sees the Negro as his competitor who wants his job, house, and neighborhood.

"No one listens to us and our problems, no one cares

about us or appreciates the contributions we have made to American life," Barbara Mikulski, Baltimore social worker and third-generation Polish-American, complained to an American Jewish Committee conference in Philadelphia late in 1969.

> I'd like to tell you why we are troubled. First, we are tired of being politically courted and then legally extorted. Second, we are sick and tired of institutions, both public and private, not being responsive or responsible to the people they were instituted to serve. Third, we feel powerless in our dealings with these monoliths. Fourth, we do not like being blamed for all of the problems of black America. Fifth, and perhaps the key, we anguish at all of the class prejudice that is forced upon us.

The combative and articulate four-foot-eleven-inch Miss Mikulski terms immigrants drawn here for unskilled labor and factory work the "urban niggers of the industrialized society."

> Those who remain blue-collar workers are the field hands and we who moved up into white-collar positions are the house niggers with all of the brainwashing that it implies. . . . The only place we feel any sense of identity, community, or control is that little home we prize. But there again we feel threatened by black people. Ethnic Americans do not feel that black people are inferior but regard them as territorial aggressors on their residential and employment turfs.

Many ethnic Americans also believe that black people, far from being beaten down by Whitetowners or anyone else, are now getting all the breaks in this country. They reject the Kerner Commission's charge that the United States is infected with "white racism."

"My family came over here to get away from the Russians," said a Polish-American machinist, drinking coffee in his sixty-five-hundred-dollar house in Philadelphia's Whitetown.

> This is reality. This is why my mother came here. If my mother, when she was twelve or thirteen years old, was strong enough to get on the boat and make a new life for herself somewhere else, I feel that these people [blacks] should have courage enough to fight for what they want and to get away from this business of, "Why, damn, man, you're screwing me."
> And this is the feeling I get. Sometimes they come out and say this. They base their whole argument on this: "We're going to beat you down. We're going to take what you got because you beat us for a hundred years"—and I don't feel that I beat them for a hundred years. I don't feel that I've ever beat them. I didn't come in contact with them until I was twenty-five years old.

Whitetowners are hostile to all outsiders, but for newspapermen and television and radio people they reserve a special animosity. They're convinced that the press, especially the "Eastern internationalist press," unfairly dismisses them all as racists, bigots, and ignoramuses without digging into the real issues to see what makes them react as they do.

There is, I think, some truth to this charge. But the Whitetowners often invite such characterizations by behaving just like bigots, racists, and ignoramuses. For example, I heard a Philadelphia Whitetowner climax a dialogue with a bartender by declaiming proudly, "I'd rather live in a tent than next to a nigger."

In another saloon, this one in Queens, after the tumultuous Democratic Convention in Chicago in August 1968, columnist Jimmy Breslin encountered two Whitetowners whose conversation he felt compelled to share with his readers. I can see why; the two made good copy and they were archetypes of the tough, blunt know-nothings sometimes found in Whitetown. The week before, Chicago's Mayor Richard Daley had converted his city into an armed camp and ordered police to crack down on protesters at the convention. Most of the press and the upper middle class were appalled at Daley's doings. Breslin discovered that the Whitetowners were overjoyed.

"He's a real American," a beer-truck driver was saying to the bartender.

"Yes, he is," the bartender said.

"We could use a mayor like that here in this city, brother could we use him," the beer-truck driver said.

"He makes sense," the bartender said. "This guy Lindsay is a nigger-lover."

"Daley don't care, he takes 'em all on, niggers, hippies, anybody," the beer-truck driver said.

As the election campaign wore on, liberal and New Left writers began to take a new—and less damning—look at the white working class.

After covering the Wallace campaign in New England for New York's Greenwich Village weekly, the *Village Voice*, Paul Cowan reported:

There is a real temptation, in writing about the working-class people who attend the Wallace rallies, to mock their lives and habits or to profess outrage at their new beliefs. . . .

But when you talk to such people you feel a surge of sympathy, for they are this decade's invisible men. They are not fascists but sad, confused human beings whose lives have turned out to be far worse than they had hoped.

Similarly, reporter and social critic Andrew Kopkind, after a visit to Cleveland's Whitetown for his muckraking weekly, *Mayday,* now called *Hard Times,* found that

> while the blacks are baited, the poor programmed, the students beaten, the elites honored, and the New Class celebrated—the white workingmen are ignored. . . .
>
> They are neither quite bad enough for slum-clearance nor quite good enough for segregation. Around them, the atmosphere is thick and heavy—with smoke and dust, boredom and frustration.

Cowan's and, to some extent, Kopkind's observations smacked of condescension. And there's nothing that white working people resent more than being talked down to. Free-lance writer Nicholas Pileggi found this out when, in an article in *New York* magazine, he used the wrong term to describe the clustering of Italian-Americans on Manhattan's Lower East Side. The term was promptly flung back into his teeth: "Ghetto! Wha ghetto? This ain't no ghetto, this is our home and we got no riots and we got no crime on the streets and we got no Cleveland here."

When John G. McCullough, editor of the *Philadelphia Bulletin*'s editorial page, visited South Philadelphia's "Little Italy" following trouble at a predominantly Negro vocational school in the neighborhood, he also got a lecture from one of the residents. "What you have now," the man told the editor, "are a lot of pointed heads and non-degree sociologists making field trips into South Philadelphia to study the natives. They've got everything but butterfly nets. . . . [They think that] we're all just bigots and racists and street fighters."

For a long time, sociologists with or without advanced degrees paid the Whitetowns of America little heed. They failed either to see the mounting problems that working-class white people faced or to find these problems interesting enough to investigate, or else hesitated to show an interest in them for fear that their peers might think them bigoted or racist themselves.

Now, as I've indicated, these problems are being examined. Robert Wood, in his remarkable but little noticed Lincoln, Mass., speech in 1967, pinpointed the issue:

> The future of city-building in America turns less on the indignation of the disprivileged [the urban blacks] or the conscience of the exceptional [well-off suburban whites] than is commonly supposed.
> The issue becomes increasingly how to dispose the working American to reorient his life from one of relative isolation and alienation and to find real aspirations in participation in a genuine community.
> We neglect the working American at our peril.

Wood also urged an end to name-calling. "To march to the core city, to preach, to scold can only serve to make the working American confront, not encounter, the urban newcomer," he said.

David Danzig, late associate professor of social work at Columbia University's School of Social Work, argued that just because ethnic birds of a feather flock together didn't automatically make them racist hawks. He also opposed rhetorical imprecations.

> Few people who live in socially separated ethnic communities, as most Americans do, can be persuaded that because their communities are also racially separated they are morally sick. Having come to accept their own social situation as the natural result of their ethnic affinities, mere exhortation is not likely to convince them—or, for that matter, the

public at large—that they are thereby imposing upon others a condition of apartheid.

Put another way, Whitetowners really don't see how they, as comparative newcomers without much power, money, or influence, can be blamed for spreading white racism in America. "They just don't understand the concept of collective guilt," said Andrew Valuchek, special assistant on minorities for the Democratic National Committee. "They say, 'We're not in a position of power. It's unfair to call us collectively guilty of discrimination.'"

Possibly the Whitetowners are no more guilty than the rest of white America—but they certainly seem blatantly culpable when they show up on the television news cursing and hooting the "niggers" and encouraging their small children to do the same.

Maybe it takes a Whitetowner to understand a Whitetowner. Dennis Clark, writer, urbanologist, and staff member of Temple University's Center for Community Studies, grew up in Philadelphia's Whitetown. A boilermaker's son, he survived "amateur bouts at the Cambria [a neighborhood fight joint, long shut down, that might have been the model for "Stag at Sharkey's"], bad booze in Spud Murphy's, choir practice at the Visitation [Roman Catholic Church] and pursuits by Reading Railroad cops."

Clark thinks many ethnics reflect "the stamp of old tribal grudges" and "the ferocious prejudices of the Old World."

"They represent failure in the great American sweepstakes and in getting the goodies," he says. "They represent a certain amount of pathology. They represent people set adrift from another culture. They represent insecurity. They represent a lot of free-floating aggression against neighbor-

ing groups, whoever the neighboring groups happen to be."
But Clark also says of Whitetown:

> The people show the marks of the punishment meted out to the lower echelons of the white working class by industrial society. If their psychology is one of self-reliance and pugnacity, cynicism and rude social attitudes, it is because they have themselves been frequently denied, punished and baffled by life.
>
> They know and respect what is closest to them: home and church. Higher education, civic betterment, government, the "organization man" corporate world are all alien. They have struggled with the industrial and technical society, not understanding it, and have often lost. They are the stepchildren of the industrial system. For Negroes, the true orphans of the system, they have scant sympathy left over.

Clark was talking about Philadelphia Whitetowners. But much of what he says I think applies to working-class ethnic Americans wherever they are. Many of them are in trouble. It is now widely recognized that the "true orphans" of our industrial society need all the help that can be marshaled for them. It is time to recognize that the "stepchildren" need help, too.

The Schools of Whitetown
—Then and Now

Any attempt to help the "stepchildren" of Whitetown should start with their schools. For in our increasingly complex and technological society education is the passport to progress. As the Transit Ads say: HA-HA (*Think school is a laugh? See how funny it is when you can't get a good-paying job.*)

To be sure, the implications of this nation-wide, hell-for-leather obsession are frightening. There's no blinking the fact, however, that to get ahead these days young people must put in the requisite years in school and college. In other words, one advances by degrees—bachelor's degrees, master's degrees, doctor's degrees. Black America generally understands this. In most of the big cities, black communities now are pressing hard to improve ghetto schools and to gain a greater voice—a controlling voice, if possible—over school supervision and management. In this effort, they often are receiving strong support from white-liberal intellectuals.

Whitetowners see what is happening. To them it is nothing less than a conspiracy to rob them of the schools they have always known and still want. In changing times, the Whitetowners oppose change. In their thinking about education, they tend to reflect what Margaret Mead, in *The School in American Culture,* termed the "Little Red Schoolhouse Ideal." Theirs is a "beloved image" of "the school in a world which did not change." They look back to a "past golden age which has been lost" (and which was never really golden but only seems so now with the passage of time). Embedded in the "Ideal," wrote Miss Mead, is the notion: "What was good enough for me is good enough for my children." And at a school meeting in Philadelphia one night I heard a hard-core Whitetowner utter those very words.

The Whitetowners' suspicions about present-day school policies are understandable if not justifiable. In fact, public schools have become instruments of social change, levers to help bring black America into the "mainstream." The role of schools as agents of change is new—and it is threatening to ethnic groups still struggling to "make it" in America. When the Whitetowners' immigrant forebears were flocking to this country, the schools served as social controls. Certainly there was no thought of turning the schools over to the immigrants.

Their children entered classrooms in strange clothes, with alien interests and foreign tongues, and came out speaking English, playing baseball, wearing knickers, eating ice cream—and often detesting their parents' peculiar ways of speaking and living. The schools thus transmitted the values and styles of older Americans (Protestants) and made the new arrivals (largely Catholics and Jews) conform. Sociologically, the schools' job was to perpetuate the *status quo* and to keep peace in the urban ghettos, which were then predominantly white.

In the process, the middle-class white school systems often were just about as callous and cruel to lower-class white children as these same systems are accused of being to black children today.

In reviewing this history, we should note that public

schools were not established in this country until immigrants started arriving in large numbers. As Arthur Mann, University of Chicago professor of American history, has written: "The era of mass migration (1820–1920) coincided with the century during which America's public and parochial schools were founded." Earlier, the Protestant churches educated their own and little was done for the rest. Massachusetts, in 1837, was the first state to establish tax-supported schools, but they were free only to the children of the poor. In many states no schools existed at all for those who couldn't afford to pay tuition. And even in Massachusetts attendance was not compulsory.

Pennsylvania's record merits study. In 1683, one year after William Penn first sailed up the Delaware, his Provincial Council set up a school "for the instruction and sober education of youth in ye towne of Philadelphia." A man named Enoch Flower was appointed schoolmaster. For eight shillings a quarter, boys were taught reading, writing, and "casting accounts."

Presumably, this was Pennsylvania's first "public school," albeit a tuition-charging one. Within a few years it shut down. In 1689, the Society of Friends opened a school of its own in Philadelphia. And for the next century and a quarter Pennsylvania's only schools were privately run by churches.

Even the American Revolution, with the democratic spirit it engendered, failed to produce true public schools. Pennsylvania's first constitution, adopted in 1776, directed that schools be established in each county and that teachers' salaries be paid by the public. But the mandate was ignored. A second constitution, adopted in 1790, ordered the legislature to provide free schooling for the poor. More than a quarter of a century passed before the first such school for paupers' children opened in Philadelphia, in 1818. Others followed in Pittsburgh and Lancaster. Thus there existed an early-nineteenth-century version of the "separate but equal" syndrome, based on economics rather than race—the poor thrown together in charity schools, the better-off youngsters clustered in private church schools. The stigma attached to the first public schools must have been almost as shattering as that clinging to today's schools in Negro slums.

Not until 1836 was a law enacted calling for a general system of free public education in Pennsylvania. By this time, concerns about the deportment of the increasing numbers of newcomers were growing. Education—what Horace Mann termed "the balance wheel of the social machinery" —was seen as a possible cure of "Irish pugnacity." Yale College's Timothy Dwight was blaming the "peculiar defects and vices" of the Gaelic people on their lack of schooling. Yet the campaign to extend the blessings of book learning to all Pennsylvania children met furious opposition. Protests came not from the Roman Catholics but from other, established church groups—the Lutherans, the Friends, the Mennonites, the Reformed—that had their own schools. They joined the largely Protestant land-owning class and the German-speaking population in battling against taxes that would pay for the schooling of immigrant children.

Public-school backers finally won the fight, but it wasn't until the Civil War period, almost two centuries after the coming of William Penn, that free public schools were established in all Pennsylvania counties. This same slow progress was the general rule. Massachusetts, because of a "unique tradition in social control," writes Arthur Mann, was the first state to enact a compulsory attendance law, in 1852. Little by little, the other Northern states followed suit. The twentieth century had dawned before the Southern states required attendance at school, with Mississippi the last to do so, in 1918. (And following the Supreme Court's 1954 decision barring *de jure* school segregation, Mississippi repealed its compulsory-attendance law.)

Although Protestants initially opposed establishment of

the "common schools," they soon took them over and made
them into something like mirror images of their own
schools. Bible reading, a Protestant custom, was required in
schools in many states, and the King James rather than
the Douay (Roman Catholic) version of the Bible was generally used. Protestant religious exercises and hymn singing
became frequent. The affront to Catholic immigrants was
pointed. In Philadelphia in 1844 the worst religious riots in
American history erupted over the issue of school Bible
reading. Native American Protestants, on the trumped-up
pretext that the city's Catholic bishop was seeking to drive
the Bible out of the schools (all he really wanted was the
optional use of the Douay version or, that failing, permission for children to skip the exercises), engaged Irish immigrants in bloody street warfare in the city's Kensington section, which was then and remains today a working-class
white area. Two Catholic churches were wrecked, fifty
houses were burned, and half a dozen men were killed. Leo
Pfeffer, the church-state expert, believes that these riots
more than anything else forced the American Catholic hierarchy to start its own separate school system.

If the hierarchy needed further reason for its separatist
educational movement, subsequent events provided it. In
1854 Bridget Donahoe of Ellsworth, Maine, was expelled
from her neighborhood public school for refusing to read
the King James version. Her father lost an appeal in the
Maine Supreme Court. In 1855, when the Know-Nothings
captured the Massachusetts State Legislature, they passed
anti-immigrant, anti-Catholic measures restricting office-
holding to native-born citizens, requiring twenty-one years
of residence for voters, and ordering the Protestant Bible
read in the Massachusetts public schools. Four years later
Tom Wall, eleven, was flogged by his Boston public-school
teacher for refusing to recite the Protestant version of the

Ten Commandments. A court upheld the flogging. (Not until 1963 did the United States Supreme Court side with the Bridget Donahoes and Tom Walls by throwing out all Bible reading and prayers. By that time, it was the Catholics who wanted Bible reading in public schools and many Protestant groups that opposed it.)

A certain amount of idealism lay behind the founding of public schools, but the underlying aim of social control and social order was never absent. "We tend to think of our American system of public schools," wrote Merle Curti, in *The Social Ideas of American Educators,* "as having been founded out of a great zeal for the welfare of the plain people. But actually this zeal was tempered by the zeal for the welfare of the employers of labor, by zeal for maintaining the political and social *status quo*." Humanitarian reaction against the social evils of industrialism certainly helped pave the way for creation of tax-supported schools, Curti conceded. But to win their fight, he said, such humanitarians as Horace Mann had to convince the ruling classes that public schools would save them money and assure their continued domination.

Mann, in his 1848 report as secretary of the Massachusetts public-school system, suggested that education would prevent the masses from resorting to violence. Children should be taught, he argued, to despise the use of bullets to effect social change. Of course there was nothing new in this idea. Back in the eighteenth century Adam Smith, the economist, had noted that "an instructed and intelligent people are always more decent and orderly than an ignorant and stupid one" and are "less apt to be misled into any wanton or unnecessary opposition to the measures of government." And Thomas Jefferson, in a letter to President George Washington in 1786, had declared it axiomatic that "our liberty can never be safe but in the hands of the people themselves and that, too, of the people with a certain degree of instruction."

What is worth pointing out here, though, is that public officials so clearly saw public schools as another weapon in their peacekeeping arsenal. Daniel Webster said schools would support society against "the slow but sure undermining of licentiousness" and against "open violence and overthrow." Edward Everett, the "other" speaker at Gettysburg in 1863, favored educating mechanics since "an intelligent class can scarce be, as a class, vicious." And United States Education Commissioner John Eaton, in his 1877 report, said that schools could train children to resist the evils of labor strikes and other violence. Capitalists, he said, should "weigh the cost of the mob and the tramp against the expense of universal and sufficient education."

Academic freedom, as we know it today, simply did not exist in nineteenth-century schools. "I know of no country," wrote Tocqueville, "in which there is so little true independence of mind and freedom of discussion as in America." On the other hand, the schools, besides being WASPish in their religious orientation, were, as Commissioner Eaton implied, openly propagandistic for capitalism, nineteenth-century style. For half a century teachers read David Page's *Theory and Practice of Teaching,* which stressed the instructors' duty to make their small charges aware of the "sacredness of all property." Likewise, the widely read *American Journal of Education* spread its gospel of economic truths. In one issue Henry Barnard, the editor, published a catechism that defended the "system" against its critics:

Q: Suppose a capitalist, in employing his capital, makes large profits, would that harm the working man?

A: No. There would be more capital to pay wages.

Q: Are you sorry, then, that capitalists should have great profits?

A: Glad.

Q: Why does the foreman get more than the laborer?

A: Because the foreman's work is of more value than the laborer's.

Q: If there are two boys starting in life, one the son of a man who has accumulated capital, the other of a man who has not, shall I be right in saying that the boy without this advantage can never be a capitalist?

A: No.

Q: But what is to make him a capitalist?

A: Saving.

To catch the full significance of this kind of preaching, one must recall what life was like for the laboring classes. In 1845, for example, the average family income for two-thirds of New York City's population, according to Horace Greeley, was fourteen dollars a week. And in the same period, forty per cent of all New England factory workers were children seven to sixteen years old, who worked twelve to fourteen hours a day under the most oppressive conditions. Most of these poor people were, of course, immigrants or the children of immigrants. Much of the "social dynamite" that James B. Conant found in the Negro ghettos of American cities in the 1960s was present in the immigrant ghettos of the late 1800s. Clearly, the schools had a big job in preventing an explosion.

And so they sermonized endlessly. Since drunkenness was a problem among immigrants, even arithmetic lessons warned of the evils of alcohol. Example from one book: "There were 7 farmers, 3 of whom drank rum and whisky and became miserable. The rest drank water and were healthy and happy. How many drank water?" (The contrast with some of today's motivational techniques and attempts to "tell it like it is" could not be more striking. When Albert Shanker, president of the United Federation of Teachers in New York, taught mathematics a few years ago, he posed such questions as: "If it takes 4 ounces of poison to kill a person, how many ounces would it take to kill your mother, your father, your sister, and your brother?" Says Shanker, "It was the only way I could get them to learn. They loved it.")

With the tremendous tide of immigration from 1890 to 1920, the city public schools were flooded with foreign-stock children from Eastern Europe. In 1909 the United States Immigration Commissioner reported that 57.8 per cent of the pupils in thirty-seven of the nation's largest cities were foreign-born themselves or the children of immigrants. In New York the total was 71.5 per cent, in Chicago 67.3 per cent, in Boston 63.5 per cent.

The schools simply couldn't cope with all these youngsters. Despite its compulsory school law, New York City estimated in 1900 that 40,000 children of school age were not enrolled in school. An official history said, "There were not enough truant officers to round up the truants and put them in school." Of 500,000 elementary school pupils that year, only 13,700, or less than three per cent, went on to graduate from high school. As late as 1920 less than one-fifth of the city's sixteen-to-eighteen age group had finished eighth grade. In Chicago rates of truancy, illiteracy, dropping out, and retardation were reported highest among immigrant children. Well over half of the ten-to-twelve-year-old public-school pupils of Polish, Lithuanian, Slovakian, and Italian parentage were at least one grade behind their age level.

In those days, the immigrants were termed "minority groups," just as Negroes, Puerto Ricans, Mexican-Americans, and other "people of color" are today. Natives tended to draw insulting comparisons between the "old" immigrants, many of whom had gained a foothold, and the "new" immigrants, most of whom hadn't. Arthur Mann quotes a "well-known educational reformer" as saying of the latter group: "Illiterate, docile, lacking in self-reliance and initiative, and not possessing the Anglo-Teutonic conceptions of law, order and government, their coming has served to dilute tremendously our national stock, and to corrupt our civic life."

By today's standards the city schools attended by the immigrant-stock Americans were incredibly primitive. But even by the standards of their own day they were pretty awful. In 1893 a free-lance writer named Joseph Rice spent five months visiting schools in thirty-six cities. Here is what he wrote in *The Forum* magazine about the schools of New York City:

> The typical New York City primary school . . . is . . . a hard, unsympathetic, mechanized drudgery school, a school into which the light of science has not yet entered. Its characteristic feature lies in the severity of its discipline, a discipline of enforced silence, immobility and mental passivity. The primary reading is, as a rule, so poor that the children are scarcely able to recognize new words at sight at the end of the second year. Even the third year reading is miserable.

Rice found Philadelphia schools "chaotic." Pupils spent more than half their time in "busywork." The curriculum was narrow, the teachers were unprepared, and the results were "miserable." "In some of the classes," Rice later wrote of Philadelphia, "the children at times amused themselves by walking around the room, or by talking so loudly . . . that the teacher could scarcely communicate with the other pupils. . . . I found the reading very bad, the arithmetic not very much better and beyond that but little was attempted."

As in many other cities in that wild and woolly era, Philadelphia's municipal government was riddled with corruption which seeped into the schools. Extortionists ran sectional school boards, hiring and firing teachers and forcing them to pay kickbacks for jobs. Classes were jammed, most children spent only four years in school, and thirteen thousand pupils had desks so big their feet didn't touch the floor.

Rice thought the schools in New York and Philadelphia were bad enough—but those in Chicago were even worse. Only a small percentage of Chicago's teachers were normal-school graduates; many had not even finished high school. Rice rated some of Chicago's teaching "by far the worst I have ever witnessed." "With the exception of a little singing," he wrote, "the pupils during the first six months do nothing but read, write and cipher all day long. There is not even a recess to break the monotony." Despite the time given to it, reading and writing were poor in Chicago, according to Rice. There was no sight reading and the city provided only one reading book per semester. As a result, the pupils read and reread the same worn volume until the term ended.

As for the public-school curriculum, it had always been far removed from actual life, but its record of irrelevancy must have reached some kind of sorry pinnacle at the turn of the century. Just as our schools today frequently teach— or try to teach—reading to poor city Negro children through exposure to Dick, Jane and Sally (the WASP waifs of suburbia), so did the schools of sixty and seventy years ago use instructional materials that were totally alien to the lives of the newcomers from Poland, Italy, Russia, and Ireland. Here is how Oscar Handlin, in *The Uprooted,* described turn-of-the-century education of immigrant children:

Falsity runs through all their books which all were written to be used by other pupils ["Jack goes to school. On the way he meets a cow. On the way he meets a sheep"]; even the arithmetic sets its problems in terms of a rural countryside. . . . They learn the songs their mothers never sang. They mouth the words of precepts with no meaning: A rolling stone gathers no moss. Make hay while the sun shines.

One hears much today of the failure of the white middle-class teacher to empathize with the black lower-class pupil. To hear Handlin tell it, the same problem existed in the schools attended by immigrants, only then it was white native-born teacher and white foreign-stock children. Of such a teacher, Handlin writes, "Casually she could twist the knife of ridicule in the soreness of their sensibilities: there was so much in their accents, appearance and manners that was open to mockery." And although a few teachers may have been touched with sympathy, Handlin states, "what these offered was pity, nobler than contempt but to the children no more acceptable. It is rare indeed to find a dedicated woman whose understanding of her students brought a touch of love to her work."

Nor is the tendency of today's educators to dismiss as inferior children who are "different" a new one. They were doing it half a century ago. Boston's superintendent, in a 1920 report, denied committing such an offense and then went ahead:

It is to our credit that in our schools we have never made invidious comparisons with respect to the children of the immigrant. . . . Still, we cannot ignore the arguments for some sort of special educational provision for immigrant children. The motive is similar to that which has prompted us to make special provision for various kinds of atypical children. We wish in the schools to furnish an equality of educational opportunity; but we can no longer deny the fact of individual variation of powers and abilities, and the schools cannot bestow an equality of benefit through the same ministrations to all children; children equipped with lesser gifts by nature must be given more by nurture.

To meet the needs of immigrant children, the schools of the early 1900s introduced some needed reforms and some questionable ones. They added kindergartens and playgrounds, offered domestic-science classes for girls and manual training for boys, hired nurses and instituted medical examinations. Teachers in slum schools gave lessons in dress, courtesy, and deportment. In New York teachers gave hundreds of baths each week. In Massachusetts twenty-six cities and towns organized "steamer classes" for immigrants just off the boat.

The schools also began segregating physically handicapped children and pupils they deemed to be mentally retarded. For hard-core troublemakers they set up special facilities. Meanwhile, the American high-school curriculum was drastically changed. Some would say it was watered down. Before mass immigration, the secondary schools were traditionally subject-centered. They saw it as their job to transmit a body of knowledge. Under the impetus of progressive-education leaders, the schools shifted their focus from subjects to students. This revolution was spelled out in the National Education Association's "Cardinal Principles of Secondary Education" in 1918. In this historic document the NEA proposed that the high schools, instead of putting all their emphasis on subject matter, begin to stress instead "health, command of fundamental processes, worthy home-membership, vocation, civic education, worthy use of leisure and ethical character."

Despite these efforts to make schools more meaningful for the new city dwellers, social-class divisions continued to separate teachers and pupils and even pupils and pupils. Until the 1930s it was largely the middle- and upper-class children who stayed in school through high school. In 1905 about two-thirds of all children dropped out before ninth grade, only nine per cent graduated from high school, and only four or five per cent entered college.

Change came slowly. "At the present time," George S. Counts wrote in *The Social Composition of Boards of Education*, published in 1927,

> the public high school is attended largely by the children of the more well-to-do classes. This affords us the spectacle of a privilege being extended at public expense to those very classes that already occupy the privileged positions in modern society. The poor are contributing to provide secondary education for the children of the rich, but are either too poor or too ignorant to avail themselves of the opportunities which they help to provide.

In *Who Shall Be Educated?*, written in 1944, W. Lloyd Warner, Robert J. Havighurst, and Martin B. Loeb similarly spotted a gulf between teachers and pupils. And in their view the problem was still one of social class, not race.

> Most lower-class children do not understand or appreciate the teacher's efforts. In turn, the teacher tends to neglect the lower-class children if she does not actually discriminate against them. They do not reward her with obedience and affection, and she does not reward them with affection, good marks and special approval. Conversely, when the teacher finds a lower-class child who does respond to her efforts, who does seem to understand middle-class standards, she is the most interested and puts in extra effort where she thinks she can do some good.

In the first decades of this century, some urban school systems came to be taken over by the immigrant classes themselves. When this happened, the usual response of the middle- and upper-middle-class liberals and intellectuals was to move their children bodily out of public schools into private ones. Such an exodus occurred, for example, among Harvard University families when the Irish seized control of the public schools in Boston and Cambridge.

Shady Hill Academy, a progressive private school, was started by a group of Harvard professors who didn't want their sons and daughters to attend Cambridge schools. And to take a specific example: When Arthur M. Schlesinger, Sr., the Harvard historian, moved his family from the Middle West in the 1920s he enrolled his son, Bud, in public school in Cambridge. The Schlesingers believed in public education and had had good experience with it in Ohio. But Cambridge, with its Irish domination, was something else. Disillusionment quickly set in. One day the boy returned from junior high school to report that his social-studies teacher had told the class about a curious country in Europe where all the inhabitants had red eyes and white hair. Albanians they were called, said the teacher.

That was enough for Professor Schlesinger, Sr. He packed Bud (Arthur M. Schlesinger, Jr.) off to Exeter, thus ending the public-school career of the future Pulitzer Prize-winning historian.* A check in 1962 showed that of more than fifty members of the faculty of the Harvard Graduate School of Education only one had children attending Cambridge public schools. Since 1964, however, when thirty-one-year-old Theodore R. Sizer was appointed dean, there has been some change. Sizer, a firm believer in town-gown cooperation, has worked hard on urban-education problems and has set an example for his faculty by sending his own children to the Cambridge schools.

But perhaps this casebook of horrors provides too bleak a picture of public education for immigrants in the United States. If the schools mistreated and miseducated great numbers of foreign-stock children, for many others they opened wide the door of opportunity. America was, after

* This story was told to me by the late Professor Schlesinger.

all, the first country in the world to establish free public schools. To many immigrants, especially the Jewish immigrants already imbued with a love of learning, the public schools became the very symbol of the precious liberties for which their adopted country stood.

"They were part of the good rhythm of life," writes A. M. Rosenthal, of the *New York Times,* "and as we grew older we believed, as an article of faith, that the public schools were an underpinning of democratic society, that it was there that rich and poor sat together, that boys and girls of 'all races, colors and creeds' learned to live together and to succeed together."

Rosenthal's parents traveled from Russia to the Bronx by way of Canada. Their son attended New York's public schools and one of its free city colleges, got a job at the *Times,* became a foreign correspondent, won a Pulitzer Prize for distinguished reporting in Poland, and is now managing editor of the newspaper. Does he think the public schools were a fraud all along? "Certainly not for the white lower middle class, sons of immigrants," Rosenthal said in an editorial-page column in the *Times* in the summer of 1968, when New York's school woes were worsening. "They gave exactly what was wanted. That, most of all, was a sense of being taken in by the country and accepted, which is why there is a particular quality of immigrant love for America, because no other country does it—'land where *our* fathers died.' "

Rosenthal concluded regretfully—"how painful it is to understand it of a warmly remembered part of life"—that the public schools were, in fact, a fraud for other children, notably Negro children. And now, he said, Negro parents are demanding what his parents did not have to struggle for: schools that satisfy them. By and large, the schools do appear to have satisfied the Jewish immigrants and to have served them well. But for many reasons, as we have seen, the experiences of Irish, Italian, Polish, Ukrainian, Greek, Hungarian, German, and Russian immigrants—the groups that inhabit the Whitetowns of America—were often less satisfying.

Having survived discrimination themselves, today's Whitetowners can't understand what all the current shouting is about. They are appalled that black students wear dashikis, call themselves Afro-Americans, and insist on attending courses in black-African history. They forget that the Irish, who once considered themselves a mystical breed apart, held "race conventions" of their own and in this century (1903) petitioned for the teaching of Irish history in New York schools. More important, though, has been the failure of Whitetowners, indeed of most white Americans, to see that black Americans are not just another ethnic group. Like the Jews, Poles, and Italians, the Negroes have had to confront the disadvantages of underclass immigrants on the urban frontier. But the problem of pigmentation has been paramount. In white America their blackness has made all the difference. On the one hand, they've been taught in school that they've got to conform to get ahead, and on the other hand, they've learned the cruel lesson that because they're black they can't conform. Hence the excruciating dilemma that whites often fail to recognize.

Beyond the fact that many Whitetowners are totally unsympathetic to Negro aims and efforts in education, there are three reasons why the school situation in Whitetown and Blacktown today is so explosive. First, education is vastly more important in this age of electronics, moonshots, instant communications, computerized everything, than at any previous time in history. When the immigrants were tipped out of school at eighth grade in 1910 or 1920, it didn't matter very much because America's relatively crude, unsophisticated economy had jobs for unskilled, undereducated workers. Less so today.

Second, the Negro thrust in education has come at the time of the first really substantial Federal spending on schools. For about a century and a quarter after the schools were started, Washington treated public education as almost exclusively a state and local responsibility. Its only aid went for vocational training. Important Federal assistance began with the National Defense Education Act of 1958 and was greatly expanded with the Elementary and Secondary Education Act of 1965. Through ESEA's Title I alone, a billion dollars a year now goes to schools with concentrations of pupils from low-income families.

The third point is that the Federal government, seeing greater educational needs and deficiencies in Negro areas, wants to put most of its emphasis—and money—there. To the extent that this is being done, it is being done at the expense of Whitetowners whose educational shortcomings are often almost as serious as those of the Blacktowners.

"For the next generation or so," Harold Howe II, then United States Education Commissioner, wrote in the *Harvard Educational Review* in the winter of 1968,

> I believe we must tip the educational scales in favor of our minority youngsters and commit a major share of our resources to providing superior educational programs for them.
> In a sense, this is inequality in reverse—an extra loading of the balance in favor of those who for generations have seen the weights on the other end.

As justification for this policy, Howe quoted President Johnson:

> You do not take a person who for years has been hobbled by chains and liberate him, bring him up to the starting line of

a race and say, "You're free to compete with the others," and justly believe that you have been completely fair.

One of the difficulties with Howe's "extra loading of the balance" is that the scales, as the examination of nineteenth-century and early twentieth-century schools indicates, have never been heavily tipped in favor of working-class white children. Not historically and not now. In his mammoth, Federally financed study in 1966, *The Equality of Educational Opportunity,* James S. Coleman of Johns Hopkins University found no significant difference in the school facilities currently provided white and nonwhite children in this country. His surprising discovery is often overlooked.

"The [Coleman] study set out to document the fact that for children of minority groups school facilities are sharply unequal and that this inequality is related to student achievement," reported Harvard researchers Susan S. Stodolsky and Gerald Lesser in the *Harvard Educational Review* in the fall of 1967. "The data did not support either conclusion. What small differences in school facilities did exist had little or no discernible relationship to the level of student achievement." *

Coleman decided that schools' physical facilities weren't of major importance in determining school "output"—despite what everybody had thought. The job ahead, as he saw it, was to "overcome the difficulties in starting point of children from different social groups."

But the children of Whitetown haven't been getting much of a head start. Since Sputnik, says Mario Fantini, of the

---

* Daniel P. Moynihan, President Nixon's Special Assistant for Urban Affairs, thinks Washington sought to conceal this crucial fact from the press and public. Its fifty-two-page summary of the Coleman Report dealt mostly with school segregation and "withheld from all but the *cognoscenti,*" says Moynihan, "any suggestions that major and, in effect, heretical findings had appeared." His article appeared in *Harvard Educational Review*'s Winter 1968 issue.

Ford Foundation, improvements in American education have merely "strengthened the *status quo,* enabling the system to serve better those it has always served best." And those it has always served best are the white middle class, now largely in the suburbs.

Certainly, one finds little to cheer about in the schools of Whitetown, U.S.A. Philadelphia's Kensington section is an example. Its schools are old, its classes large. Its dropout rate is very high and its college-going rate is very low. Kensington has more cases of pediculosis—nits and lice—in pupils' hair than any other section of Philadelphia, and a greater proportion of underweight children and children with cavities.

Most significantly, the administrative district comprising Kensington and adjoining black North Philadelphia regularly ranks last among the city's eight districts on all measures of academic promise and achievement, from the Iowa Test of Basic Skills to the California Test of Mental Maturity. Some inner-city districts that are ninety per cent or more Negro produce slightly higher test scores than does Kensington's district. Despite its glaringly obvious deficiencies, Kensington is excluded from such Federal programs as Model Cities. Many of its schools fail to qualify for aid under ESEA. The neighborhoods, though poor, are not quite poor enough.

The Whitetowns of other cities evidence similar inequities. "Boston's poor whites," says Assistant Superintendent of Schools William L. Cannon, "face the same educational deficiencies as the 'soul brothers.' " He sees a "very high correlation" in the test scores of black and white pupils in low-income sections. Says George Thomas, assistant dean of Harvard's Graduate School of Education, "The poor whites in Boston are less well served than the poor blacks. Less money goes into their areas—partly because of Federal directive. The whites are prouder and more quiescent, the blacks more concentrated. Only in rare cases have the whites learned a lesson from the hustling black community. There's more action in [black] Roxbury than in the white areas. In general, Roxbury is much more together."

Charlestown's Harvard School is testimony to what has been permitted to happen in that old section of working-class Caucasians. The school was built in 1871, its outside fire escapes are rusty and its wooden doors creak, it is a certified firetrap. (In an interview, its principal defended the school's continued use on grounds that "schools almost never burn on school time.")

The Harvard School is dimly illuminated. In one room, when I was there, a lone light bulb (it appeared to be sixty watts) dangled from an eight-foot cord that ran from the high ceiling to a point just above the teacher's desk. The building is a rabbit warren of little closets and rooms tucked planlessly here and there off corridors. You encounter the dusty auditorium by surprise on the third story. There is one toilet seat per floor. There is no play yard.

An elevated line linking Charlestown to downtown Boston, five minutes away, rattles nearby. The school sits back from a busy commercial street and heavy trucks trundle past all day long. (The trucks run within six feet of the living room of a Charlestown resident who has an important job in the Boston city government. Like so many Whitetowners, he's proud of the old place and is damned if he will move.)

The principal of Harvard School is responsible also for two other Charlestown elementary schools, one built in 1866 and the other in 1893. All three schools are small, enrolling a total of only about eight hundred children, mostly of French-Canadian, Polish, and Italian descent. In the next few years they are to be replaced by a single new building. The point is, though, that the "morbid, desolate crumbling" school of "rank smells" and pervasive gloom that Jonathan Kozol, in *Death at an Early Age,* found destroying the hearts and minds of Negro children in Boston's Roxbury section, exists in white Charlestown, too.

Some of the oldest schools in Cleveland serve its polyglot West Side. This is a section in advanced stages of decay. It lost four thousand people between 1960 and 1965, now counts twenty-seven thousand, 96.9 per cent of them white. You still see Polish delicatessens, Ukrainian social clubs, and Russian Orthodox churches there. In the last fifteen years, however, many of these ethnic groups have moved to suburbs like Parma (using freeways that slice through their old neighborhoods to get back and forth). In schooling, employment, and family income, the West Side rates under Cleveland city averages.

Especially hard hit is the so-called Near West Side, across a smoky, industrial valley from central Cleveland. In this dingy, trash-strewn neighborhood many of Cleveland's estimated fifty thousand Appalachian whites live in urban hillbilly squalor. Despite their poverty, these people, like all Whitetowners, have pride. To them, the public-welfare program is nothing more than a huge black boondoggle. Staying off relief, therefore, becomes a badge of distinction. Stay off they do—and their schools suffer.

"We measure poverty by welfare cases," explains Mrs. Rose Cira, research associate in the Cleveland Board of Education's division of educational research. "Because they lack welfare cases, the Near West Side schools often fail to qualify for Federally financed programs. They are not considered target schools. They don't get the concentration of moneys and services that the [predominantly black] East Side does. There is a discrepancy that we're constantly trying to eliminate."

Another reason why Appalachian whites don't sign up

for welfare is that they're often on the move—down to West Virginia and Kentucky, and then back again. They don't stay put long enough to qualify. The result is that their schools have the highest pupil-transiency rates in the entire city. When I visited the Kentucky Elementary School on the Near West Side in June 1968, its pupil turnover stood at 130 per cent—and climbing. The school enrollment was nine hundred but twelve hundred boys and girls had been admitted or transferred out since the previous September.

"No sooner do we get children working to an acceptable pace," complained Mrs. Mary B. Diggs, the principal, "than they're gone. Many of the families still own farms back in the hills or have relatives there. They go 'home' for the spring plowing and we don't see them for six weeks."

Principals and teachers report the Appalachian white youngsters now are falling behind Negro pupils not only in attendance but in effort and achievement. "Negro parents," said Miss Mary Gulmi, principal of the Tremont School, which dates from 1875, "are aware of the importance of education. They take advantage of the opportunities offered them. The poor whites are satisfied with truck-driver jobs paying ninety to a hundred dollars a week. They don't stress education, they don't push, they're not too concerned that their kids aren't doing well. We've made the Negroes conscious of the need for education but not the poor whites. One of these days they're going to be outstripped."

At the one-hundred-fifteen-year-old Hicks Elementary School, teachers said the twenty-five per cent Negro enrollment was, on the whole, more interested, curious and aware than the fifty per cent Appalachian-white enrollment. "The Southern whites are ignorant of the help available to them," said one teacher, "or else they refuse it. They want to go back to the hills. They don't talk to teachers as Negroes do —that is, as equals. There is less parental participation among the whites."

"Motivation of family is greater among Negroes," agreed Mrs. Marian B. Harty, a principal who has served in poor-white and poor-black schools. A veteran teacher saw a psychological difference: "When I first came here thirteen years ago," she said, "the Negro was hangdog. Now he'll fight, push, he's very aggressive. It's the Appalachian whites who are insecure. It's hard to motivate them. The best readers are the Negro children. Not that they're brighter; they've just got more drive."

Bill G. is a blue-eyed ten-year-old with dungarees and a faded striped shirt open at the collar. His blond hair is cut short. Bill's father is in the Army somewhere. His older brother is going to high school in West Virginia. Bill lives with his mother, who is a waitress and has a drinking problem, and with his sister and Cecil. Cecil? "He's livin' with us now." Bill was born in West Virginia, was taken to Texas at the age of two, returned to West Virginia, then moved to Cleveland with his mother when he was in second grade. They frequently drive back to the old home town, Webster Springs, West Virginia. The three-hundred-fifty-mile trip takes seven hours.

When he first moved to Cleveland, Bill was "sceered" of his teachers, but now his schoolwork has improved. His long-range prospects are dim, however. Comparatively few Appalachian whites get through high school and fewer still go to college. At Cleveland's twenty-two-hundred-student Lincoln High School more than twenty-five per cent of the enrollment was Appalachian white but only one Appalachian white student ranked in the top ten per cent of his graduating class in 1968.

As is so often the case in black slum schools, Near West Side school officials blame pupils like Bill and parents like his mother for the children's failure to achieve. "They don't like school rules, they don't see the reason for homework," Miss Gulmi said of the parents. "If you ask for a note explaining a child's absence, the parent will say, 'Well, we overslept.' They are kind of free spirits. Any ordinary demands that a school would make—they just don't like to do it."

Besides appearing lackadaisical and apathetic, the Appalachian whites also exhibit the ferocious prejudices and free-floating aggression that Dennis Clark finds in the ethnic Americans. Mrs. Annette J. Maddox, Hicks School principal, told of a twelve-year-old Kentuckian who, after two weeks at Hicks, announced bluntly, "I hate niggers. I hate all niggers. I ain't never met no niggers like niggers at this school. These niggers are the worst I ever met."

Mrs. Maddox warned the boy not to speak that way. "You have to go to school with 'niggers,' as you call them," she said. "There are colored teachers in this school and I am colored. You'll find the colored here as nice as those in Kentucky." The boy was adamant: "Ain't nobody gonna make me like no niggers." And at the end of the school year he refused to join in the promotion exercises because so many of his classmates were black.

It is this kind of poor-white boy who needs special help. But as Federal aid is allocated in Cleveland, he's not getting it.

Detroit's Ruddiman Junior High School serves a predominantly Polish neighborhood in the northwestern part of the city near the militantly all-white suburb of Dearborn, where police teach housewives how to shoot guns. Many of Ruddiman's families would like to move to Dearborn but can't afford to. A large public-housing project gives the school its only Negro pupils—about ten per cent of the enrollment of almost eleven hundred.

Ruddiman dates from a one-room school built in 1861

that is still standing and is still used. Four additions have been tacked onto it and all are under one roof. The inevitable freeway carries motorists within fifteen yards of Ruddiman's front entrance. For two-thirds of Ruddiman's families incomes range from six to nine thousand dollars a year. The other third are in the three-to-four-thousand-dollar poverty range. Since the school neighborhood ranks just above Detroit's poverty level, Ruddiman doesn't get a dime under Title I of ESEA.

When I visited Ruddiman, its principal, Mrs. Dorothy P. Cooper, a peppery little woman with glasses, an upswept hairdo, and a sense of outrage, was scrounging around for half a dozen spotlights for the school's upcoming fine-arts festival. "If this were a Title I school," she said bitterly, "I could order these lights and have them in a week. But as it is, we'll just have to go without."

Even among Ruddiman whites with the highest family incomes cultural deprivation is acute, although not always obvious, according to the principal. Of the Polish parents, she said:

> Many have enough money but lack the cultural background of selectivity. They are permissive, indulgent, well meaning but poorly advised. They let their children make course decisions, and it's the children themselves in many cases, not their parents, who elect not to take college preparation.
>
> Social life is limited. Many of our children have never been downtown [six miles away]. Shopping centers are their social gathering places. When they take a summer vacation trip they come back talking about how many miles they covered, how many states they passed through, not what they saw. This is the way people out here think. They visit Disneyland but not the Grand Canyon.

Mrs. Cooper's indictment extends across the board of American society generally. Her point was, however, that although most Ruddiman children aren't poverty-stricken, they still need special programs to lift their sights and their values. The school offers none. There is much racial prejudice in the neighborhood (and one suspects it might exist within the school faculty and administration), but there are no special intergroup education efforts aimed at improving the racial climate at Ruddiman.

Ruddiman is a typical Whitetown case: its constituency is poor but not poor enough. Its problems, while genuine, are hidden. Its people are, in the main, uncomplaining. "They don't ask for anything," said Mrs. Cooper, who seemed both admiring and vexed. "They have pride. This is the one thing these people have. They plug along as best they can. They don't expect help and they don't get any."

At Detroit's school-administration building, Assistant Superintendent Louis D. Monacel recognized the problem. Dr. Monacel directs state-Federal projects for the Detroit schools. "We're not programming Federally for these [white] people," he said. "The criteria are tightly woven to the ghetto."

What this means, he suggested, is that the sons and daughters of white factory workers are probably getting shortchanged. "We assume too much," he said. "We assume that we don't have to counsel them, push them, make sure they take advantage of every opportunity. But without that counseling they drift out of school. I've kind of ignored these people and assumed they were doing fine. They aren't. We've got to take some of the responsibility."

Monacel contrasted the expectations of a young, bright, ambitious black student today with those of a white trade-unionist. "If the Negro has anything he can make it," said Monacel:

Colleges and universities all over America are running for Negroes. They've got to have them. In a way, this is shabby.

Where were the colleges ten years ago? But it's also good because Negroes who want to and have ability can get into the best universities.

Meanwhile, the white unionist feels the ground being cut from beneath him, or thinks he does. The one thing he has is job security and the new rules are changing that, too. Detroit is a union town and Detroit schools deliberately close apprentice training classes if they're not racially integrated. It is only right and just that we do this. But think how it effects the white unionist.*

Detroit, with about three hundred thousand pupils, is the nation's fourth largest school district. Its superintendent is a thoughtful, pipe-smoking, career educator named Norman Drachler. Dr. Drachler worries about the schools' lack of support in white ethnic neighborhoods.

"In the so-called Polish corridors," he said, "we lose millage and we lose it consistently." He meant that these areas vote against school-tax increases. "They're concerned that every dollar goes to the Negro," Dr. Drachler continued. "They're concerned about law and order, about vandalism. In these areas I don't hear questions about the relevancy of the curriculum, as I hear in the Negro communities. Maybe it's a key that we don't have a single representative of ethnic groups on our [elected] school board. Not a Pole or an Italian. There was a thrust and they didn't make it."

Dr. Drachler believes the estrangement is temporary. In his opinion, the white ethnic groups "more and more iden-

* In a letter to the *New York Times,* August 3, 1963, a white unionist offered a classic defense of the apprenticeship system. "Some men," he wrote, "leave their sons money, some large investments, some business connections, and some a profession. I have only one worthwhile thing to give: my trade. I hope to follow a centuries-old tradition and sponsor my sons for an apprenticeship. For this simple father's wish it is said that I discriminate against Negroes. Don't all of us discriminate? Which of us when it comes to a choice will not choose a son over all others? I believe that an apprenticeship in my union is no more a public trust, to be shared by all, than a millionaire's money is a public trust." (Quoted by Robert Wood and others.)

tify with the white Protestant culture that prevails in our textbooks and in our schools.

"I don't think they want to be different," he said. "They want to assimilate and become Americanized. But they are very suspicious of our so-called Negro alliances. And they are bewildered, as all of us are, by the strange change of pace in our society."

The Adlai E. Stevenson School in Chicago's Scottsdale section serves a different kind of Whitetown. Here the people have, in effect, fled to the suburbs, even though their postwar community in southwest Chicago is just inside the city limits. All of the houses are new, most are in good repair and most are single-family, owner-occupied dwellings. The first houses built in the 1950s sold for thirteen thousand dollars, but recent ones of brick with basements and two-car garages bring twenty-five plus.

Only four per cent of Scottsdale's population is foreign-born. Virtually every European nationality group is represented: Poles, Irish, English, Norwegians, Swedes, Germans, Czechs, Austrians, Hungarians, Russians, Italians, Canadians, Dutch, Lithuanians. There are a few Chinese but no Negroes or Puerto Ricans in Scottsdale. There never have been and, if the present population has its way, there never will be. About fifty per cent of the men are blue-collar workers. Many police and firemen live there. Scottsdale is two-thirds Roman Catholic and heavily Republican. There are no "first families" and there is no real "establishment." What unites many of the people is the fact of their mutual "displacement" from their former homes in racially mixed neighborhoods downtown and their determination that "this shall not happen again."

There's nothing very attractive about Scottsdale's setting

on the once forbidding prairie, but its people enjoy many advantages. Serving Scottsdale and surrounding communities are three public elementary schools, a large parochial school, a public high school with junior college attached, seven churches and a synagogue, two shopping centers, two hospitals, two movie houses, a public library, a bowling alley, and four parks.

Stevenson School (named, by the way, for the Chicagoan who was Vice-President in the second administration of Grover Cleveland, not for his grandson, the late Ambassador to the United Nations) opened in 1955 with 685 pupils. It has since been enlarged and its enrollment in kindergarten through eighth grade has doubled. The neat, trim two-story school has twenty-eight regular classrooms, five mobile classrooms, three full-time kindergarten rooms, a library, a cafeteria, a combination gymnasium-auditorium, and a home-economics room. The school playground is large and well equipped.

The building is not without defects. It heats unevenly. The gym is inadequate and both the teachers' room and parking lot are too small. Maintenance and repairs are behind schedule. When I visited the school in May 1968 a surprising number of windows were broken, the result of troublemaking by rowdy neighborhood youths, I was told. Compared to other schools in Chicago, though, Stevenson's problems are minimal. And that's just the point: Scottsdale wants to keep it that way. What it fears is change, racial change, change "forced down our throats" through school bussing or other integration devices.

Stevenson School's principal, Eleanor R. Coghlan, is a Scottsdaler in spirit, although she lives some miles away. She said Stevenson pupils consistently score above national norms on standardized tests—and she produced records to prove it. "Stevenson compares very favorably with the highest-income schools on the North Shore," she said. "We know how much higher we stand than the inner-city schools. And we know it's not just a matter of teachers or supplies. You find some marvelously dedicated teachers in inner-city schools. And those schools are loaded with help. They've got people walking around with nothing to do."

Mrs. Coghlan, a spruce, well-organized widow, said that, as a representative of the Chicago school system, she couldn't condone Scottsdale's openly segregationist views. "But I can understand," she said. "I have empathy. I am as aware as anyone of a need for a different climate. I take in-service courses on this very subject. But this community is certainly not ready. If they bussed in colored children we'd have riots. They know this at the Board of Education."

Earlier, I had talked to Dr. John Byrne, district superintendent in Chicago's predominantly white Uptown section. "Rightly or wrongly," Dr. Byrne had said, "there is a feeling that we're carrying the ball for the Negro people." He argued that the anti-Negro prejudices of Scottsdalers and others in Chicago's "White Crescent" were socioeconomic in origin rather than racist. "These people live in small neat bungalows," he said. "They manicure their lawns and put pink flamingos out front. They buy this baloney about property values declining [when Negroes move in]. They see themselves losing their hard-earned investment. Middle-European people especially are land- and property-conscious. So this makes it hurt all the more."

Despite Chicago's efforts to raise the quality of Negro education, Dr. Byrne thought the school board was actually spending less in the ghetto than in white areas. His explanation was that in the black sections many of the teachers were new and at the bottom of the salary scale, while veteran teachers filled white schools. In other words, it's cheaper to run a school with novices than old-timers. City-wide, only seventy-two per cent of Chicago's teachers in 1968 were "assigned"—that is, fully certified and with tenure. In some white schools, however, ninety-five per cent or more of the teachers were assigned.

When I told Mrs. Coghlan what this district superintendent had said about spending in black and white schools, without identifying him by name, she blew up. "What was that?" she demanded. "Who was it? I'll bet he's a new superintendent and I'll bet he's colored. I'll bet those two things."

She was half right—Dr. Byrne was newly appointed. But her angry reaction showed how high feelings run in school systems seeking social change. What she said next was also typical talk for Whitetown school administrators: "The Negro element is very vocal. No one is looking at this side at all. We are the forgotten men. We don't get one cent from the government. We get the bare minimum. We aren't given a thing."

It was a fact, however, that Stevenson School's staff consisted almost exclusively of veteran teachers. Indeed, the principal herself counted sixty teachers in other Chicago schools who were then on a waiting list for transfer to Stevenson. Some had been waiting for seven years. And virtually all wanted to transfer out of black schools. When and if they transferred out, their places would, in all likelihood, be taken by new teachers. Dr. Byrne seemed to have a point.

In Los Angeles, you will search in vain for an old ethnic neighborhood. There are no ancient Charlestowns or hard-bitten Kensingtons or other Eastern-style Whitetowns of any description. Despite the sprawl and the smog, everything's up to date in this incredible 710.6-square-mile school district—almost two-thirds the size of Rhode Island. Every year more than a thousand new classrooms are built and a forty-year-old school is considered obsolete. (In Cleveland, by contrast, more than half the schools are over fifty years old.) To an Easterner, even the L.A. slums look good. "We have," said a school official, "the world's richest poverty areas."

Appearances are misleading. To find space for 27,500 additional pupils each year, Los Angeles has had to cut school costs to the bone. In building after building you find a principal, a secretary, and a fixed number of classroom teachers, but no other staff or extra help of any kind. That's all the exploding school system can afford. Most of its Federal aid under ESEA's Title I provides "saturation" help for 60,000 poor Negro and Spanish-American children. Working-class white areas are generally excluded from these special programs. An example is the Valley East Elementary District, which includes the less affluent parts of Hollywood and North Hollywood. In 1968, Valley East enrolled 40,711 pupils—eighty-six per cent of them white—in fifty-four schools: a good-sized city school system, all by itself. Yet serving these 40,711 children was one art supervisor but no art teachers, one physical-education supervisor but no phys-ed teachers, one music supervisor and thirteen music teachers. There were libraries in the schools but no certified librarians. Federal funds supported a project for gifted pupils in Valley East and one to teach English to Mexican-American children who made up eleven per cent of the enrollment. They also helped maintain the librarianless libraries. But that was it.

"We're a fringe district," said Mrs. Helene C. Lewis, administrative assistant to the district superintendent. "We need help but don't get it. These are forgotten people. [Shades of Scottsdale's Eleanor Coghlan.] They need that little push. We keep telling them downtown that these kids are almost as badly off as those in the ghetto. But nothing happens."

Just a block from Hollywood and Vine—crossroads of the celluloid world—is one of the schools that Mrs. Lewis was talking about. The Selma School sits on a back street seldom seen by tourists. Seventy-five per cent of its pupils are white. Many of their parents were drawn to Hollywood by the bright lights. Almost invariably, dreams of stardom turn into nightmares of marriage tangles, drinking, often narcotics. Failing to strike it rich, these rootless people move on. So kids come and go at Selma School. It's like a revolving door. Of all schools in the entire Los Angeles district in 1967–1968, Selma had the highest rate of pupil transiency. It also ranked near the bottom in reading.

The principal, Miss Sarah Macaluso, saw a correlation. "When the transiency rate is so high," she said, "you can't blame reading disabilities on the teachers. We don't have the children long enough to teach them anything."

At the seventy-four per cent white Grant School on Santa Monica Boulevard, in Hollywood, newly appointed principal Edith Dury said she was "floored" to find so much poverty and so many divorced and separated parents. In 1966–1967, Grant had the city's third highest pupil-transiency rate. "We have many families on public assistance," Mrs. Dury said. "We have many emotional problems —both children and parents. A mother was in this morning. She neglects her child shamelessly, yet she's flying to Germany for a vacation with some man. That's the kind of value system and morality you find here."

By skimping on such schools, Los Angeles educators are, in effect, perpetuating such ways of life. Nor is Valley East unusual. Twenty-five miles south of Hollywood, in the city's Harbor Area Elementary District, I talked to Superintendent Jack R. McClellan. He served in Watts before taking over the predominantly white Harbor Area in February 1968.

"The low-income Caucasian community is not demonstrating," he said. "It's not demanding space in newspapers or on TV. These people are doing their best to meet their problems within their income. But they are saying to me, to principals, to teachers, 'We want what the others are getting.' "

Dr. McClellan thought they had a point. He was surprised that a drive to get money for working-class white schools had not been organized. "Apparently there is no leadership," he said. "The churches haven't picked it up."

One of the schools I visited in the Harbor Area was the Carson Street School, just off the Harbor and San Diego freeways in Torrance. Carson Street School is in a tough white neighborhood. Knifings, shootings, car thefts, and narcotics addiction are common. About one-eighth of its families are on welfare and the bulk of these are one-parent families. Maybe half the parents were high-school dropouts; very few have had any college experience. Carson Street enrolled almost fifteen hundred pupils, two-thirds of them white, most of the others Mexican-American.*

To run this forty-nine-classroom operation, the principal, a New Englander named Minnie Queenen Wallace, could call on, besides regular teachers, one vice-principal, one music teacher, a corrective physical-education teacher, one day a week; a counselor one day a week; and a speech teacher three days every two weeks. That was the extent of supportive services for a big school bursting with problems.

* California requires all school districts to conduct racial and ethnic surveys every year with pupils placed in categories designated by the State Department of Education. In Los Angeles the 1968 breakdown was "other whites" (the designation for all Caucasians except those with Spanish surnames), 54.1%; Negroes, 21.4%; Spanish-surname students, 20.3%; Chinese-Japanese-Korean, 3.5%; American Indians, 0.1%; "other nonwhite," mostly Samoans, 0.5%. Such racial distinctions, though invidious, are required under the Civil Rights legislation. These studies help Washington determine whether or not school districts are segregated in fact if not in law.

Because of overcrowding, Carson Street was on a "divided day," some children attending classes from nine A.M. to two P.M. and others from ten to three.

Mrs. Wallace seemed proud of the fact that her parents rarely registered complaints. "These people aren't asking for anything," she said. "The others have their hand out all the time." It was clear to whom she was referring.

At noon the day of my visit, the principal and new officers of the school Parent-Teacher Association had an end-of-year lunch at a near-by Howard Johnson's. There were nine mothers, all of them white and most from the Southwest. I heard no gripes about the school. The women were too busy talking about firearms. Eight of the nine said they had guns in their houses; the only unarmed officer of the P.T.A. was the lone college-trained one. The outgoing president said her husband was teaching her how to shoot both a .30-caliber rifle and a .22. "I think this is good," she said. Whitetown all the way.

In every big city, you find Whitetowners working in public schools as teachers and principals. They may have moved to the suburbs, but they remain Whitetowners in spirit. Their sympathies are with the working-class whites. And for them the conspiracy theory is genuine—and frightening.

An example is San Francisco's John P. Ward. He's principal of the Douglas Elementary School, just over the hill from Haight-Ashbury. In 1968, when I was there, Haight-Ashbury was a national symbol of youth in rebellion. On June afternoons, its sidewalks were thronged with freak-outs, copouts, loafers, lovers, exhibitionists, dilettantes, mystics, musicians, nihilists, Marxists, hippies, Yippies, pseudophilosophers, phonies. Everything that Haight-Ash-bury stood for John P. Ward detests. He's convinced that because the Douglas School is 71.3 per cent white it is being discriminated against. He's convinced that because he's white he's being discriminated against.

Ward, a new principal, runs a ten-teacher school for three hundred pupils, many from broken homes and living on welfare. Six of his teachers were new the previous September. A seventh is a long-term substitute replacing a teacher on sabbatical leave. Ward's only office help is a secretary who works six hours a day. He has, as he puts it, "two-fifths of a speech teacher" (meaning one teacher two days a week) and two-fifths of an instrumental-music teacher. Ward's guidance file is bulging. He must handle all discipline, all counseling, all special problems, plus the avalanche of paperwork and statistics-gathering required of principals these days.

All this seems to leave him little time for staff development or curricular innovation. So these jobs go undone. Douglas Elementary, in San Francisco's Eureka Valley, receives no ESEA help or Federal aid of any kind. Ward's chief advantages are that the school is small and the building, which opened in 1954, is in good shape. But Douglas pupils, in the middle rank in reading, fall in the bottom ten per cent nationally. Compared with children across the country, all but the very best readers at Douglas are subpar.

As a result, Ward is a bitter man. "I spend too much of my time on social-welfare work," he said. "I spend more time on social welfare than I do on education. Society is deliberately dumping these problems in our laps. If that's the way the game is to be played, I need help. All of this is detracting from my educational role. It's taking its toll."

Ward considers Harold Howe's plan of tipping the educational scales in favor of minority-group pupils "absolutely discriminatory." "It's discrimination in reverse—discrimination against the productive elements of society. I've been getting complaints from parents, but they're fearful of being called racially prejudiced. They're scared to death of it."

What really outrages John P. Ward, though, is the over-all racial atmosphere in San Francisco. He sees the press, the politicians, the business establishment, and the school system bowing to pressure from minority-group militants and actually conspiring to hurt the white working class. He specifically includes white principals among those being hurt. Ward, seventeen years in the system and an assistant principal for almost nine years, formerly headed the San Francisco Principals Association.

Of himself and his fellow Caucasian principals, he said, "We're living a life of hell. It's getting to the point where the work isn't worth it. You can be doing the finest job in the world and you're driven to your knees by false accusations. We're fed up with the injustice of it."

Ward went on to complain about something that is irking white principals and middle-echelon school administrators in big-city school systems across the country: that, in their efforts to promote black administrators, city school boards sometimes appear to be discriminating against whites.

"Someone somewhere has to stand up with the moral courage for what is right," said this San Franciscan.

If the Negro has the stuff he's going to make it. But only if he gets there on his own ability will he gain respect. Superficial attempts to advance him won't solve anything.

The Board of Education should say exactly this: "If you want to get ahead, buddy, you have to prove your worth and prove your responsibility." But as it is they're going to scuttle us [white school administrators] by forcing us to knuckle under. This is a compromise of principle. So what's going to happen? Top-flight people are going to the suburbs. They won't come here and subject themselves to the indignities and abuse.

Of course, Ward overlooked the fact that race, religion, and national ancestry have always been crucial factors in selection of school personnel. Historically, capable Negro school men have been held back because of their color, and white incompetents have advanced because of *their* color. Ethnicity and religion also can be important. To get a top school job in Boston you must be Roman Catholic and you should be Irish. In most other cities white Protestants have dominated the school superintendencies. In San Francisco itself an open though unofficial quota system has operated to guarantee that the three major religious faiths are represented on the city school board. Such was the case in New York City, too. Its board traditionally consisted of three Jews, three Protestants, and three Catholics until Negroes and Puerto Ricans were given representation in an enlarged board during John V. Lindsay's mayoralty.

Ward said he knew all this but believed that Catholics and Jews earned their right to good jobs in the San Francisco school system without resort to violence or Black Panther tactics. Maybe so. But the point is that group conflict and ethnic lobbying are a way of life in American schools and other institutions.

San Francisco pours most of its Federal funds into minority-group schools. In 1967–1968, only twenty-seven out of 105 elementary schools received a share of the city's $3.25 million ESEA Title I grant. Of the twenty-seven, seventeen were predominantly Negro, three predominantly Chinese, three predominantly "Spanish surname," and four mixed— that is, no single racial or nationality group accounted for fifty per cent or more of the enrollment. With its 1968–1969 ESEA funds cut, San Francisco reduced the number of aided schools from twenty-seven to nine. Of the nine, six were predominantly Negro and three Spanish surname. The reduction caused protests.

"We got calls from everybody," said Victor Rossi, coordinator for compensatory education. "They all said they needed help. I had to tell them that although they're eligible, they couldn't have it because of the shortage of funds."

The other side of the coin is that in San Francisco, as in other cities, you find white schools that need help but don't know it or won't admit it. The Ulloa School is one. It serves San Francisco's Sunset section near the Bay. Lower-middle- and middle-class families live there in stucco row houses, which, because of the city's skyrocketing real-estate values, cost upwards of $25,000. Ulloa is 76 per cent white; its only Negro pupils are bussed in. On Stanford-Binet reading tests, Ulloa's midpoint ranks in the bottom 15 per cent nationally.

"When the test scores were published, to cover our embarrassment, we said our poor showing was due to the bussed-in children," said Mrs. Leona Lee, 1968 president of the Ulloa P.T.A. "But it wasn't. Their scores were published separately. We face the same problems as other areas and we need compensatory education just as badly as they do, but our people won't admit it. We've been fooling ourselves too long."

Ulloa parents spurn extra help because they consider themselves superior to Negroes. And this false pride, this prejudice, is not restricted to whites in the Sunset section. "Chinatown," said Mrs. Lee, who grew up there, "is one of the most prejudiced areas of San Francisco. Chinatown looks down on the Negro people. I can remember how my father used to say, 'Don't associate with this or that Negro.' "

Of course, this kind of thinking cuts both ways. A month later, I heard Robert B. Core, community coordinator for Opportunities Industrialization Center in New York and a Negro, report to a conference on ethnic America: "My parents in Pittsburgh told me not to kiss little Italian girls because they taste like garlic. Well, I checked—and it's not true."

After my visits to the Whitetowns of American big cities, I paid a call on Harold Howe II in his Washington office. It was a hot day in August 1968. The United States Education Commissioner's tie was loose and his half-smoked cigar was unlit. His feet were up on a coffee table, where they remained as we talked.*

About the school concerns of Whitetown, U.S.A., Howe professed to be stumped. "It's a hell of a perplexing thing," he said, "using Federal dollars to bring about social change. This process is bound to cause abrasions. We're living in a very abrasive time and I see no likelihood of a letup."

Howe said there was no question but that the working white American identified by Robert Wood needed help. "But if you have to make a hard choice in deciding who will get Federal education aid," he added, "you're forced back to the zero-to-three-thousand-dollars-level group."

Under Title I of ESEA, the biggest and most comprehensive Federal school-assistance program ever devised, about nine million students in 16,400 school districts have been served. Howe's office had no racial breakdown. He thought that, including all programs in suburban and rural as well as urban areas, more white than nonwhite children were aided but that the proportion of black children served was much higher.

"In any program," Howe said, "you have the problem of the cutting point. It's pretty clear to us that if you disperse funds among a very large number of youngsters, much of the money will just be frittered away without doing much good. We have pressed for concentration. Without much success, I might add. The natural tendency is to give everybody a little, and that's what the school districts have done."

* Howe resigned as Education Commissioner on Dec. 31, 1968.

Commissioner Howe favored reducing sharply the number of children served so that more money could be spent—a critical mass, he called it—on fewer pupils. In 1968–1969, the districts averaged $110 per pupil in Title I programs. Howe wanted this raised to maybe $250 per pupil, with no increase in Washington's outlay. "We want to move from our present position of serving nine million children under Title I to a point where we will be serving only six or seven million," he said. "We will deny help to some youngsters but more will get solutions to their problems. The trouble is that at present Title I's billion dollars are spread too thin."

In Howe's view, working-class whites were "really hurting, particularly in terms of expectation. What they tend to do," he said, repeating a point I had heard in several cities, "is deny themselves necessities in order to respond to what they see in magazines and on television. There's an element of tragedy about this."

Black people, said Howe, have historically been denied mobility in American society. The doors now are opening, but Howe did not fear "overcompensation." He considered it inevitable and probably necessary that city school systems should favor black administrators over white ones of comparable training and experience. "Since central-city school systems are full of black children," he said, "there is some sort of vague rationality in having black administrations. If in doing that you awaken feelings of resentment among those who haven't been able to use the mobility always available to whites, I guess what you have to say is, 'That's too bad.'

"That's where the element of tragedy comes in. I don't know what you can do about it."

Reflecting later on what Howe had said and what I had seen and heard in the big-city school systems, I concluded that the failures of urban education—and suburban and rural education, too—can't be blamed on money alone. Perhaps they can't be blamed on money at all. Lack of money didn't cause the basic problem today and a surfeit of funds won't solve it. It's much more complex and more difficult to deal with. Historically, the job of the schools has been to transmit the American culture as a coherent and credible system of values and ideas from generation to generation. As long as the national life style, with all its imperfections, proved generally acceptable to most Americans the schools seemed to do an adequate transmission job.

But what we appear to be witnessing now is a mass rejection of this culture by Americans of all ages. The schools, and especially the colleges, are thus caught in a bind. They can no longer be mere transmission belts because the things they've been transmitting are now widely discredited as shoddy and second-rate. They must therefore seek to improve the culture by reforming the society. Hence their role as social-change agents. But in seeking to perform this function, the schools have managed to alienate everybody. Those favoring social change are convinced the schools, as currently constituted, are doomed to failure if, in fact, they ever really make the effort. These critics point to self-serving educational bureaucrats of narrow vision and social and racial biases—I saw many who fit this general description—as Exhibit A. Such limited people, they say, simply could not effect social change even if they wanted to. And there's some doubt that they want to.

Yet the schools are also distrusted by those opposed to change. They see school reformers seeking, however clumsily, to effect change. And they don't like it. These are the Whitetowners. They are ubiquitous and their number is legion.

Kensington
Against the World

DECEMBER MORNING IN PHILADELPHIA'S WHITETOWN:
A pale winter sun shines wanly on rows of drab houses, almost all alike. The houses are soot-gray, as are the nearby stores, factories, bars and churches. Even at this early hour, the section looks tired.

In the houses, men get ready for work. Millhands, mechanics, machinists. Longshoremen, teamsters, policemen. Office workers, teachers, beauticians. Bartenders sleep on. (In this section, one taproom for every 472 people.) In other households, no one up. Families living off public assistance ("On the welfare," they call it). Many idle youths who later will be "bumming" school, hanging on the corner, making trouble.

Down the street, children form lines to enter the Neighborhood Elementary School. A classic turn-of-the-century fortress: three dingy stories of stone with five-foot iron fence on three sides. Obscenities scrawled on walls. Half a dozen classroom windows broken. Custodian stokes coal furnace, but in top-floor rooms the temperature reads fifty-one.

Teachers lead pupils inside. Wooden floors creak underfoot. All classrooms jammed. No auditorium. No lunchroom. Makeshift gymnasium in basement. Also in the cellar: the only toilets for 950 pupils. The stench is strong. It rises.

Wearing coats against the chill, teachers start teaching. Many frustrations. In reading and arithmetic, this school is one full year behind national norms. In a fourth-grade class, all thirty-seven boys and girls struggle with first-grade readers. In one sixth-grade class, half a dozen stumble over the primer.

As the morning wears on, pupils misbehave. From two rooms, shrieks of *"Shut up!"* Five boys to the principal's bench. Two sent home. Counseling teacher leaves building to fetch ten-year-old truant. His house is only a few doors away. It's a mess—paint splashed on walls, furniture chopped up, TV set wrecked. The boy's mother is pale, distraught. Her older son was recently sent away for residential psychiatric care. Last night the younger boy, missing his brother, went on a rampage in the house. Now the mother doesn't know what to do. Cowering in the tiny backyard is her son the truant. He seems terrified of the adult world, of authority, of his own mother. He's a misfit at home and in school, a loser in life at a very young age.

This is the start of a more-or-less typical school day in Philadelphia's Kensington section, a factory district two miles northeast of City Hall. Kensington is a community in crisis. In many ways it looks, thinks, and acts like so many of the Negro ghettos festering in American cities. Its educational, political, social, and economic problems are almost as great as those found in the black slums. It, too, has failed to solve these problems, and failure has made it sullen, surly and suspicious.

Like Harlem and Watts, Kensington is filled with bitterness, but this is a case of white rage. Kensington is 99.7 per cent Caucasian. It is home for a hundred thousand proud, irascible, tough, narrow-minded, down-to-earth, old-fashioned, hostile, flag-waving, family-oriented ethnic Americans. There you find living, often in nationality enclaves, the first-, second-, and third-generation descendants of Irish, Polish, Ukrainian, Italian, Hungarian, German, even Scottish and English immigrants. Kensington's adults average 8.6 years of schooling. Fewer than four in a hundred are college-educated. Kensington's population is falling and its people are aging. But it remains Philadelphia's last large stronghold of the low-income white man. There are other, smaller pockets of resistance, yet in this city of two million most of the low-income areas are either integrated or overwhelmingly black. Not all of Kensington's hundred thousand people are poor. Indeed, many live comfortably in neat, well-furnished, mortgage-free houses. These are the proud, solid Kensingtonians who spurn the mounting debts and rootlessness of suburban life. They like the place just as it is.

Many other Kensington families, though, live in poverty. There are more poor whites in Kensington than anywhere else in Philadelphia. And the 1960 census found twice as many poor white families as poor nonwhite families in Greater Philadelphia. The total was 97,000 white families with incomes under $3,000, against 45,000 nonwhite families.

Kensington's air is polluted, its streets and sidewalks are filthy, its juvenile crime rate is rising, its industry is languishing. No more than a handful of new houses have been built there in the last third of a century. Its schools are among the oldest in the city. Its playgrounds—the few that it has—are overrun with young toughs. Industry is moving out. Social workers and clergymen often give up in despair. (A Protestant minister has written of his five years in Kensington: "There is nothing here that I wouldn't like better someplace else.")

Yet nothing much is being done to get the old mill district back on its feet. Federally financed urban-renewal programs and the Model Cities project stop just short of Kensington. In a 1967 study, Dr. Murray Friedman of the American Jewish Committee found that the city's own capital building program for 1966–1971 included no new parks, playgrounds, swimming pools, libraries, or health centers for Kensington. It desperately needs all of these facilities. Friedman suggested that neglect of Kensington and other white, urban ethnic communities was "as much of a national scandal as similar failures in Negro ghetto areas." He thought, though, that Kensingtonians themselves had to bear some of the responsibility for this neglect. "They harbor an Old-World or ethnic suspicion of authority," he said, "and hesitate to bring government into their lives."

Kensington's physical decline has been accompanied by an erosion of spirit. When Peter H. Rossi, the sociologist, surveyed the district in 1950 for his book *Why People Move,* he was both appalled by living conditions there and astonished by the Kensingtonians' remarkable sanguinity. He discovered that nearly everybody living in Kensington at that time liked Kensington. Indeed, among residents of four Philadelphia neighborhoods studied by Rossi and his staff, Kensingtonians had the fewest complaints about their own section, although Rossi's objective measurements ranked Kensington third in the list of four as regards actual living conditions. "The objectionable features of land-crowding, heavy industrial noise and air pollution," Rossi wrote of Kensington, "count little to the inhabitants of this area."

In 1968, when I asked the parents of children at a Kensington public school what they thought about the place, their replies differed sharply from those reported by Rossi eighteen years before. Most thought Kensington was going downhill:

"This is nothing but a dump. It's dirty and a slum area."

"I come from a foreign country and I have never seen such destructiveness and dirt as in this neighborhood. I do not expect my children to live in Kensington. I hope for better times and I will move out."

"All the homes that are being torn down in center city are pushing the white trash up this way. They are the people who don't know what a broom is for, or what soap and water is for."

"Kensington is going downhill fast and nobody seems to care. The teen-age children are wild and unmanageable."

The Kensingtonians made no bones, either, about why they thought their neighborhood was on the skids.

"The trouble is with crooked politicians who are after the vote—any vote. They promise anything just for the vote. It is this search for position and power more than anything else that is ruining our city and our country."

"The city and state government and the board of education spend too much time and taxpayers' money attempting to appease a minor class of people in our city while our community and others like us practically are forgotten."

"The city builds playgrounds and other recreation places in North Philadelphia and South Philadelphia because they think this will keep the Negroes happy. Well, they should do something for Kensington too. Maybe if the people of Kensington would riot they would get what they wanted. But they're more sensible and don't act like a bunch of animals. So they just have to wait and hope that they get what they ask for."

"We are lost and forgotten here in Kensington. God only help us now."

While Kensington's plight is similar to that of many other Whitetowns, it is, in certain ways, different from all the rest. Kensington is in a class by itself simply because Philadelphia —for better or worse—is in a class by itself.

Brilliant city government between 1952 and 1962 helped Philadelphia shed its old corrupt-and-contented label, but it remains, I'm afraid, a laughingstock nationally, the butt of countless warmed-over jokes relating to its stodginess and stuffiness. The fact is Philadelphia *is* rather stodgy. It *is* square. It thinks small. A zinging, hustling, fast-buck boomtown it is not. And it never has been. Its citizens are anything but flamboyant. Its mayor, James Tate, lives quietly in a row house in a working-class white section uptown, and its reputed Mafia boss, Angelo Bruno, lives quietly in a row house in a working-class white section downtown. Philadelphia lacks Boston's brains, New York's bounce, Chicago's brass, and San Francisco's press agent. But it has other, less-obvious assets. On being transferred to Philadelphia from other cities, business executives shudder at the prospect and then, often, find themselves gradually won over by its surprising beauty and charm, its stability, its sense of history, its diversified economy, and its livable pace. Many of us who love Philadelphia would agree with Louis I. Kahn, its internationally acclaimed architect, that the City of Brotherly Love still has "a character of personality, not impersonality."

Christopher Morley's Kitty Foyle spoke of Philadelphia as a "grand homey old town," and even in a time of racial tumult and unrest there is some truth to this characteriza-

tion. Philadelphia is America's fourth largest city and its
129.7 square miles lie deep in the heart of Megalopolis, the
huge supercity stretching from above Boston to below
Washington. Outside of its central business district, however,
Philadelphia seems less like a city than a vast collection of
neighborhoods. It is these neighborhoods with their thousands of single houses and hundreds of churches that have
helped to give Philadelphia its sobriquet, "the world's
largest small town."

There are neighborhoods in Philadelphia for every taste
and pocketbook. Places like Manayunk and Southwark,
Germantown and Nicetown, Tacony and Torresdale,
Frankford (Kitty Foyle's home) and Fox Chase, East Falls
(where Princess Grace of Monaco grew up) and West
Oak Lane, posh Chestnut Hill and racially integrated
Mount Airy. And Kensington, the legendary factory area
where white makes right.

Kensington dates its founding from 1730, when an English
sea captain and merchant named Anthony Palmer bought a
hundred ninety acres along the Delaware River two miles
northeast of Philadelphia's present City Hall, laid out
streets, sold lots, opened a burial ground, and named his
settlement after the fashionable Kensington section of London. Palmer's development became a riverfront fishing village, and Charles Dickens, who visited Philadelphia in
1842, is supposed to have dubbed it Fishtown. At any rate,
that is what a small, tightly knit section in lower Kensington
has been called for generations. And despite the inevitable
newly constructed expressway that has now cut it off from
the river, Fishtown survives today as a quaint urban hamlet
of narrow, twisting streets, neighborhood groceries, corner
bars, and row houses occupied by men and women who

consider themselves the old, original Kensingtonians and who yield to no one in their pride in their community or in their determination to keep it white. (In the summer of 1960 Fishtowners successively routed from houses or apartments two Negro families, two Puerto Rican families, one dark-skinned Portuguese family, and a Cherokee Indian from North Carolina. In the fall of 1966 they joined in five days of rioting against a Negro family that moved into a near-by Kensington section.)

The larger area that now calls itself Kensington generally shares Fishtown's racial antipathies, its fierce loyalties and fear of change. But this more comprehensive section is impossible to pinpoint exactly on a map. Kensington is more a state of mind than a geographic entity; its boundaries shift as housing patterns shift.* Pride and pugnacity—these are marks of Fishtown, of Kensington, and of Whitetowns generally. It was ever thus. From the beginning Kensington seems to have been home for combative working people. The upper classes always spurned the place. As they made money, most gentry moved to Frankford or Torresdale or some swankier section. But the little man stayed.

Even the earliest Kensingtonians seem to have been crotchety craftsmen with a penchant for insulting outsiders. As far back as 1770 a Kensington linen-printing firm was pledging that its blue-and-white handkerchiefs would be "as durable in washing and color as any imported from Europe," and certainly the equal of those made by the "boasted Britons." Actually, the first Kensingtonians were themselves British—thrifty, industrious workers who kept their small houses spotless and raised their children to be patriotic and

* This is often true of Whitetowns. The *New York Times,* in describing racial and ethnic changes in Flatbush, an old Jewish section of Brooklyn, asked a community leader to define its borders and got this answer: "If you want to know the truth, today when people say 'Flatbush' they mean the place where the Negroes aren't." Kensington likewise.

God-fearing, as well as, one suspects, xenophobic and bigoted.

For a few years after the Revolution Philadelphia was the United States capital, and for many years it was the new nation's largest and most important city. Kensington, though not a part of the city proper, became a bustling district. A census of buildings in 1810 showed 869 in Kensington. Fishtowners caught fish and built boats, while in the rest of Kensington weaving was the principal occupation. A Kensingtonian named William B. Mayer, who later became a Philadelphia court administrator, was a boy of five in 1821, when there were smokehouses near the river. "The men caught great numbers of herring and the women pickled and smoked them," * Mayer reminisced seventy years later. "Even to this day the place is known as Fishtown, but I tell you they were a steady and reliable lot, and what great sailors the men were. . . . I feel like taking off my hat whenever I mention the name. Do you know I believe Washington had the Kensington men in mind when he said: 'Put none but Americans on guard tonight.' The men up there helped win our great naval victories in 1812. They are— and always were—so staunch in their Americanism. The women, too, were steadfast and true, and took to the water as readily as the men. Philadelphia has reasons to be proud of the district of Kensington."

However, Kensington in this period was also a hotbed of religious intolerance and rowdyism. As there were no mills in those early years, the English weavers hired Irish immigrants to work on hand looms in their homes. The weavers were Protestants, the immigrants Catholics. Feelings ran high—so high, in fact, that the anti-Catholic Native American Party flourished in the soil of Kensington. The result

* *Kensington, A City Within a City* (Philadelphia: Keighton Printing House, 1891).

was that East Kensington became nativist and West Kensington Catholic. "Against the Roman Catholics," one Philadelphia historian has written, "there was general prejudice born of old struggles in Europe. Their religion as well as their nationality made them objects of hatred to many of their neighbors." "The Jews," wrote another chronicler of the period, "were not nearly so unwelcome an ingredient in the population as the Catholics."

In 1820 Kensington broke off from the Northern Liberties district, of which it had been a part, and became a separate and distinct municipality, albeit a badly fragmented one. Despite William Mayer's assurances, these were trying times in Kensington. Violence erupted regularly at local elections. Much of the trouble was spawned by the volunteer fire companies, which were fiercely competitive and influential and seemed to attract the worst elements. The fire fighters, said one historian, were nothing more than "bands of ruffians who found in organizations of this kind license for the gravest misbehavior." There were riots, murders, ceaseless rivalries. "Pistols, knives, iron spanners, and slingshots were freely used. The volunteer 'Jakey,' coarse, swaggering, drunken, became a type of the town."

In 1828 a tavern brawl over a disparaging remark about "bloody Irish transports"—i.e., immigrant weavers—set off several days of rioting in Kensington between Irish and anti-Irish factions. In 1843 four companies of militiamen were summoned to restore order following fighting between striking and nonstriking weavers. Those who kept working were assaulted by the strikers. Houses were entered, warps cut, looms destroyed. Then in May and July of the following year the Bible-reading riots spilled blood on streets all over Kensington. Although school-board records show that Catholic Bishop Francis Kenrick simply sought fair play in Bible reading and an end to the overwhelmingly Protestant bias in most school religious exercises, Know Nothings packed the grand jury that was impaneled to investigate the trouble. Its subsequent presentment blamed the riots on "the efforts of a portion of the community to exclude the Bible from the public schools." The grand jury said that when "a new party" (the Know Nothings) met in Kensington their sessions were "rudely disturbed and fired upon by a band of lawless, irresponsible men, *some of whom had resided in the country only for a short period.*" After showing its nativist colors, the grand jury report declared: "This outrage, causing the death of a number of our unoffending citizens . . . was followed up by subsequent acts of aggression, in violation and open defiance of all law." [Emphasis added]

Despite the hostility in this period, the Irish kept coming. From 1839 to 1855 an estimated seventy-five thousand Irish immigrants poured into Philadelphia. Fleeing famine back home and traveling in the steerage of overloaded lumber ships, many took housing in such areas as Kensington's old Seventeenth Ward—housing almost as abject and miserable as what they had left. The Philadelphia Board of Health blamed the high death rate from smallpox, tuberculosis, and other diseases on "the manner in which they [the immigrants] live in crowded apartments, in narrow streets, blind courts, alleys amid dampness and filth."

While the Irish were having their problems with nativists in Kensington, the Negroes were having their problems with Irish downtown. In 1830 there were only 15,624 Negro freedmen and slaves in Philadelphia's population of 204,585, but antiblack bigotry often led to violence. Race riots began in 1829 and continued spasmodically until 1840. "There is probably no city in the known world," wrote a visitor to Philadelphia in 1842, "where dislike amounting to hatred of the coloured population prevails more than in the city of brotherly love."

Following disorders in South Philadelphia in August

1834, in which whites wrecked a Negro church and at least twenty houses occupied by Negroes and killed at least one Negro man, there was convened what may have been the first officially appointed riot commission in the United States. It consisted of fifteen citizens of the city of Philadelphia and adjoining districts, including one man from Kensington. Its job was "to inquire into the origin and progress of the late riots in Philadelphia, and the means taken to suppress them."

The rioting had raged for three nights. Of eighteen white men arrested, fourteen had recognizably Irish names—John M'Laughlin, Mich. Cavenah, Hugh M'Intyre, etc.

In its report in September 1834, the commission termed it an undisputed fact that "the object of the most active among the rioters was a destruction of the property and injury to the persons of the colored people, with intent, as it would seem, to induce, or compel them to remove from this district."

Of the second night's disorders, the committee said, ". . . the mob did much injury to property, breaking into houses, destroying the furniture, and greatly abusing and beating the inmates, all colored people, many of whom, after having labored hard through the day, had retired to rest, without a thought that their dwellings would be invaded, and their lives endangered by the inhumanity of persons to whom they were strangers. We record such facts with deep regret, but trust that their record will act as a warning, and deter other persons from being seduced into a participation in such an outrage."

In view of the Chicago "police riot" of August 1968 and criticism of alleged police overreaction in other cities in recent years, the 1834 riot commission's comments on the performance of citizen posses and volunteer corps called out to help quell the Philadelphia disturbances is worth noting. The commission said that virtual hundred per cent attendance of those summoned "affords gratifying evidence of the general determination of our citizens that the laws should be respected and the public peace preserved."

"If any additional evidence was required," continued the report, "it is to be found in the obedience, discipline and good order which was at all times preserved whenever the citizens were called out, wherever they were directed to go, and whatever they were ordered to do, by those under whom they were organized. It is due to these citizens and to the volunteers, horse and foot, who were out during the riots, to remark that, notwithstanding their determination at all times to do their duty they were in no instance guilty of a wanton exercise, but were as forbearing as they were resolute."

As analyzed by the commission, the riot's cause too had a contemporary ring. "An opinion prevails, especially among white laborers," said the panel, "that certain portions of our community prefer to employ colored people, whenever they can be had, to the employing of white people; and that, in consequence of this preference, many whites, who are willing and able to work, are left without employment, while colored people are provided with work, and enabled comfortably to maintain their families; and thus many white laborers, anxious for employment, are kept idle and indigent." In other words, Philadelphia Negroes over a hundred and thirty-five years ago were thought to be taking jobs from white workers, many of whom were no doubt immigrants.

One of the results of the urban unrest was a demand for law and order. The State Legislature in 1845 required the city and surrounding districts to establish and maintain police forces with a ratio of at least one policeman for every one hundred fifty taxable residents. Another demand was for more coordination between city and suburbs in law enforcement. Under conditions then existing, one authority stopped where another began and when rioters crossed boundary lines it was difficult to prosecute them or halt their depredations. The obvious step was to create one big municipality, and in 1854, after years of debate, this was done. The Consolidation Act of 1854 brought Kensington, Northern Liberties, Southwark, Spring Garden, and other outlying districts into the city and gave Philadelphia its present boundaries.*

While all these events were taking place and despite the turmoil in its own backyard, Kensington was growing. Carpet manufacture started there in 1830, and thirty years later Kensington could claim 124 carpet makers with 2,500 employees. The first American textile mill opened in Kensington, and for some time this district enjoyed a monopoly in the tapestry trade—ten million dollars a year. It was home for the world's largest lace factory and the world's largest hat factory. Kensington built ships, caught fish, and loaded coal for export at the world's largest coal piers. To assist home purchasers in Kensington the first building-and-loan association in the United States was established there, and the Salvation Army in 1880 picked Kensington as site for its first American headquarters. By this time, Kensington housewives had established the custom of scrubbing their front steps early every morning. The place was widely recognized as the "stronghold of the respectable workingman and his family," a community that looked after its own.

Small wonder, then, that an anonymous Chamber-of-

* Dennis Clark argues that this expansion, besides strengthening Philadelphia's police force in dealing with immigrants, also added non-Catholic sections to the city proper, thus helping to forestall a Catholic political takeover for more than a century.

Commerce-type tub-thumper took a look at Kensington in 1891 and liked what he saw. "A City within a City," he wrote of Kensington in the book of that name, "nestling upon the bosom of the placid Delaware. Filled to the brim with enterprise, dotted with factories so numerous that the rising smoke obscures the sky, the hum of industry is heard in every corner of its broad expanse. A happy and contented people, enjoying plenty in a land of plenty. Populated by brave men, fair women and a hardy generation of young blood that will take the reins when the fathers have passed away. All hail, Kensington! A credit to the Continent—a crowning glory to the City."

This is the kind of pride Kensington engendered in its people. Though true-blue Kensingtonians would never invoke such phony imagery, they would approve of the general sentiments expressed. The place must have had something. True, just as the Irish had to claw and bully their way into Kensington, so did all succeeding white ethnic groups. But little by little the Poles, the Italians, the Ukrainians managed to carve out their own neighborhoods. There was even a tiny "Jewtown" occupied by merchants from Kensington's bustling business district. (The name has stuck and two long-abandoned synagogues are still standing but Jewtown is now Kensington's only Negro section.)

Despite its rich diversity of cultures, however, Kensington did not become a true melting pot. Its nationality groups kept to themselves, closing out the rest of the world and the rest of Kensington. Each had its own siege mentality. Even within the enclaves there was parochialism. On your own block you knew everybody; in fact, you might all be related. But the people two "squares," as Philadelphians call blocks, distant were total strangers. And all strangers were feared and detested.

On Kensington's Waterloo Street the neighbors waged a

"battle" almost every Saturday night. Throughout the district there was too much drinking, too much venereal disease and tuberculosis, too much illegitimacy and juvenile delinquency, too many dirty streets and smelly factories.* But none of this overly dismayed the Kensingtonians. Even with its divisions and discriminations, its alarums and excursions, its pettiness and prickliness, they loved the place. And there was a kind of muscular and earthy ethnic style to Kensington, a sense of sharing common joys. The soccer games at Lighthouse Field—Philadelphia's best soccer players have always come from Kensington. Boxing bouts at the raucous, smoke-filled Cambria A.C. The soft pretzels— under the El at K&A (Kensington and Allegheny avenues, the principal business section), you could buy this Philadelphia delicacy for a penny or two while placing a numbers bet with the pretzel vendor.

What Norman Mailer, writing in *Harper's* about the 1968 Democratic Convention in Chicago, said of Chicagoans would apply, I think, to working-class Philadelphians of maybe fifteen or twenty years ago, before the great sadness set in:

> . . . they were simple, strong, warm-spirited, sly, rough, compassionate, jostling, tricky and extraordinarily good-natured because they had sex in their pockets, muscles on their backs, hot eats around the corner, neighborhoods which dripped with the sauce of local legend, and real city architecture . . . vistas for miles of red-brick and two-family wood-frame houses with balconies and porches, runted stunted trees rich as farmland in their promise of tenderness the first city evenings of spring, streets where kids played stickball and roller-hockey, lots of smoke and iron twilight. The clangor of

* As recently as 1962, a Temple University study of Philadelphia sections found Kensington second in venereal disease and tuberculosis and first in juvenile delinquency.

the late Nineteenth Century, the very hope of greed, was in these streets. London one hundred years ago could not have looked much better.

What's more, until the Great Depression, Kensington continued to enjoy growth and relative economic well-being. In 1920 this factory district was said to lead entire United States cities in the value of its felt hats, carpets, rugs, tapestry, hosiery, and knit goods. In 1922 the opening of the fifteen-million-dollar Frankford Elevated Line sparked further business and commercial activity. The El linked Kensington to downtown Philadelphia and West Philadelphia and thence to suburban Delaware County.

Of course, the thirties brought chaos to Kensington as it did to virtually all industrial sections. Banks closed, factories folded, jobless men walked the streets and soup kitchens opened. (There's still a soup kitchen in Fishtown.) Strikes were frequent.* Kensington's "happy and contented people" faced hard times. Over the entire area hung a pall of despair as thick as factory smoke. Visiting Kensington in January 1933, a *Philadelphia Bulletin* reporter wrote: "Here are darkened mills, here are shivering people crying for clothes and shoes those mills could give. But no money."

Four bitter years later conditions were not noticeably better. A Federal Writers Project, reporting on Kensington in 1937, found little to cheer about:

> The massive factory here dwarfs the rows of workers' homes, which are tiny, in need of repair and unrelieved by any sign of vegetation. Most of them were built during the industrial boom in the early 1900's, but construction im-

---

* Kensington's turbulent labor history has helped shape the anti-Negro views of its unionists. They built labor organizations that extracted better pay and working conditions while Negro workers were often exploited as strikebreakers. The whites remember this.

provements during recent years have left their dreariness unaltered.

Although the Kensington population has remained virtually the same in its makeup for decades, there has been considerable migration out of the area by families whose incomes are now derived from employment in the landscaped "new technology" plants in the Greater Northeast and the suburbs.

Just when Kensington seemed to be going down for the count, World War II came along. Kensington revived. Its shipyard expanded enormously. Its factories worked overtime. Its biggest and most famous firm, the Stetson Hat Company, employed almost five thousand men and women and maintained a hospital for them. Kensington's restaurants and taprooms were thronged with free spenders. High-school dropouts—Kensington has always had more than its share of them—got jobs in the mills at twice the pay of schoolteachers. And thousands of young men left Kensington as soldiers, sailors, and airmen. For just as Kensingtonians, in William B. Mayer's words, helped win the War of 1812, so have they pitched in, with unshirted enthusiasm, in every succeeding war. War is something the Kensingtonians understand, and while it might be wrong to say that they enjoy fighting, it would be correct to say that they inevitably acquit themselves with distinction, be it a neighborhood brawl or a world conflict.

It seems clear now, though, that the seeds of Kensington's destruction were sown in the war it supported so spiritedly. Military service widened the horizons of young Kensingtonians. So incredibly parochial was Kensington that before the war many residents had never taken the ten-minute subway ride downtown. A socio-economic psychotherapy study of Kensington by Harry Slutsky of Temple University's medical center reported only seven years ago: "The principal of Welsh School at Fourth and Dauphin Streets [on Kensington's western boundary] stated that the first thing she did when she assumed the principalship was to organize a mother's group to take them on a visit to Center City. They had never been there before." As World War II fighting men, though, a whole generation of Kensingtonians found a new world beyond K&A. In this country and abroad they saw sights they'd never seen and dreamed new dreams. After the war their "home town" never looked quite so good again.

Following the war, too, with the GI Bill of Rights paying college fees for veterans, young Kensingtonians became commuters to Temple and Villanova, LaSalle and St. Joseph's colleges. It was the first time that college doors had opened wide for substantial numbers of young people in Kensington. Previously, almost all Kensingtonians started work in their teens, many quitting high school to take jobs either because of economic need or because they wanted pocket money to buy cars, clothes, and other goods providing instant gratification. (According to Freud, maturity is the postponement of self-gratification, but you don't find much of this in Kensington.) Their subsequent exposure to academic life forced many Kensingtonians to look at their mill district through new eyes. They decided it had few charms for college-educated men.

In addition, Kensington's "war brides" had ideas of their own. In Kensington a "war bride" was a girl from anywhere outside Kensington, be it Sydney, Australia, or South Philadelphia. Before getting married, most of these newlyweds had never seen Kensington. What they saw displeased them. Many soon convinced their husbands that Kensington, with its soot, its trucks, its noise, its lack of green space, recreation facilities, and good schools, was no place to raise children.

And so the exodus, which started in the thirties, accelerated. Soon it became a headlong flight. Not that Kensington was unique. From almost every American city after World War II white families moved to the suburbs. The reasons are well known: mass-produced, relatively cheap suburban housing (lower Bucks County's 17,311-house Levittown opened in 1952 just fifteen miles from Kensington with prices within the range of the average truck driver); easy credit (the Federal Housing Administration readily guaranteed mortgages in the all-white suburbs while refusing them in black and integrated city neighborhoods); cars for everybody and more and better highways to drive them on; the American itch to move up the ladder even at the cost of abandoning old friends, old haunts; the new affluence putting this "good life" within reach of working-class white people (as long as they didn't mind being saddled with twenty-five-year mortgages), and, most significantly, the white city dweller's fear of being inundated by Negroes.

Of course, many Kensingtonians stayed put. The older ones, pensioners and widows, couldn't afford to move. Others stayed because, despite everything, they still loved Kensington and were loyal to it. And some, after moving to the suburbs, couldn't adjust to life there and so returned to Kensington. Still, the out-migration was steady. And, of course, whites occupying the Kensington houses vacated by those seeking greener pastures were generally poorer and less stable; often they were refugees from racially changing districts downtown.

Kensington's decline was gradual and newspaper Sunday supplements continued to refer to its "respectable workingmen" and its "quiet dignity." For a long time, the people themselves refused to admit that anything was wrong or that their old factory district was out of step in the shiny new age of cybernetics. "Kensington has been on the downgrade for sixty years," old-timers would scoff, "but it hasn't fallen yet." When Peter Rossi made his survey in 1950 he encountered this slightly wonderful-if-wacky Kensington-against-the-world attitude which has prevailed there down through the generations.

"This district," Rossi wrote of Kensington, ". . . is a residential peninsula surrounded on the north, south and east by large industrial establishments. On the east a freight rail line runs its heavy cars on tracks in the middle of a wide avenue. On the west, another freight line runs in a cut. . . . Its structures crowd the narrow streets and are built side by side in the monotonous row pattern. There are few open spaces in the area and . . . the narrow streets restrict escape from the street noises. . . . The freight trains rumbling by on southern and eastern borders contribute to the noise as do the factories in the area itself and on its other borders. Smoke from nearby heavy industries leaves a gritty film on the visitor's car and, when the wind is favorable, factory odors pollute the air."

On the other hand, Rossi found that Kensington's two-story, five-room brick row houses were "neat in appearance, newly painted and in good repair," with "colorful awnings" to protect their front windows from the summer sun. Sixty-two per cent of Kensington's households, reported Rossi, had no complaints about its physical aspects, sixty-four per cent had no complaints about the size of their small houses, and fifty-nine per cent considered the community "extremely friendly." Only three per cent had attended college, seventy-five per cent held blue-collar jobs, and family incomes averaged $3,197 a year, but seventy-six per cent owned their houses, only fourteen per cent were newcomers to Kensington within the previous two years, and fewer then half wanted to move.

All in all, the picture Rossi drew was of a hard-bitten

working-class community that was managing to hold together despite overwhelming odds. That was 1950. Two decades later Kensington seems to be falling apart. Its population declined alarmingly—from 155,347 in 1920 to 98,598 in 1960. And the slippage continued in the decade of the 1960s.

Despite the tremendous increase in college-going nationally, Kensingtonians continue to spurn higher education. Of 20,901 Lower Kensington and Fishtown adults over twenty-five who were reached in the 1960 census, only 2.6 per cent had attended college for as long as a year and only 1.3 per cent completed four years. By contrast, 7.9 per cent had no more than four years of school and 56.9 per cent dropped out before ninth grade. In this census tract, the median of school years completed was 8.6, one full year under the Philadelphia mean and almost two years behind the metropolitan Philadelphia (including the city and four suburban counties) mean of 10.5 years.

Twenty per cent of the Fishtown–Lower Kensington houses were reported as substandard. The median value of the houses was $5,800, but only one per cent was said to be worth over $10,000. Meanwhile, Kensington's churches were in deep trouble. Protestant church membership there declined an average of twenty-four per cent between 1950 and 1960. In Episcopal churches alone membership fell off from over 4,700 in 1945 to under 1,100 in 1965. Many churches either shut down or were merged. Few of those that were left could survive without subsidies from central church funds.

For Kensingtonians the one statistic in the census data which they could point to with pride was the one relating to racial composition of the population. Lower Kensington–Fishtown was 99.7 per cent white; in a population of 36,358 there were said to be twenty-six Negroes and sixty-eight "other races." About 25 per cent were foreign stock, most from Poland, the United Kingdom, Germany and Ireland.

In recent years, Kensington has managed to hold the line racially, but in other categories it has often lost ground. While many houses continue to be well kept, increasing numbers are deteriorating; and although many blue-collar workers make good money, poverty in Kensington is growing. Old people, especially, are barely able to survive. As in other sections, crime is rising. A Fishtown school-community group, seeking to awaken the neighborhood to the "deplorable conditions" there, reported: "Schools have been vandalized and defaced. It is not safe to walk the streets even on necessary errands, whether night or day. Hoodlums roam the neighborhood to incite racial incidents and damage businesses and homes. The [city's] curfew is a joke."

To its credit Fishtown, in 1969, finally managed to organize itself with some effectiveness. More than twenty groups joined together and got from the City Council a promise to build a recreation center there. Meanwhile at Fishtown's junior high a brilliant new principal, Mrs. Marion Steet, made major strides toward reducing tensions inside the school and out.

Yet gains come slowly in Fishtown and in Kensington generally because so many of the people are so fractious. "These people," said a ten-year resident, "are about as friendly as a rattlesnake." Another couple told of moving into Kensington with their mentally retarded daughter. "The Kensington community does not strike out at the colored people alone," the father later reported. "They will strike out against anyone, even parents like us, of a little girl with problems like hers."

Although many observers believe mental illness is a major problem in Kensington today, there are no mental-health facilities in the entire community and no way of reaching the mentally sick. Kensington is a breeding ground for the manufacture and swift dissemination of racist gossip. Indeed, the old mill district is now one vast rumor factory. Nearly every week fabricated stories of shootings, stabbings, murders, or rapes spread through one or more of its neighborhoods. To halt the spread of such inflammatory reports, parents at one Fishtown school opened a Rumor Control Center with a phone number that neighbors could call to check the latest gossip. But the factory kept grinding out rumors. "In one week," said a healthy, physically unmarked, junior-high principal, "I was beaten, shot, knifed, and slugged in my office—according to the baseless stories that circulated in our community."

With Fishtown and Kensington deteriorating, one might think that city planners, social workers, and community organizers would be hard at work there. But such, of course, is not the case.

"The real significance of Fishtown," reported Lyle Yorks, a native Kensingtonian who studied the section in the summer of 1968 as part of his graduate work in psychology at Vanderbilt University, "is the existence of a group of working class whites in trouble who are unrecognized by professionals in the field of urban social problems."

He predicted that nothing would be done to help Fishtown until its decline becomes "blatantly noticeable through the development of a highly visible skid row district or violent racial clashes."

One difficulty is that sociologists, social workers, all who express a wish to help improve Kensington immediately become *personae non gratae*. "What's the matter?" they are asked. "Aren't we good enough for you?" Another, perhaps even greater, difficulty is that many Kensingtonians themselves even now refuse to recognize the existence of problems.

"Kensingtonians," said Charles Morgan, director of the Philadelphia Health and Welfare Council's North-Central Office, "are psychologically unable to face up to their social, cultural, and economic deprivation. Pride prevents them from taking advantage of social services. For them to accept these services might be to admit that they're not all they claim to be."

"Nobody knows how to work in the white community," commented James Oliver, a native Kensingtonian, who directs Temple University's Student Community Action Center and who would like to extend his operations there. "Kensington doesn't want us. It refuses to admit it's a poverty area. It won't go into programs with Negroes. Kensingtonians suspect college kids. The college student's vocabulary is greater. If he wears a beard, he's out. A Jewish accent is suspect, too."

Besides social workers, Kensingtonians are wary of politicians, educators, and preachers. The reason is simple: they suspect all three of wanting to integrate Kensington when all Kensington wants is to be left alone. "I believe that religion is getting too powerful," said a Fishtown carpenter. "Because these ministers are coming out and these priests are coming out, 'Love the colored.' Why, all of a sudden, is that being brought about? They didn't love the colored before. Now, all of a sudden, they're changing their religious principles."

Under this kind of pressure from their parishioners, not many Kensington churchmen—Protestant or Catholic—do say, "Love the colored." Most of them simply ignore the racial crisis and the battle for social justice in the cities. As a result, a Kensington school principal could say of her pupils' parents, "Some of the worst bigots here are Bible-toting, hymn-singing churchgoers and Mass-attenders." And a Fishtown father, a rare liberal in that community, could say of his fellow communicants at the local Presbyterian church, "The ones who sit up front every Sunday are the most biased 'nigger' haters."

The churches thus see themselves as hamstrung. School people also are closely watched. One mother of two daughters told of anxieties in the planned change of principals at her neighborhood grade school. She liked the female incumbent because "she wants to teach the three R's the way we think they should be taught—without any influence from socialistic viewpoints that a lot of the colleges and professors and so forth have. But we don't know who will take her place. You have a lot of administrators who have gone to college with people who are leaning in a direction that we as Americans have never believed in. Now you could get an administrator to come in and start changing the curriculum in such a way that the children would have a slanted idea on democracy, and so on."

Anti-intellectualism has deep roots in Kensington, as, indeed, it has in Philadelphia generally. At the opening of Kensington High School for Girls in 1910, residents who questioned the desirability of such an institution are said to have chanted, "We don't want no high school for girls. Girls is our pearls." Kensington Girls High has survived and its alumnae, including Nora Levin, author of *The Holocaust,* are proud of the place. But the two comprehensive high schools serving Kensington regularly register the highest dropout rates in Philadelphia.

Many Kensingtonians simply do not accept the notion that every qualified student should go to college. One young mother of four, a third-generation Kensingtonian, spoke for herself and her closest friend: "We seen so many that have gone to college and have come out—I don't know what they go to college for, really. It's not to learn. Now I'm not knocking anybody that wants to be a doctor or a lawyer or has something definite in mind. That's an altogether different story. We also know that type. But there are a lot that just go to college, I think, for the say that they went to college. And so they don't have to go to work for a few more years. Of course, I'm not saying college isn't work. I don't mean that. But, but . . . I think also because we didn't go to college, that's why our attitude is more or less it's not necessary."

Beyond that, though, some Kensington parents actively discourage their children from aiming for college even when the youngsters have ability and are eager to go. "When I first brought up the subject of college to my father," said a policeman's daughter, "he looked at me as though I was nuts."

"Really," exclaimed another high-school student, "some parents want their kids to go through high school and that's it. If they're still living with their parents, that's money coming in. That's how I think some parents think. 'Cause there's money coming in for them. 'Cause you're working, making your own money, and then you're living there. You're getting your food there so have to pay room and board."

Because of Kensington's extremely conservative views on education, some teachers pick that section. They prefer working with children whose parents are relatively unschooled themselves—and hence no threat to the teachers—over pressure-packed suburban areas where anxious mothers prod schools to prepare their first-graders for college-entrance examinations. On the other hand, teachers' dress and deportment is probably more closely watched in puritanical Kensington than in most other sections. Of the elementary school attended by her three children, one mother said, "It's fine but I think the teachers should dress a little better. They don't help the children out by wearing go-go ear rings and mini-skirts. Don't get me wrong, if they like dressing like that fine but outside of school not inside. My kids come home and say you should see Miss So-and-So. Boy was her dress short, Mom. That's why the kids start wanting to dress like that so young. They say, 'My teacher dresses like that.' "

In a taped interview, another Kensington housewife voiced the same concern: "The younger girls that are coming out of college to teach now are really too much. Their manner of dress for one thing. I don't think it's fitting. I don't know. . . . Maybe I'm getting old. [She was thirty-five.] The thing is they're wearing clothes that the children think a teen-ager would wear. Therefore, they [the children] don't give the younger teachers the respect that they would give an older teacher. All the [younger] teachers have on their mind is, 'When are we going to get married?' or, 'Let's go in the bathroom and have a smoke.' "

While pensioners, widows, old-maidish schoolteachers, white-collar workers, a few lawyers and other professional men still live in Kensington, its tone is set by blue-collar workers, largely Irish, Italian, and East European, predominantly Roman Catholic, who comprise the bulk of its population. They are the ones who fill its bars and start its anti-Negro riots. In thought, word, and deed, these rough, tough Kensingtonians strikingly resemble another group of Americans who lived far from Philadelphia many years ago. J. W. Cash described these other Americans in his classic study, *The Mind of the South*. They were the "common-white" dirt farmers who lived in the Piedmont in the period between the Civil War and World War I. These rural Southerners, said Cash, were anti-Negro, anti-Red, anti-Jew, anti-Modern, anti-Liberal, Fundamentalist, and vastly Moral. This description also fits the urban Northerners in Philadelphia's Whitetown.

At its best, in Cash's view, the Old South of these com-

mon whites was "proud, brave, honorable by its lights, courteous, personally generous, loyal, swift to act, often too
swift but signally effective, sometimes terrible in its action."
And at its worst, he said, the Old South espoused "violence,
intolerance, aversion and suspicion toward new ideas, an in-
capacity for analysis, an inclination to act from feelings
rather than from thought, an exaggerated individualism and
a too narrow concept of social responsibility, attachment to
fictions and false values, above all too great attachment to
racial values and a tendency to justify cruelty and injustice
in the name of those values."

Again, it seems to me, Cash inadvertently produced a
good catalogue of Kensington's virtues and vices. His "hell-
of-a-fellow" Southerner lives and breathes in many Whitetowns. The violence, the intolerance, the racial cruelty and
injustice that Cash found in the Old South certainly exist in
Whitetown today alongside the pride, the bravery, the loy-
alty, the swift and signally effective action.

Like the Old South, Kensington is best (or perhaps
worst) known for its "too great attachment to racial
values," but in other respects its people seem a complex
mixture of contradictions. Kensingtonians like new cars and
TV sets, but they oppose Modernism in all its forms. Some
won't even use credit cards or charge accounts for major
purchases. They are often cowed by Authority (schools, the
police) but are contemptuous of it. They exhibit a harsh energy at work and play yet put great store by the "American
Way of Death." Indeed, funerals are important social events
in Kensington and undertakers, along with taproom owners,
are among its most affluent citizens.*

Most Kensingtonians are Democrats in a Democratic-
controlled city, but they totally lack political power and

---

* Kensington's Congressman, Rep. James A. Byrne, is an undertaker,
known to his constituents as "Digger."

seem as distrustful of City Hall as are black North Philadelphians. Although many of Kensington's workers are loyal union men, they reflect none of the idealism that was once associated with trade-unionism, and they consistently oppose public school-bond issues. (This results from both Kensington's Catholic vote and its conviction that most school moneys go to Negro neighborhoods.)

Toward their children Kensingtonians often seem overprotective and overindulgent. Even the poorest kids always have money for candy, and at Christmas parents who can't pay their water bills fill their houses with presents. Yet they're often tough with their children. "If you get hit by a car," a Kensington mother told her young son as he went out to play, "I'll break your arm!" While they can be cruel to outsiders and newcomers, Kensingtonians are often warm, friendly, and helpful to those they know and trust. For returning servicemen whole blocks hang out flags and make a special event of their safe homecoming. For the needy, they collect food baskets. And despite the district's disintegration, the family feeling in Kensington is still probably stronger than in most other parts of the city.

Said a thirty-seven-year-old commercial artist who has lived all his life there:

> In Kensington you live by blocks. You know the people down the street but you never know anybody on the next block. If a family moves in—I don't care whether it's white, black, green, or red—it will take about four months to get any kind of welcome. It'll start with a nod, a slight movement of the eyes and, finally, after four months, maybe hello. But after you've lived here for a while, it's great. You're working on your car at three in the morning, and some fellows come out to talk or help.

In their dealings with outsiders, Kensingtonians are direct. There's certainly nothing devious or two-faced about them.

On any given issue you generally know where they stand. Or if you don't they'll be glad to tell you. For example, a principal new to the district soon discovered that Kensingtonians frown on some of the social niceties. After a school-community luncheon he sought to help a Kensington woman on with her coat. From her reaction he sensed that his attentions were unwelcome and, sure enough, he later was told in so many words that Kensington women don't like strangers to help them with their coats.

I kept running into rare and wonderful ladies whose speech was sprinkled with expletives. After seeing a Fishtown milkman's wife at half a dozen community meetings, I complimented her one day on her activity in civic affairs. She beamed. "I get around," she said, "—like horseshit." Another time I entered a corner store to buy some shaving cream. Reaching for a tube on the shelf, I nearly brushed against a toothless old crone—she must have been at least seventy-five—who was seated in the shop talking to the proprietor. When I tried to joke about my near-accident, the septuagenarian snapped, "If you hit me, I'll hit you back, you son of a bitch." Bless her, she would have, too.

In contrast to this cranky candor is the persistent refusal of Kensington's most important civic organization, the Kensington Community Council, to talk straight and face facts. Because it neither sees nor hears evil in Kensington, the council has never lifted a finger to halt the creeping blight. It invariably blames "outside agitators" for race riots, crime, and other nuisances there. A good example of Kensington's ducking responsibility for what happens in Kensington was contained in the following news story, printed September 14, 1966, in the *Philadelphia Bulletin:*

> The Kensington Community Council has voiced alarm over the high incidence of vandalism that has occurred in the area in the past several months.

It cited damage to vacant houses, spilling of trash, street litterings, paintings of obscene words on buildings, sidewalks and rail bridges.

Hoodlum elements from *outside Kensington* have been blamed by council officials for the wave of vandalism.

"It grieves us," said a council official, "to see litterings, scribblings on walls and paint-swabbed buildings. We're out to keep our spick-and-span reputation."

Kensington's "spick-and-span reputation," of course, was lost long ago even though the Kensington Community Council won't admit it. But the council, while it speaks for Kensington, is not really in and of it. It represents the views of some school officials and businessmen who live outside the area but meet monthly for lunch. It has no strong area-wide grass-roots support—but then no organization in Kensington has. Indeed, Kensington's inability to organize itself is at the root of its failure to deal with its problems, or even to recognize that they exist. And at the root of its organizational gap are the suspicions of many Kensingtonians that civic organizations mean change and change means racial integration.

Of course, Kensington's big problem, the one that transcends all others, is the race problem. We know now, following the Kerner Report and other revelations, that the entire white population of the United States has been overly attached to racial values. But in Kensington this attachment has reached its extreme. For years an unofficial but effective "curfew" was enforced. Negroes who worked in Kensington knew they had to get out before sundown or risk a beating. Even today solitary Negroes are rarely seen there after dark. Negro students at Kensington secondary schools generally walk home in groups for self-protection.

Kensington's intolerance is so savage because its people are so insecure. Just to the west, the huge black North Philadelphia ghetto is slowly, inexorably inching eastward. In the last decade the black-white boundary has moved at least six blocks east. There seems to be no stopping it. Kensingtonians look at North Philadelphia. They see housing that is shabbier than their own. They see more crime, more gangs, more broken homes, more joblessness, more poverty of mind, body, and spirit. The causes of these abominable conditions don't concern them. They simply write off Negroes as hopeless and ask to be left alone.

As a result, between white Kensington and black North Philadelphia there is an almost total lack of communication. Not long ago a group of black and white students and adults attended a series of meetings in Fishtown. The aim was to get the two sides talking together. At the first meeting, whites and blacks were told to shake hands—a traumatic experience for some Kensingtonians who had never before pressed the hand of a Negro. Then they talked. They got to know a little about each other. After it was over, a white student said, "All my life I've been told not to speak to black people. Tonight I spoke to a Negro man. He was O.K."

In Kensington this was progress. But progress is slow because the obstacles are great. One is plain ignorance. Few Kensingtonians ever get to know educated Negroes. The most visible ones in Kensington are the garbage and trash collectors. They tend to reinforce the old stereotype of black people as hewers of wood and drawers of water. "I have no objection to colored," said a Kensingtonian, with this stereotype firmly fixed in his mind, "but half of them are too lazy to work and earn a living."

Kensington has no leaders of its own to admire, nobody speaking for it in the press. But almost every night the drinkers in its neighborhood taprooms see black faces on the television news. This infuriates them. And it has helped convince them that there's a conspiracy afoot among the press, the politicians, the clergy, and other white liberals to elevate the blacks at the expense of the working-class whites.

One of Kensington's tragedies is that the decent people there with a sincere desire to improve race relations don't dare speak up. They fear reprisals. In one of Fishtown's neat row houses I met a refinery worker whose family has lived there for four generations. He bitterly assailed his neighbors for bigotry and ignorance and said their closed minds could only lead to disaster. Yet when rioting erupted in October 1966, over a Negro family's move-in near by, this young man did nothing and said nothing. He was perfectly frank about his failure to act or speak up: "I didn't want to get involved. I might have said or done something that would have offended the rioters. I know these people. . . . I would be afraid to expose myself as a leader in this neighborhood. I am afraid to expose my family to this. I have been called a nigger lover in my own church because of my attitudes."

The riots in question raged for five nights after the Negro family rented a fifty-five-dollar-a-month house in a down-at-the-heels section not far from Kensington Girls High. Hundreds of singing, cursing demonstrators paraded in front of the house, throwing rocks, eggs, and bottles and booing Catholic priests who tried to disperse them. As usual, Kensington's defenders blamed outsiders for the lawlessness. Philadelphia's Commission on Human Relations looked into the question. It found that of one hundred fifty persons arrested in the disturbances, fifty per cent were Kensington whites, thirty-five per cent were Negroes living outside Kensington, and fifteen per cent were "outside whites." Six months later, and after continual harassment, the Negro family quietly moved out. Once again Kensington, like

Cash's South, had proved itself "signally effective . . . in its action."

While Kensingtonians have been roundly denounced for this kind of behavior, some observers have sought to get at the underlying causes. One is Donald Hamilton, executive director of the Lighthouse, a settlement house on Kensington's western border. Many Kensingtonians, he said, are trapped in poverty. They can't move, their backs are against the wall and so they "shoot the works." Hamilton said the riots gave these people a chance to explode, to let off steam and release their pent-up frustrations, to say openly "what they thought and what was in their guts."

> They kind of spilled out. They allowed themselves to do something that they shouldn't have done—but they're no worse than the Main Liners or the Chestnut Hillers—the whole kit and caboodle.
>
> I don't say I agree with them. I think they were wrong. But I understood why they did it. They see no other choice. They have to fight. Just as the Negroes in Newark resent their situation. They both resent it. They say, "The hell with this. Let's shoot the works." I think I'd do the same thing if I were in their place.

Others have made the point that Kensington's all-too-evident biases, its straight-from-the-shoulder prejudices, are no more contemptible than the kind of sneaky discrimination Negroes encounter in the shifty all-white suburbs. A Filipino-American living on the outskirts of Kensington said the area's attitude toward nonwhites reminded him of the Old West's view of Indians: The only good Indian is a dead Indian. Yet as this college-trained man saw it, bigotry was a greater problem among the educated than among the ignorant.

"The ignorant speak their minds," he said. "They say it out. The educated let you down easily."

The Road to Fishtown

In the Depression year of 1937 George Orwell visited the mining towns of northern England to report on conditions there. He found families trapped in wretchedness and poverty. He described "labyrinthine slums and dark back kitchens with sickly aging people creeping round and round them like blackbeetles."* He told how miners, stooped and bent, sometimes crawled five miles through a narrow, mucky passage from pit bottom to coal face, there to begin their daily seven and a half hours of "savage labor." Bitterly, Orwell wrote of the house where he took lodging: four men in a single, squalid room with dust hanging like fur from a giant chandelier and with all windows jammed shut so that every morning the place "stank like a ferret's cage." To the dirt, the smells, the vile food, and the full chamber pot under the breakfast table was added the sense of "stagnant, meaningless decay" that finally drove Orwell out.

The fact was Orwell had very little in common with the "common people." He had grown up in the "lower upper-middle class." He had been taught to despise the workers'

* *The Road to Wigan Pier.* Victor Gallancz, 1937.

"coarse faces, hideous accents and gross manners." As a boy, he had considered the workers' sons "almost sub-human," and he could never understand why they resented this and hated him for it. But his stay among the coal miners gave him new insights and deeper understanding. He put aside the bigotry learned at his mother's knee and came to see the miners as people. He never got "really intimate" with them but he benefited from exposure to their way of life. "The essential point," he wrote later, in generalizing about a middle-class person's experience in rubbing elbows with members of a lower social class, "is that your middle-class ideals and prejudices are tested by contact with others which are not necessarily better but are certainly different."

In another land and another generation I had an experience similar to Orwell's. As a middle-class suburbanite and a WAP (White Alsatian Protestant), I, too, was an outsider in the wilds of industrial, working-class Kensington. Like Orwell, I, too, suffered from cultural shock, though perhaps not as traumatically as he did. Kensington in 1968 wasn't as grim and forbidding as Wigan in 1936 (or even as Kensington itself was in 1936). And Americans aren't as conscious of social class as the English. Despite profound changes in recent years, the lines of social demarcation are still more tightly drawn in Britain than they are in the U.S. and the barriers to advancement are higher. Even so, the difference between a run-down ethnic-American factory district and a shiny suburb may be greater today than ever before. In Kensington, I found my middle-class ideals and prejudices tested daily by contact with others which were certainly different.

So join me for a trip to that far country. We're at City Hall, Old Philadelphia's geographic center. It's six o'clock

on a Friday evening in March 1969 and workers are
homeward bound. The road to Kensington lies underground. There is no direct route by car. Philadelphia is laid
out in William Penn's grid pattern, but in Kensington, and
particularly Fishtown, the grid is skewed. Streets which run
east-west in the rest of Philadelphia suddenly swing north-
south as they near the Delaware River. They twist and turn
erratically. Most are one-way streets so narrow that, with
cars parked on one side, you scrape the far curb getting by.
Street signs are often missing or twisted, and it's difficult for
strangers, even those with street maps, to get oriented.
When the mighty Delaware Expressway is finally finished,
Kensington will be easier to reach by car from downtown.
Not that Kensington's needs and interests are of much concern to the highway builders. They're putting down the con-
crete to speed travel between central Philadelphia and lower
Bucks County. Kensington just happens to be in the way.

But right now driving to Kensington is out of the question. I'll take the Frankford El. The El (an elevated-subway
line) is a key element in Philadelphia's vast and decrepit
mass-transit system. It is sixty years old and looks it. At that,
it is probably no more neglected or bedraggled than most
high-speed lines in American central cities. Those seeking
evidence that American capitalism reserves most of its ben-
efits for the well-to-do and merely trickles down aid to the
workers would do well to examine mass-transit facilities.
Compared to London's underground, the Paris Métro, and
Moscow's subway, transit lines in Philadelphia and other
United States cities are third- or fourth-rate. They are older,
dirtier, less efficient, worse in every way—and their fares
are higher.* For a long time it was fashionable for Ameri-

* Of course, the rate of automobile ownership among United States
workers is higher than that in most other industrial countries, but the
demand for cars is stimulated and maintained in part by consistently
dreadful public transportation.

cans to hold Moscow's massive subway up to ridicule and derision. Certainly, Soviet architecture in the 1930s, when the subway was built, lacked grace and charm, as it still does. But the subway itself is spotless and a joy to ride in.

It's no joy to ride on the Frankford El. At City Hall there are no maps to direct you. The concourse lighting is dim. The place stinks of urine. And before going downstairs to board your train you must make sure that you have exactly thirty cents in change. Otherwise, you can't get through the turnstile. Subway cashiers ceased making change in 1968. The idea was to cut down on holdups of transit employees, and it worked. But now the former change makers merely sit in their cages passing out transfer slips and seeing that the turnstiles function properly.

Walking downstairs to the elevated-subway line, I move from one world to another. Behind is the business and financial heart of Philadelphia. Here buildings dominate people. City Hall itself is no raving beauty. Former Mayor Richardson Dilworth, a WASP liberal who won the Whitetown vote simply by being the most daring, creative, outspoken, and colorful mayor in Philadelphia's modern history, once suggested that the big stone pile be torn down, but it still stands and has recently been sandblasted.

City Hall was built for an estimated twenty-four million dollars over a thirty-year period ending in 1901. Atop its tower is a 37-foot high, 53,580-pound statue of William Penn. The statue faces toward Penn Treaty Park on the Delaware River in Fishtown, where, under a towering elm since fallen, the founder is said to have reached a historic accord with the red men that kept the peace in the City of Brotherly Love. The top of Billy Penn's hat reaches 547 feet 11¼ inches above the street, and the city has decreed, unofficially, that no building in Philadelphia shall be as tall.

All around City Hall are the lesser structures that make

up the city's core. Here are the glistening new office buildings in Penn Center, Philadelphia's too hastily conceived
and not very well executed answer to Rockefeller Center in
New York. To the south are the smart Chestnut Street
boutiques. To the east, Wanamaker's, proper Philadelphia's
favorite department store. Near at hand, the big banks—
Fidelity, First Pennsylvania, Girard Trust, Philadelphia
National. The hotels—the old Bellevue and the new Shera-
ton.

And scattered amid the commerce and the money-chang-
ers are the private clubs, those bastions of social control that
defend, as Nathaniel Burt wrote in *The Perennial Philadelphians,* "the purity of Philadelphia bloodlines against the
nouveaux riches." Some of the clubhouses, like the Grecian-
style Union League, are widely known landmarks. Others,
like the Philadelphia Club and the Rittenhouse Club, are
unpretentious to the point of being unrecognized by the
shoppers and office workers who stream past their entrances
every day. The Philadelphia Club is the most exclusive. To
get in you have to have "old money," and in Philadelphia
many of those with old money go back to the Revolution.
Their Tory ancestors wined and dined British officers in
Philadelphia in the winter of 1777–1778 while George
Washington and his men froze at Valley Forge. Even Dilworth, a Yale man with good social connections, had to
scrap like hell to get into the Philadelphia Club because he
came from Pittsburgh.

The Philadelphia Club, with its high ceilings and nineteenth-century paintings, its underplayed opulence and casual discrimination against Jews, Catholics, Negroes, and all
but the most upper-crust WASPs, tops the hierarchy in a
city where, according to sociologist E. Digby Baltzell in
Philadelphia Gentlemen, "social connections are perhaps
somewhat more important than elsewhere." A Whitetowner

would no more aspire to membership in the Philadelphia Club than a Proper Philadelphian would consider joining the Mummers.

The Mummers. Now there's a Whitetown institution for you. Mummers clubs are scattered throughout the city's white working-class sections, and club members seem to spend half the year getting costumes ready for their big parade on New Year's Day, when they pour whisky into their horns and strut up Broad Street to the music of string bands. The origins of mummery are lost in history, but sequin-bedecked, flowing-caped Mummers have been marching in Philadelphia for over a hundred years—and with the city annually donating thousands of dollars in prize money for best costumes, bands, and clowning, the event shows no signs of extinction. So far as I can determine, there has never been a Negro Mummer. For years Mummer clowns wore blackface and entertained the crowds with Amos-and-Andy type of routines. Finally, the courts ordered a halt to this practice, so mummery is now pristinely white. And very few of the Mummers themselves realize that their theme song, "Oh, Dem Golden Slippers," was written by a Philadelphia Negro named James A. Bland.

In any event, the subway is a fit place for Mummers but not for Philadelphia Clubbers. I board a Kensington-bound train at Fifteenth and Market streets, the western side of City Hall. It is rush hour and the subway car is jammed with secretaries, students, blue-collar workers, a few prim-and-proper white-collar types. There's a lot of jostling but no camaraderie. Most of the riders sit and stare in silence. A few read newspapers (generally the tabloid *Daily News*) or paperback books. The subway lurches east under Market Street toward the Delaware River. There are stops at Thirteenth Street, Eleventh, Eighth, Fifth. Fifth and Market streets—Independence Hall. Nobody in the subway thinks of the architectural jewel where it all began in the United States or of the cracked Liberty Bell in the back room or of the founding fathers who lived and breathed there almost two centuries ago. Few have even visited Independence Hall since their school days, if then.

The subway runs to Second Street, just two blocks from the Delaware in the oldest section of old Philadelphia. There it turns north and comes out of the ground. It becomes an elevated line running parallel to the riverbank. It swings under the approach to the Benjamin Franklin Bridge, which connects Philadelphia with Camden, New Jersey. Now the El cuts in from the river and rumbles up toward the factory district. The view out its soot-gray windows is of the backside of dingy mills, vacant lots, parked cars, rows of houses, TV aerials, chimneys. The scene could be an English or Scottish factory town. Not in Orwell's coal country, but perhaps in Manchester or Leeds or Liverpool or Glasgow.

The subway stations, named after streets, are English, too: Berks, York, Huntington, Somerset. Other names are indigenous to Philadelphia, a prominent one being Girard Avenue at the lower end of Fishtown. It honors the crusty, one-eyed, nineteenth-century skinflint and opium trader who left his shipping and banking fortune—then the largest in the United States—to found a boarding school for poor, white, male orphans. Stephen Girard's anti-intellectualism —he opposed the teaching of Latin and directed his school to stress "facts and things rather than words or signs"—may have been at the root, Nathaniel Burt thinks, of Philadelphia's long-standing resistance to belles-lettres. Girard was a no-nonsense, practical, courageous man, a Whitetowner in spirit if not in pocketbook, and his exclusion of blacks from Girard College was stoutly defended by twentieth-century Whitetowners. Not until 1968, more than a century and a quarter after Girard's death, did the courts finally rule the ban illegal. A handful of Negro children was subsequently admitted to the school, whose ten-foot wall separates it from the surrounding black slums of North Philadelphia.

The subway train stops at Kensington and Allegheny avenues, K&A. This is the heart and center of Whitetown. Or it used to be. Now it has lost a lot of its juices, its zest and guts. But K&A is still Kensington's hub. As the air pressure opens the subway doors, I step to the platform and walk down a rusty, rickety staircase to the street. There, over the entrance to the station, is a faded and torn Wallace sticker. At the curb is the inevitable pretzel vendor. It's six-fifteen and he's getting ready to quit for the night. But five cents still buys a soft, salty, doughy, warm pretzel with mustard slopped over it—the best food bargain in Philadelphia. Soft pretzels are democratic, appealing to the tastebuds of rich and poor. To my palate, they are far superior to such Philadelphia indelicacies as scrapple, which is found on the menu at the Union League but not on the street in Whitetown.

What I notice first about K&A is the people. Downtown it's the buildings that impress and dominate, but here it's the people. The buildings of Kensington are less than nothing, hardly one is of more than passing interest and there simply aren't any new ones, good or bad. But the people are something else. K&A is a shopping district, and on a mild Friday night in late March it's alive with people. Many have just been paid—Friday is holdup day in Philadelphia for this reason—and spirits are high. Stores, restaurants, and bars are full. I go into a bar. Bars are easy to find in business sections, but they also dot Kensington's residential neighborhoods. These little corner tappies are a refuge for the hell-of-a-fellow Whitetowner as well as the unassuming, nontroublemaking worker who enjoys male talk and conviviality over a glass or two of beer or a couple of whiskies. Some of these men say bar whisky actually tastes different— and better—than stuff from the same bottle when taken at home. Like Kensington itself, the bars are old-fashioned, and above the rear door of many still hangs the sign: LADIES' ENTRANCE. But nobody pays attention to that any more, not even in Kensington.

The mood and atmosphere in a neighborhood tappie depends on the mood of the bartender, who usually lives above or behind the barroom, and on the mood of the drinkers. These moods, in turn, depend on the time of day and the day of the week, the weather and the season, and also the news in the paper and on television, not to mention the ups and downs of the personal lives of the dispensers of drink and the drinkers. Before the Presidential primaries in 1968, I entered one of these small, neighborhood taprooms as the barkeep and his lone customer were exchanging views on a favorite subject: niggers. The bartender was a heavy-set, reasonably well-spoken man who looked to be of German extraction. The solitary drinker was a white-trash nigger hater. The bartender wanted the man's money but wasn't going to put up with a lot of nonsense.

"There's good whites and good niggers," the bartender was saying as I walked in. "Bad whites and bad niggers. There's some whites you can have. And you know what we're getting in this neighborhood," he said, looking his white-trash customer in the eye, "—white trash."

The point was lost on the white-trash drinker. "Niggers is takin' over," he said. "Look at this." He pointed to a headline in the afternoon paper: ROMNEY VISITS N. PHILA. "Them politicians," he snarled. "Comin' here to visit the nigger slums. They're all the same. They'll do anything for votes.

"How about that Rusk's daughter marryin' a nigger. She started goin' with 'im when she was fourteen. What kind of father is he? He's runnin' the country and he can't even run his own family."

"Aw, you're just a barroom orator," snapped the bartender, who, by this time, was fed up. "Whatya ever do but talk?"

"I'll do somethin'. Just wait." And with that, the drinker buttoned his coat against the rain and walked out.

It was an ugly scene on a dreary day. No doubt it has been repeated in countless Kensington bars. Wars and rumors of wars, assassinations, changes of national administration make no great difference. You can always hear that kind of talk somewhere in Kensington. But now it is March 1969 and payday. People have money in their pockets and in the Kensington Avenue bar that I select the atmosphere is warm and friendly. On the wall behind the bar are four photographs of John F. Kennedy, two in color, and three pictures of Robert F. Kennedy; and there are American flags. In one corner is the ever-present television set, and, though it's on, nobody is watching. Today's bar special is PM, workingman's whisky. A single shot is thirty-five cents, a double, sixty-five. A plate of sharp cheese and crackers costs forty cents, and a dollar will get you a "boatload" of fried shrimp.

Here is the camaraderie that the subway lacks. There's a barroom hum, what James Agee, writing of a workingman's bar in *A Death in the Family,* called "the thick quietude of crumpled talk." Down the bar a voice calls out, "Yo, Harry. You not workin' tonight?" Several stools away, Harry airily dismisses the notion. "I never work Friday nights. Peons work Friday nights." Next to me is Al, a foreman at a Kensington firm that makes storm windows and doors. Every Friday night after work Al stops at this bar for a few beers. He tells me this and a lot of other things about himself. In fact, he falls on me, a willing listener, with all the enthusiasm of a man who lives alone, has few friends and few people to talk to. He explains that he's been working for the same company for "going on twenty-six years," makes good money—sometimes over two hundred dollars a week—and likes the place and his bosses.

It turns out, though, that this is a crucial weekend in Al's life. But Al talks very rapidly and the barroom is getting noisy. Although I answer every punctuating "Right?" or "Understand?" with a knowing nod, I'm not sure I do comprehend. Or at least I find what Al seems to be saying hard to believe. It goes like this:

Al is responsible for the production of forty machine operators at his plant. They've always gotten along well, "understand?", and no problems. But now the company is adding to Al's responsibility. It's bringing up another forty workers from South Carolina, "right?" These South Carolinians are to be paid a dollar an hour, which is below the minimum wage in Pennsylvania and a dollar and a quarter less than the pay of the other machine operators at the plant. Besides the dollar an hour, the Southerners will get room and keep in some kind of company facility.

These arrangements seem strange to Al, but they are not what's bugging him. Nor does he appear troubled by the fact, revealed in an answer to a question from his listener, that the newcomers are all black. No, what's gotten Al stirred up has to do with men and machines. Now, the machines in the plant are set up to be run by right-handed workers, "understand?", and this is important, "right?", because have you ever tried to write with your left hand? I am now beginning to get the drift, incredible though it seems. Of the forty new workers due on Monday not one is right-handed; they're all lefties. They've been running left-handed machines in South Carolina and now they're coming up to Philadelphia to work right-handed machines, "got it?" Well, the mess will hit the fan on Monday morning, and Al won't take responsibility for what's going to happen. In fact, he plans to meet tomorrow, Saturday, an off day, with some other foremen to decide what to do. All he knows is that those left-handed South Carolinians aren't competent to run his right-handed machines, "right?".

When I recounted this story later to a liberal friend, she immediately smelled a rat, the same one I thought I had sniffed. "He wasn't really worried about left-handers," she said of Al. "He's thinking about all those niggers coming into his plant." Well, Al was certainly in his cups the night I talked to him, right? But the following week I took a run up to his factory. And believe it or not, everything he told me was more or less true. There was a problem of left-handed workers from the South and right-handed machines up here, but the company thought it was getting straightened out.

There is much, much more from Al that Friday night as he drinks beer and chain-smokes cigarettes and eats sparingly from the sharp cheese and crackers I offer him and refuses shrimp from my boatload. He wants to tell his life story but it is time for me to go.

I start to walk to Fishtown. I leave Kensington Avenue and head down the narrow back streets, two-story houses clustered in rows on each side. On the better blocks, the houses have front porches, but only rarely do I see a tree or a patch of grass. Inside the houses television tubes are alight. On front sofas people sit watching.

After a few minutes' walk I reach a block that is festively decorated with banners and bunting strung over the street: red, white, and blue. To anyone at all familiar with the

Whitetowns of America, the message is obvious: one of the neighborhood boys is returning from Vietnam. In this case it's Jimmy. WELCOME HOME, JIMMY, read the hand-lettered pennants. Jimmy's house is easily identified by the lights and signs. Jimmy's mother answers the door. She is a slim woman, about forty, with a thin face, glasses, upswept hair, and no make-up. She stands on the stoop talking easily about Jimmy when I explain my interest but not inviting me in. Jimmy, she says, is twenty-one, he has been serving with the "First Air Cav—the best," and he's due home Sunday. His friends put up the decorations two weeks ago. There will be parties for Jimmy for thirty days; besides his friends, he has sixty-four aunts, uncles, and cousins, all but a handful live near by and all want to drink to him and wish him well.

Jimmy dropped out of Mastbaum Technical High, the vocational school which most Kensingtonians prefer over the academic high school. They prefer it not only because the academic high, Edison, is mostly black and is located in black North Philadelphia but also because Kensingtonians, like Stephen Girard, have always preferred vocational "facts and things" over academic "words and signs." Jimmy's mother went to Mastbaum. His father, a waterfront checker, went to the Catholic high school. Both parents are native Kensingtonians.

After dropping out of Mastbaum, Jimmy worked as a machinist and then was drafted. In Vietnam he served in seventeen different locations. He spent a month in a Danang hospital after being hit in the neck by a bullet or a piece of shrapnel that ricocheted off his squad leader's helmet. Jimmy got himself a "Gook rifle." He is "all for his outfit." The only complaint he wrote home about related to "mistreatment of some of the colored fellows" in the Air Cavalry Division.

When I ask how the house is fixed up inside for Jimmy's return, his mother invites me to come in and see. There in the front room is a Christmas tree, reaching almost to the ceiling. It looks green and fresh, considering it is artificial, and is gaily festooned with Christmas balls and tinsel. On the floor around the tree are neatly and colorfully wrapped presents. Most of the presents, says Jimmy's mother, are clothing, including a number of Italian knit shirts, which Jimmy especially likes. The family is also giving the boy money and a ring.

The tree has been standing in the living room since Christmas Eve, almost three months. The living room itself is filled with red, white, and blue streamers. On the front wall near the tree are two tinted photos of Jimmy in uniform, one of his older brother, a Navy veteran, and one of his younger sister. Scurrying about the room is Jimmy's tail-wagging basset hound, Sinbad.

The tree, the presents, the photos, the streamers, the faithful dog—a working-class family's welcome home for its beloved soldier son. All this is enough to bring a lump to my throat. But what I find most notable about Jimmy's mother as she describes the party plans and points out the decorations is her dead-pan seriousness, her complete matter-of-factness. There is not a drop of maudlin sentimentality here, she seems to be saying. No need for tears. This is just what Kensington people do when their boys come marching home. It happens all the time.

I'm heading now for Wanda's house. Wanda—I've made up the name but not the person—is a short sharp-featured, gray-haired Fishtowner, one of its many Polish immigrants. I've been renting a room in her house in order to learn more about this distinctive community. The house is typical of many in Fishtown: a front room and kitchen, where Wanda eats, on the first floor, two bedrooms and a bathroom on the second. Wanda is sixty-two, lives alone, and keeps the house spotless. There are no books or magazines in the living room, but a big color-TV set stands in one corner, as well as bouquets of plastic flowers, religious figurines, and embroidered exhortations to God to bless this house.

In some ways I have found Wanda to be a typical White-towner and in other ways not so typical, but in all ways she is a gritty human being. She's at work when I open her front door with my key, and I have time to reflect on some of the things she has told me about herself.

She was the second oldest of twelve children of poor Polish peasants. Neither of her parents had had any formal schooling in Poland and her mother never did learn to read or write. When Wanda was young—and before most of the other children were born—the family emigrated from eastern Poland to Pennsylvania's hard-coal country around Scranton. Her father took a job in the mines. He labored as a miner for a number of years—Wanda wasn't sure how many—until a "big explosion" in No. 11 mine caused injuries from which he never fully recovered. After the family moved to Philadelphia, Wanda's father died of the dreaded "black lung" disease that continues to strike miners even today.

As the oldest girl in the family, Wanda had to stay home whenever anybody got sick. Still, she managed to get through four years of school before her mother forced her to find a job. She was twelve years old. ("Among the Polish people, you know," she had told me, "they don't think you need school.") She took work in the mills of Kensington, and for the next fifty years, with time out for bearing three children of her own, she toiled as a millhand. When I met her she was still working five days a week from two o'clock in the afternoon until ten at night, on a stand-up job twisting, reeling and winding carpet yarn. Eight hours on her feet was exhausting, Wanda acknowledged, and her boss must have been trained in Dickens-era sweatshops. But she stuck with it.

Wanda had lived in Fishtown for thirty-three years and in the house where I found her for seven. Her husband was dead and her three children were grown. One of her two sons, after a stint in the Marines that "made a man of him," had moved west with his wife and four children. He was running a repair garage near Hollywood and was apparently living quite comfortably. Or so it seemed to his mother the millhand. The younger son, also married and with children, was a mechanic in a Philadelphia repair garage. Wanda also had a married daughter who lived in Connecticut. The daughter had eight children—the oldest boy was attending college. Wanda didn't know what college, but she was pleased. This grandson was the first member of her family, as far as anyone could remember, who had ever gone to college. And what's more, he was planning to become an English teacher. Wanda thought that was wonderful.

From her husband's savings and her own economies, Wanda had built a modest nest egg. She was making only a dollar-ninety-seven an hour at the mill, yet she had spent more than six thousand dollars on improvements to her small house. She knew she'd never get that much money out of the house if she sold it, but that didn't seem to trouble her. The house suited her and that was enough. She planned to retire at sixty-five and thought she would have enough money to live without burdening her children. Much depended on her health, which wasn't good; she had a liver ailment that required treatment from time to time. The doctor said she shouldn't be working on her feet eight hours a day, but that couldn't be helped. And, anyway, she wasn't complaining.

I am still musing about Wanda's life in Whitetown when she walks in. After completing her eight-hour stint, she's had to take two buses—thirty cents for the first ride, five cents for the transfer (and don't forget to have exact change!). Far less taxing than Orwell's miners crawling five miles back to the mine shaft, but wearisome enough for a fifty-year veteran of the mills. Wanda's tired, her feet hurt, and if I weren't there she'd probably flick on the TV. But she seems to welcome somebody to talk to. We go into her small kitchen. Living alone as she does, she keeps her housekeeping as simple as possible. Instead of squeezing or-anges for juice in the morning, she puts a spoonful of Tang in a glass of cold water. Now, instead of percolating coffee, she boils water for instant. We sit at the breakfast table a few feet from the gas stove and talk. I ask about Fishtown. She laughs and says the place doesn't seem to have changed much in all the years she's been here.

"What do you like about it?"

"Well, I've lived here so long. No colored."

"Why don't you want to live with colored?"

"I've got nothing against colored. I've worked with col-ored girls. They're very nice. I wouldn't have nothing against them. As long as they left me alone. That's all I want. I work with colored girls and colored men, and they're very nice."

When I ask Wanda about Fishtown's deficiencies, she cites the shortage of recreation facilities for young poeple. "It doesn't even have a playground," she says. "That's what they should have around here, a playground. The poor kids. When they play on the street, why, they get chased. Where else are they gonna play? And people holler. In the summer, people holler. Well, I never sit outside. I don't have any time. But other people holler."

Wanda is pleased that there are very few beatniks or hip-pies in Fishtown. Most of the youngsters, she says, are just "normal boys." They're all "very nice boys" and quite a few have never been downtown on the Frankford El. "They couldn't even get there," says Wanda, laughing again. "They'd get lost. As far as they get is Front Street [at Fishtown's western extremity]. You can do all your shopping on Front Street. To tell you the truth, I ain't been in town in two years—up until last week. I went to the doctor's and then I stopped at Eighth Street and did some shopping. I ain't been down there for two years."

Still, Wanda sees a generation gap. Even in Fishtown, the children are different. "We're old-fashioned," she says of the parents. "They [the children] want more. They want to live better." None of this impresses Wanda. She doesn't play bingo, as so many Fishtowners do. She doesn't play cards ("Too dumb," she explains with another laugh). She doesn't have many friends and doesn't want many. "I don't like anybody running in and out of my house. I think it's my business. I don't have time for coffee breaks and all that stuff."

Wanda acknowledges that Fishtown might not be as safe a place to live as it once was. "When I lived on Cabot [pronounced ka-BOTT] Street," she says, "I never even closed the door. The door was always open. This was fifteen years ago. We never even had a key. Everybody did that then." Now she never leaves her house unlocked. She'd be afraid to because of "the stuff that you read in the papers." You know, "sometimes you're not safe in your own house."

Despite its inadequacies, though, Fishtown suits Wanda. She has a house, a job, reasonably good health, and a certain pride that goes with being self-sufficient. She has achieved an admirable peace of mind in Fishtown that she might have lacked elsewhere. "I'm contented here," she says. "I think I've done pretty good for only going as far as fourth grade."

I go up to bed. And as I mount the stairs I think that

Wanda *has* "done pretty good." Much of what is exciting and stimulating about America has passed her by, but she has kept a firm grip on her sanity while making ends meet. Given the handicaps under which she has labored all her life, perhaps that is all one could hope for or expect.

My bedroom is at the head of the stairs. It has no door—you simply walk into it. Across the entranceway, Wanda has strung a curtain for privacy. Beside the bed is a long, plain dresser against one wall. The single overhead light is so weak that I can't read in bed without straining my eyes, but everything is tidy and I sleep well.

Tidiness is on my mind next morning when I awake. Tidiness, in fact, is the hallmark of Wanda's house—tidiness and a kind of mausoleum *décor*. These are common characteristics of the better Whitetown houses. In the larger ones you sometimes see completely furnished rooms that seem never to have been lived in. You find upholstered chairs and sofas carefully covered with plastic and obviously not intended for use. Their importance seems to lie in their simply being symbols of a secure and stable household and evidence of material wellbeing.

There is no mirror in Wanda's upstairs bathroom, so I go to the basement to shave over a laundry tub. The basement, too, is far cleaner than my dirty cellar in suburbia.

Wanda is still asleep. I boil an egg over her gas stove and make some instant coffee. Stacking the dishes in the sink—something I suspect Wanda would never do since she seems to clean up after every meal or snack—I leave the house and resume my wanderings.

A dozen blocks from Wanda's house is a particularly slummy section of Kensington, where wooden houses built on stilts look ready to collapse or to burn up at the striking of a match. It is drizzling as I walk down this street. In one house a family is preparing to move out. Children are carrying kitchen supplies down the long, wobbly outside staircase to a ten-year-old station wagon with a rented trailer hooked to the back. Standing on the sidewalk directing the packing is a small, hollow-cheeked man with a dead cigarette stuck onto his bottom lip in the manner of a French workman. I fall into conversation with the man and he tells this story:

He is a house painter. He and his wife and seven children formerly lived in Cleveland. Each of the past several winters he had come east alone to work in Philadelphia, where he found he could earn a hundred and sixty dollars a week against a hundred at home. The previous fall, rather than make the trip by himself again, he decided to relocate his entire family and take up a new life in the East. The family moved to Kensington. Four children were enrolled in the neighborhood elementary school and two in junior high. The oldest child, a seventeen-year-old boy, got a job.

Within two months, the couple's dream of happy family life in Kensington had turned into a nightmare. The oldest son took to drinking and cutting up. He couldn't hold a job. The junior-high kids played hooky, hung on corners, hid in vacant stores to smoke and sniff glue. School authorities warned the parents about the need of controlling their children. But the painter and his wife, also pale and tired, simply could not cope. Finally, the two junior-high youngsters disappeared for three days. Police picked them up downtown in the company of pot-smoking hippies.

For the harried parents that was the last straw. They decided to go back home. And as I walk by they are loading their battered furniture, their kitchen gear, and their seven children into their ancient auto for the drive west. I go inside the house and find a disaster area. Holes in the walls, trash and garbage strewn on the floor. Junky pieces of furniture left behind. Wanda would have been appalled.

As for the parents, they look like Okies from the 1930s

dust bowl. And the older children could be bit players in *Bonnie and Clyde*. Just before getting behind the wheel, the father steps over to me. We shake hands in the rain and I wish him well. He hangs his head in despair.

"They just went wild," he says of the kids, now all peacefully assembled in the car and eager to begin their trip. "We'd never seen anything like it back home. Now we're goin' back." And with that, he gets into his car. I wave goodby to them and they drive off.

I keep walking and soon reach one of Kensington's main arteries. Not far along this wide avenue is the house and law office of a man I'll call Tom. Tom is a third-generation Irish Kensingtonian, a rare bird who not only graduated from high school but went on to "the University" (in Philadelphia, that's Penn) and Temple Law. Tom was first in his Kensington parochial-school class, and he caught hell for it. Academic eager beavers were disliked by their classmates. Tom is one of those Kensingtonians who continue to live in Kensington not because they're trapped but because they love it.

Tom invites me into his house, which is something to see. There are fine carpets, a nicely paneled basement children's rumpus room, three beautifully furnished bedrooms. No mortgage, no grounds to keep up, no hidden costs. So Tom is banking thousands of dollars each year for the future college education of his five children. Like many Kensingtonians, he doesn't believe in credit buying or charge accounts. When he needed a new car recently, he withdrew the money from the bank and paid the dealer in cash.

Tom has another law office downtown. Many of his clients are Kensingtonians, and he notes, as Wanda had done, that they are often lost and bewildered when they leave Kensington. "About once a month," says Tom, "I get a phone call from someone who can't find my office. Many of them just don't know their way around the city."

But his neighbors' provincialism doesn't dismay Tom. Nor, apparently, does it trouble his wife. Tom says that, although she grew up on the Main Line, she likes Kensington for the same reasons he does. Besides their comfortable house just three blocks from Tom's parents and two blocks from the site of the old grocery that his grandparents ran for years, they have a place at the Jersey shore and a growing bank account. Meanwhile, most of their suburban friends, says Tom, are weighted down with big mortgages. In the spring and summer they have a lot of grass to cut (Tom has none) and all year round they have a long commute to town. Tom concedes that only one of the fellows he grew up with is still living in Philadelphia. But Tom is "damn proud" of Kensington, thinks it's a "great neighborhood," and plans never to move out. "To get some of us out of this neighborhood," he says, "they're going to have to carry us feet first in a box."

A client comes in to see Tom and I leave.

I abandon the main drag and walk up into another residential section of Kensington. Suddenly a beer truck whips around the corner and I recognize the driver's assistant. He is a public-school teacher whom I had met previously. I had known this teacher worked on a beer truck on Saturdays but had never before seen him on the job.

Unlike Tom, the teacher, whom I'll call Ed, is a native Kensingtonian who has moved out. He grew up in a Ukrainian section and attended a Ukrainian parochial school. When he yawned in class one afternoon, he once told me, the nun threatened to crack him in the mouth. To this day, Ed never fails to cover his mouth while yawning.

Ed's father is a welder and his mother is a sewing-machine operator. Both had ninth-grade educations. They still live in a conventional row house thirteen feet wide. His parents remember the Great Depression and continue to worry about money. Not Ed. He seems much more relaxed and sure of himself. He has reason to be more self-assured: he and his wife are making more money than Ed's parents. His wife works for a bank and Ed, in addition to his regular teaching job, also teaches summer school and works Saturdays and holidays on the beer truck. He and his wife moved from Kensington to a $14,000 house in Philadelphia's lower-middle-class Northeast. Before World War II, this section was largely farmland. Now it is filled with thousands of houses. It is almost entirely white. Many of its homeowners fled from Kensington or lower-income "changing neighborhoods" closer to the center of the city.

Ed isn't worried about finances, even though "all my neighbors are in debt." He says, "I don't believe in killing myself over money. After we have children we want to be home with them." For the present, though, Ed wears several hats. He enjoys hustling cases of beer into Kensington houses. Often his customers give him an earful. "The bigotry is tremendous," he says. "You have to hear it to believe it."

As the beer truck disappears down the street, I head over to Kensington Avenue and walk under the El. I'm in the neighborhood now where I'd been drinking beer with Al, the right-handed foreman, last night. Because of the rain this morning, Saturday business is poor in the shopping district. This is old-school shopping—no giant department stores or sleek plazas, just block after block of small storefronts. Kresge's, candies, shoes, shoes, shoes, shirts, shoes, a five-and-ten (where nothing costs a nickel or a dime any more), fashions, shoes, fashions, wigs, lamps, drugs, loans, lunch, flowers, frocks, paints, gifts, shirts, a bar—in fact, the bar I was in last night.

I leave the avenue again and walk several blocks to one of Kensington's typical elementary schools. It's a three-story monstrosity that should have been torn down years ago, but the section didn't complain very much. Nothing would have been done had it not been for a young Protestant minister serving a small church in the area. He and his wife, who had two children in the school, mounted a drive to get it replaced. Their case was so convincing that the Board of Education revised its capital building program to speed up the school's replacement. But the new building is still three or four or five years away.

Directly across the street from the school live a couple whom I'll name John and Connie. I've gotten to know them through the minister who recruited them to help in the new-school campaign. John is thirty-six, Polish, a $165-a-week machinist at a Federal installation. His mother completed four years of school in Poland, his father six years in Philadelphia. John went through Catholic high school. His wife, a few years younger than John, is English and also a high-school graduate. They have two children in elementary school.

They urge me to come in out of the rain. In size and shape, their house is almost identical to Wanda's, but with children living there its furnishings and atmosphere are totally different. In the living room, their son's bicycle is leaning precariously against one wall. No other place to put it, John explains, unless you take it down to the basement. And it's a pain in the neck getting the bike down the cellar stairs. Also, John and Connie have interests far different from Wanda's. They have books, records, camping gear, a rock collection.

John and Connie are more middle class in living style and outlook than many Kensingtonians. Yet John, a husky, thoughtful man with glasses, hasn't tried to break out and maybe he never will. We sit in the kitchen drinking coffee and he talks about it. He speaks slowly, picking his words carefully and forming perfect sentences.

"We couldn't afford that tent we have," he says, "if we lived in another neighborhood. We couldn't afford the car I had to buy. For myself, I would like to move out. We stay here primarily because our parents are here. They're old and no one else stayed so we stayed. This is my wife's rationalization for staying. This angers me. I would like to move out. But the reality is: Why bring up a family fight over nothing? I do have it good here. There are some minor things. I can go down in my basement and bang my head against the pipes. Every time it happens, I swear, I curse. I love flowers. I love dirt. I don't have anything. If I go out in the yard, it's all cement. But generally I can be a little freer with the dollar than if I did move out.

"My anger is not with the poorer people moving in. It's with the older people who don't want change. These people are passive. They won't get involved. They're so old that they're afraid. All the fight has been driven out of them. It's not fear that you should be ashamed of, it's inaction. My anger with these people is that they let their fear master them. There are ways of overcoming fear and one of them is facing up to it. I was never as active as I am right now. There was a couple of times when I spoke before the whole auditorium of people over in school. I was terrified but still I did it. I felt there was a need for it and when I get up again I'll be terrified again."

John says that he grew up frightened of Authority and cowed by it, whether that Authority was the mother superior or the cop on the beat. Those in authority never sought out his views on anything. Now he finds the public school doing just that: inviting the people in and soliciting their opinions on whether a new school should be built and where and how big.

"Whether they listen or not, to me with my background," John says, "I would say that this is amazing. To be able to talk back to Authority—this is something that I have to get used to. And this is one of the things also that retards me as a leader—that I cannot talk to Authority without any feelings of fear or whatever, whatever feelings I have. It's a compound feeling, not only fear, respect for Authority and everything else."

John may be too introspective to be the prototype Whitetowner. But he understands Whitetowners. He does not know his neighbors well, but he shares their feelings on many issues.

On city politics: "People feel they are being shortchanged. I think it's more than a suspicion. I feel that people . . . my attitude is that in a political year they'll take from one to give to another. My feeling is that this is a political reality. Whether it's necessary or not I don't know. I'm angered by this. I don't like it. But I don't know what to do about it."

On Negro gains: "The colored are evening up a big score. They're getting a lot more attention. My feeling is that we [Whitetowners] don't squawk enough. The squeaky wheel gets the oil, and it's a Depression axiom. Why should you have to scream and holler to get things done? If you lack leadership, if you lack drive, you won't get things yourself. It's not just a feeling that the Negro is getting it. There's also a feeling that the richer whites are getting it."

On patriotism: "I'm an American and proud of it. When I put on a uniform [John was a draftee, serving from 1952 to 1954], it was an American uniform. People may call me a Pollack and I'll laugh at them, but I don't feel myself as being Polish. I'm an American. If you were to come with a [peace] placard down Kensington Avenue, this would get people mad enough to throw rocks at you."

On ethnic relations: "A race riot when I was a child was trouble between the Polish and the Italians. The Italians came up from South Philly and they bought right on our street corner. And there was a big fight. Now the Polish and the Italians intermarry. My sister married an Italian. And values change. Not that I would like to see the whites and colored—I still have that feeling—I don't know that I would like to see it. But, like I say, values change and they're not as horrifying when the change does come as the way people fantasize them."

On integrating Kensington: "I find myself being prejudiced. I do have the feeling that if the Negro comes in that it will deteriorate. The professional class will not move into this neighborhood. The middle class wants to move to Germantown. So what we are going to get is the lower class. I don't hate the Negro, I don't love him. But he's got to prove himself. And I don't feel that he's proving himself."

Before leaving Kensington there's one more stop to make. It's in tiny Fishtown, at the lower end of the Kensington district and just a couple of blocks from Wanda. It is the house of one of the leaders of Fishtown's unit of the Neighborhood Schools Association. She and her husband, a construction worker, have spearheaded the drive to keep Fishtown just as it is and to keep Fishtown's elementary school just as it is.

The couple is expecting me. They are ready to give me an earful. With them are a construction worker whose children are grown but whose feelings run high, and a repair-garage operator who is Jewish and a Mummer and whose children attend parochial school because his wife is Catholic.

The talk goes on for four hours. They express themselves with varying degrees of vehemence, but it all adds up to the same thing: they don't want any outsiders tinkering with their lives or with their schools.

My hostess and her husband are Italian-Americans from South Philly. They are converts to Fishtown and, just as converts to a religion often are more rabidly devout than the birthright faithful, they are more loyal to Fishtown and its traditions and prejudices than most native Fishtowners.

I had previously met a fourth-generation Fishtowner whose great-grandfather had seen Abraham Lincoln's funeral train pass through Philadelphia and through Kensington on its way to New York. This young man was thoroughly embittered. "Everything we have here," he had told me, "is anti—anti-Negro, anti-Jew, anti-everything. I don't see anything but doomsday as far as keeping the Negro out is concerned. There will be violence—blood on the sidewalk. There has been already."

But the people I'm talking to today, while acknowledging the possibility, even likelihood of violence, make no apologies for it.

Construction worker: "No son of a bitch—when it comes down to plain language, pardon me—no son of a bitch is going to tell me who I have to sell my house to. I'm not prejudiced against the colored race, believe me. I believe a man has a right to live, to make a living, a decent living, a decent home to live in—but to live decently, too. Not to be foul mouthed, and not to be a bunch of booze hounds, which three-quarters of them are. They haven't got a stick of furniture in the house, but they've got a brand-new car out there, a television in the house, and that's it. And you're trying to ram down my throat that I have to rent to one of them, or sell to one of them, no."

My hostess: "I think all intellectuals should stick their

heads in a bucket of mud. It's you intellectuals that are trying to tell us we should change. And I don't think we should
change. I think there's nothing wrong with trying to be a
true-blue American."

Her husband: "I want my children to grow up to be
good Americans, get a nice, fair education. I don't want
them to have the best; I don't expect my kids to be Einsteins.
I want them to live a normal life. I want them to come home
to me after school [he has two daughters] and not tell me
that someone molested them. And I worked in a lot of
schools where I saw a lot of white girls being molested,
buddy. And God forbid if my kid should ever come home
and tell me that one kid laid a hand on her."

Construction worker: "What gets me is this here business you read in the newspaper, you hear it all over the
place—it actually gets under my skin and irritates me—that
the Negro doesn't get the same education as the white person. I've been in those schools. I've seen whole classes doin'
nothin' but reading comic books because the teacher
couldn't tolerate them. They didn't want to hear the teacher.
They go crazy.

"I was workin' down at Seventeenth and Wharton, the
Barrett School, when they snuck that bird in from down
South there, that King. They kept it quiet till he came in
there, but that school went crazy when they brought that
bird in. Now why should a school bring somebody like him
into our district here? Let him be praised when he flaunts
the law as much as he does. You mean I should respect him
when he gets away with the stuff he pulls?"

Before going into Fishtown, I had been told that it was
probably the most bigoted neighborhood in Philadelphia.
"It's isolated and insulated," a school principal had told me.
"There has never been an effort on the part of Fishtowners
to do anything—except keep Negroes out." The conversation in the living room is not reassuring. The picture I get is

of people who like their neighborhood, like it overly much, really, but that is because they are under attack and hence defensive. They like it white, they're afraid of the implications of integration. They tend to reduce all Negroes to the lowest common denominator since it is the lowest-common-denominator Negroes whom they see most often. And so they stand firm against change and against integration. It's almost as simple as that. They can talk in generalities, as my hostess does: "People in this neighborhood want to keep it provincial. There's a very dyed-in-the-wool atmosphere where a mother can reach out and see all her chicks." Or they can spell out their opposition to integration in dollars and cents, as the garage owner does: "My mother bought her home for six thousand dollars. She put five thousand dollars into it and eight years later she sold the home for twenty-one hundred to get out of the neighborhood."

These are bitter, suspicious people with very evident prejudices. It seems clear that the attitudes one finds in Fishtown go back a long way, not only to past ethnic conflicts there but back to attitudes that George Orwell saw in *Wigan Pier*. What Orwell said of English middle-class attitudes toward English workers fits perfectly, I think, lower-middle-class Fishtown's attitudes toward black working-class North Philadelphia.

"Every middle-class person," wrote Orwell, "has a dormant class-prejudice which needs only a small thing to arouse it; and if he is over forty he probably has a firm conviction that his own class has been sacrificed to the class below. . . . In his eyes the workers are not a submerged race of slaves, they are a sinister flood creeping forward upwards to engulf himself and his friends and his family and to sweep all culture and all decency out of existence."

The conflict that Orwell analyzed in Britain in 1937 in

terms of social-class differences is both a class and racial conflict in the United States in 1970. Since a person can change his class but not his color, the conflict is more firmly rooted here. It is much more difficult to resolve here and much less likely to wither away. For this reason, I conclude, as I bid my hosts good-by, the spirit of Fishtown is likely to long endure even if the neighborhood itself disintegrates.

The Making
and the Breaking
of a Whitetown Teacher

In the spring of 1967 I decided to take a look at the schools of Kensington. It was about time. As a newspaper education writer, I had, over a period of many years, visited schools in all the big American cities. I had traveled extensively abroad, poking into classrooms from Cairo to Capetown and from London to Leningrad. Locally, of course, I had spent many hours in Philadelphia's black ghetto schools, where conditions were critical. I knew well the best academic schools, public and private, in the city and suburbs. And I'd even inspected some of the few remaining one-room schools in Pennsylvania's antique Amish land. Yet I had almost completely overlooked a big chunk of the population, locally and nationally. Only rarely had I wandered into schools, in Philadelphia or anywhere else, that were attended by the non-college-bound children of truck drivers, policemen, longshoremen, factory workers—the Whitetowners.

Nor had anybody else been paying much attention to these schools. There just didn't seem to be any reason to. In education as elsewhere, as my Kensington friend John observed, the squeaky wheel gets the oil. And the working-class white parents, if they were not entirely pleased with their schools, were at least quiescent. On matters relating to teachers, textbooks, school facilities, "relevancy" of curriculum—matters about which many black parents were up in arms—there was hardly a word from the whites. Three years earlier Philadelphia Whitetowners had emerged from their lethargy long enough to question the bussing of a few hundred Negro children from decrepit, overcrowded North Philadelphia schools into a handful of previously all-white schools in Kensington. But when it became clear that the bussing was temporary and the number of pupils being bussed small, the excitement died down. After that, nothing.

Of course, it was not safe to assume from Kensington's silence that all was well in its schools. But until 1967 there was no way of knowing. There was no way of knowing how good or bad any Philadelphia public schools were because the Board of Education refused to administer nationally standardized tests. The only tests it used were prepared by its own staff. And even in the case of these tests, it never made public the school-by-school results. So it was impossible not only to rate Philadelphia's schools against United States norms but also to rate individual Philadelphia schools against Philadelphia norms. And when their Board of Education president, J. Harry LaBrum, insisted publicly that Philadelphia schools were "second to none" in the nation, there wasn't much his critics could say or do—even though they were sure he was wrong.

Fortunately or unfortunately, depending on one's point of view, this policy of shielding Philadelphia schoolchildren from invidious comparisons with pupils elsewhere or even with one another abruptly ended in 1966 when a new, reform school board took office. In the fall of that year the Iowa Tests of Basic Skills were administered to all fourth-, sixth-, and eighth-graders in city public schools. At a press conference on February 1, 1967, the test results were announced. These results convinced me that I had been missing a big story.

Philadelphia, the nation's fifth-largest school system with 275,000 pupils, is divided geographically into eight administrative districts. In each district there are 30,000 to 40,000 pupils and twenty-five to thirty-five schools. Kensington is in District 5. In 1966–1967 District 5 enrolled almost equal numbers of black North Philadelphia children and white Kensingtonians. The Negroes live in the western half of the district and the Kensingtonians in the east. In the middle is the only integrated section—poor blacks, poor English-speaking whites, and poor Spanish-speaking whites, mostly Puerto Ricans. Overall in 1966–1967 District 5 was 52 per cent black and 48 per cent white. I examined carefully the fourth-grade test results. In fourth-grade reading, District 5's average was one year and two months behind national norms and three months behind the Philadelphia city average. Indeed, District 5 and two other districts posted the city's lowest average in fourth-grade reading. One of the districts with which District 5 tied for last place was 84 per cent black, the other was 65 per cent black. Two districts that were 91 per cent and 86 per cent black ranked a hair above Kensington's District 5 in fourth-grade reading.

In fourth-grade arithmetic the results were similar. District 5 was again in the basement, tied with the district with 65 per cent black enrollment. All the other districts outperformed District 5. It was three months behind the city average in fourth-grade math and nine months behind national norms. Its composite score, representing the average for vocabulary, reading, language skills, work-study skills, and arithmetic skills, again placed District 5 in a triple tie for

last. And the other two door-mat districts were not only
blacker but also slightly poorer economically.

It was true that among District 5's twenty-five elementary
schools, the ten predominantly white schools generally outscored the ten predominantly black and five mixed schools.
But the margin was very slight and seemed to match the
income spread, Kensington being slightly better off than
North Philadelphia. Furthermore, not one of District 5's
schools, white, black, or mixed, measured up to national
norms in either fourth-grade reading or arithmetic. In reading, only three of the twenty-five schools managed to exceed
the city average, which was itself almost one full year behind national norms. One of the three was a special "magnet" school, drawing pupils from the entire district and even
from outside the district. In arithmetic five schools exceeded
the city average but none could get within shouting distance
of national norms.

One other result caught my eye. Of 195 elementary
schools then in Philadelphia, the one with the lowest fourth-
grade reading score was located dead in the middle of District 5. And this school's enrollment in 1966–1967 was
listed as 21 per cent black, and 79 per cent white. The white
total included a sizable minority of Puerto Rican pupils with
special reading problems that were then—and continue to
be—largely unmet in the schools of Philadelphia. But the
total performance of children in this school was abysmal.
And the school enrolled many youngsters from the poorest
families on Kensington's western fringes.

It was the Iowa Test scores, then, that unmistakably dem-
onstrated the lamentable state of Kensington's schools and
got me interested in observing conditions there close up. My
timing was fortuitous. A few years earlier, Philadelphia's incredibly inbred, insecure, homegrown school system never
would have tolerated a reporter in its midst. Certainly not

one masquerading as a teacher, as I decided I would try to do.

Until roughly 1963 the entire city school system was more or less run by its business manager, a man with a tenth-grade education who, over almost three decades, built up the power to pick board members, set tax rates, prepare budgets, and dominate instructional matters while controlling school business operations with an iron hand. With the death of this remarkable school official in the summer of 1962 conditions gradually changed. The fresh air of reform blew through the system. Outsiders took high positions. The stodgy House-of-Lords school board, whose average age at one time exceeded sixty-five, was deposed. In its place came a younger, smaller, far more energetic board that cut all ties to the past and welcomed new ideas. When I sought permission to view the system from within the bureaucracy the superintendent was forty-year-old Mark R. Shedd, a native of Maine with a Harvard doctorate who was just getting his feet wet in Philadelphia. He had been hand-picked by the school board president, Richardson Dilworth, former Mayor of Philadelphia. Together, Shedd and Dilworth gave Philadelphia its most dynamic, progressive—and controversial—school leadership in a hundred and fifty years. But that is another story.

With the blessing of these two officials and with a grant from the Carnegie Corporation of New York, I took a leave of absence from the *Philadelphia Bulletin* and signed on as a substitute teacher for the 1967 fall semester. It was agreed that I would take an assignment in a Kensington elementary school and teach fourth grade as long as I could stand it—or as long as the kids could stand me. My teaching credentials were hardly impressive. I had never taken any professional education courses and had never taught for a day in a public school. My experience was limited to a brief Sunday-school teaching stint in the late 1940s and a couple of years as a journalism instructor at a women's college outside Philadelphia. Still, I thought that with luck and a lot of help I might be able to stick it out in the classroom without too much damage to the children's education or my own self-respect.

In August 1967, after being mugged, fingerprinted and X-rayed (innovations put into effect over union protests after a few persons with police records succeeded in getting hired as teachers), I joined a "survival course" for new teachers that was already under way in a North Philadelphia junior high school. In the group were hundreds of liberal-arts college graduates like me (though most were about twenty years younger than I was). They had been given provisional certificates permitting them to teach while studying for the required credits.

Attendance at the five-week orientation was voluntary, yet nearly fifteen hundred new teachers showed up. The reason was obvious: Philadelphia got almost a million dollars through Title I of ESEA to run the warm-up sessions and it paid teachers five and a half dollars an hour to attend. So attend they did, in vast numbers. Most agreed, though, that the orientation was a disaster. It was badly planned and calamitously run. The new teachers never got a crack at teaching nor even a chance to talk to living, breathing boys and girls. All we could do was watch "master" teachers at work with "demonstration classes." And very few of these teachers lived up to their billing.

The first "master" teacher I observed was an older white woman working with sixteen black children. They seemed to be of first- and second-grade age, but the teacher didn't know. She hadn't been given any information about them. "I am absolutely beside myself with this class," said the teacher in a loud voice to the observers sitting in folding chairs along one side of the room. "We go from nonreaders to children who are ready for Book Two." She turned to a smiling girl in pigtails. "This little lady," she said so that all could hear, "doesn't even know how to make a circle."

If this was an example of white racism, it was at least partially offset by the actions of the orientation director. A big, deep-voiced high-school principal who happened to be black, he ran the sessions by the numbers and by the book. Each morning there was conveyed to all classrooms over the intercom system an electronic "Thought for the Day." The medium ruined the message, which invariably was trite anyway. A typical thought: "The greatest thing in the world is not so much where we are but in what direction we are moving." Hmm. As if this kind of pedagogical pontification weren't enough, the director proceeded to place the novice teachers on a par with the lowliest students in his high school. Despite the August heat, he required the men to wear jackets and ties, protested short skirts on women, complained about cigarette smokers outside the building, and tirelessly policed the auditorium during TV lectures to make sure that people were paying attention. "Any of you behave like this in *my* school," he warned when participants grew restive and inattentive during one particularly boring lecture, "and you won't stay there long."

Attending the orientation were some seventy-five ex-Peace Corps Volunteers about to try their hand at being school teachers in the United States after completing assignments in Asia, Africa, and South America. They were among two hundred former PCVs who had been recruited by good pay—$7,090 to start—and the promise, in a letter from the school board, that "all of a sudden in urban education, Philadelphia, of all places, is where the action is." As teachers abroad, the Peace Corps workers had enjoyed the kind of respect and deference accorded instructors in school systems that are more autocratic than America's. What's more, many of them had grown to like this special treatment. These teachers most bitterly resented the orientation director's tight rein. "Screwups I'm used to," a New Englander who had served with the Peace Corps in Africa growled after being told to straighten his tie. "Condescension I'm not."

Little by little those of us attending the sessions were exposed to the minor mysteries of classroom management. We took a blitz course in filling out forms—from free streetcar-token authorizations to gymnasium-apparel receipts. We learned how to write report-card comments. My instructor's advice: "Always start with something positive." As an example, she suggested the following comment on the report of a third-grader who can't read: "John is punctual and pleasant in class. He needs help in reading."

From various sources came other snippets of information and advice for beginning elementary-school teachers. We were taught to distinguish opaque projectors from overhead projectors and stencils from dry photocopiers. We reviewed initial consonant blends and commutative properties of whole numbers. We learned that antonyms and homonyms are not from *Gulliver's Travels*. We wrote number lines and experience charts. We decided to try to develop "word-attack skills," to avoid a "mind set," to seek out "resource persons." We practiced writing lesson plans and conducting informal reading inventories. We skimmed popular magazines for pictures to brighten bulletin boards. Indeed, we soon discovered that for elementary-school teachers illustrations and advertisements make some magazines better than others. By this measure, the best magazines for teachers, we were told, are *Life, Look, Ebony,* and *Seventeen. Saturday Review, Harper's, Atlantic Monthly, Commentary* got short shrift.

Over the full orientation period we received teaching tips which later proved to make sense:

—To quiet a noisy class, try switching off the light.

—Be prepared to explain everything to small children, even something as simple as how to move a chair. Be prepared to repeat everything, too.

—Don't talk too much. Many teachers think that if they're not talking every minute they're not earning their money. Maybe what teachers need most now and then is a sore throat.

—Above all, be a ham. Good teachers are good actors. They love to do preposterous things for a purpose. Kids love to watch them and often learn while watching.

By far the most outspoken and unbureaucratic piece of advice, however, came from a non-Philadelphian and a non-public-school person. It came from Jacqueline Grennan, then president of Webster College in Missouri, who had just left her Roman Catholic religious order to free the college from church control. In a taped TV talk, the former nun* belted out her lines like Ethel Merman:

"We have to give people the right to fail if we are going to give them the right to experiment. . . . If we want a swinging, singing [school] system, we'll have to expect a lot of noise and stripped gears. . . . Little children in Head Start must learn to be skeptical of the political-economic order, even as they respect the potential of our roots. . . . The issue is whether we vote for a tradition-focused world or an evolution-focused world. . . . Teachers have to be involved in the messy insecurity of a changing world. . . . A school administration must be patriarch, matriarch, autocrat, and door mat."

* Now Mrs. Jacqueline Grennan Wexler, president of Hunter College in New York City.

For new teachers, fearfully entering a big, amorphous urban school system, this was red meat, and those at the orientation ate it up. There were few such moments, however. The last day of the training session, I said good-by to my friends from the Peace Corps. I was going to a white school; most of them had been assigned to black schools. Many seemed apprehensive. They feared restrictions on their freedom.

"I don't think," said one, "that I can do much here. I get the feeling that we're going to be watched." Another said, "My biggest worry is that they won't leave me alone." As a group, the ex-PCVs were neither radical nor conservative but genuinely liberal and idealistic. Militancy was not their style, but many seemed "change-oriented." Asked if he thought teachers should be revolutionaries, one replied, "I prefer to say 'evolutionaries.'" Clearly, the returned Peace Corpsmen would not be happy in teaching positions which, as one said, "pay us nicely but demand that we remain quiet, invisible men doing quiet, invisible jobs."

I learned later that in the year that followed, the Peace Corps teachers had tough sledding. For many, disillusionment and despair set in before the end of the first semester. A number quit within a few weeks. Their dropout rate over the course of the academic year matched the over-all Philadelphia teacher average. Some had never intended to stay. Others got fed up with the bureaucracy. Many more found the contrast between the stiff classroom discipline overseas and the relaxed, often chaotic conditions at home too great.

As for the orientation itself, the school administration scrapped the discredited format and instituted an entirely new course the following summer. The revised orientation was tied to the city's regular summer-school program. The new teachers thus were given a chance to work with pupils under actual classroom conditions. This made a lot of sense. The only trouble was that it came too late to help me.

I was assigned to the Lewis R. Elkin Elementary School, D and Clearfield streets, Kensington. Elkin was vintage Whitetown—old, honorable, and obsolete. It opened in 1903 and was named for a millionaire businessman, philanthropist, and Philadelphia school-board member who had died two years earlier. In its day the school was no doubt a splendid structure; it dwarfed the countless row houses whose families it served and withstood the years better than many of the neighboring factory buildings. By the time I got there, though, Elkin had clearly outlived its usefulness. Its all-too-sturdy, soot-blackened walls, creaky wooden floors, and rusty fire escapes belonged to the era of canings, slate writing tablets, and *McGuffey's Fifth Eclectic Reader*. Elkin had no auditorium or gymnasium and no washrooms on its three classroom floors. The only toilets for nine hundred pupils were hidden in its smelly basement, along with a large coal furnace and an open area where neighborhood mothers held daily pretzel sales.

Years ago somebody had tried to give Elkin a little chic by hanging cheap prints of French impressionist paintings on the wall outside the principal's office. Unfortunately, these sun-splashed landscapes of Provence only made the Kensington school seem gloomier and shoddier by contrast. Yet its massive bulk brooding behind an ugly iron fence is typical of what one finds in working-class white sections of American cities. Certainly Elkin's condition was no more shameful than that of the Harvard School in Boston's Charlestown, the Hicks School on Cleveland's Near West Side, or the Frank H. Beard School in southwest Detroit. And in white Kensington there were at least four other schools as decrepit as Elkin.

Elkin's twenty teachers showed up two days before the start of classes, to fix bulletin boards, put desks and chairs in order, obtain textbooks, check pupil records, confer with the principal, and generally prepare for the school year ahead. I joined a fourth-grade teacher named Maria Hoffman. She was a tall, attractive twenty-five-year-old brunette from El Paso who had taught there and in Army schools abroad and was starting her third year at Elkin. Under the plan developed by Elkin's principal, Herman Witman, Mrs. Hoffman was to teach for a week or so while I watched and then I was to take the class on my own. Or try to.

As we puttered in empty classrooms that first day, I discovered that conditions in Philadelphia's Whitetown astounded teachers new to the district. "I had no idea," one said, "that urban white childrer in the North were so limited."

Elkin's Iowa Test scores bore this out. Although its fourth-graders the previous year had ranked just ahead of the District 5 average in reading and arithmetic, they fell below city averages in both categories. In reading they were a full year behind national norms and in arithmetic they were a year and two months behind. And Elkin was ninety-two per cent white. Its only black pupils were transported from North Philadelphia in the temporary bussing program to relieve overcrowding there. Meanwhile the city's elementary schools, with better performances in reading and arithmetic, were only about thirty-five per cent white.

Of course it wasn't only Elkin's fourth-graders who were experiencing trouble. Checking files on those two preschool days, I found that of 121 children entering the second grade, 90 were already behind in reading. In other words, seventy-five per cent of Elkin's first-graders—all of them white, since only children in the upper elementary grades were bussed—failed to make normal progress in reading in the previous year. But under Philadelphia's "Continuous Progress Primary," Elkin's principal was required to advance all of these children into second grade.

On paper the C.P.P. is a beautiful concept, intended to help children move at their own speed without facing failure in the lower elementary grades. The first three years of school in Philadelphia are technically ungraded. In those three years, pupils are supposed to master nine reading levels, each a little more demanding than the one before it. They can't be forced to repeat an entire year. If every elementary school had nine teachers, one for each of the nine reading levels, and if children advanced to Level 2 only after thoroughly mastering Level 1, and on to Level 3 only after truly completing Level 2, and so forth, *then,* the C.P.P. might make sense. But at Elkin and at countless other Philadelphia schools, white and black, it wasn't working that way.

Instead, the same first-grade, second-grade, and third-grade teachers were functioning in a system that prohibited flunking anybody. Even those youngsters who were still nonreaders after one year's exposure to formal schooling found themselves pushed into a second-grade class. Although they hadn't really gotten the hang of Reading Level 1, they landed with boys and girls ready for Levels 3, 4, and 5—and with a teacher who was unprepared to teach beginning reading. And so the slow readers fell farther and farther behind. I found that one-third of Elkin's sixth-graders in September 1967 were as much as three years below grade level in reading. And six of the sixth-graders could handle nothing more difficult than the primer—the book that should be read midway through first grade. The following June I was to discover that even these functional illiterates would be shoved up and out to seventh grade. For by the time slow children reach sixth grade there's nothing their elementary school wants more than to get rid of them.

Classes at Elkin were large. Close to forty pupils were expected in each sixth-grade class. Mrs. Hoffman and I looked for thirty-seven children in our fourth-grade class.

Moreover, teacher turnover had been very high. Of the twenty classroom teachers from the previous year, only nine were back. Eleven had left. Of these eleven, three had moved out of the state with their husbands who had been transferred by their companies or taken new jobs; four had shifted to other schools in Philadelphia; one had gotten married and taken a suburban teaching job near her home; one had had a baby; one had gone on sabbatical leave; one was participating in a teacher exchange which sent a Negro teacher to Elkin. Witman, the principal, though a veteran of the Philadelphia school system, was beginning only his second year at Elkin. Despite the crush of more than nine hundred pupils in a school built for seven hundred fifty, he had no assistant or vice-principal and no help in working with his new teachers.

So a bumpy beginning seemed inevitable. But all went smoothly at first in Room 22, where I sat, because Maria Hoffman proved to know her business. On that first day, I learned two essential teaching skills for Whitetown or Blacktown or suburbia. One is patience. The other is painstaking attention to minutiae. I discovered that before grappling with global concepts a teacher must master the mini ones.

Beforehand, I had had visions of giving a brotherhood lecture to the thirty-one white children from Kensington and the six black children from North Philadelphia who comprised Room 22. On the blackboard I had taped a collage of faces clipped from magazines—black, brown, and white faces, faces of children and grownups, at work, play, and in repose. Included was a blown-up photograph of Albert Einstein. Also a poster of the smiling Negro boy eating a slice of bread over the caption: YOU DON'T HAVE TO BE JEWISH TO LIKE LEVY'S. At my request, the advertising agency which held the Avis Rent A Car account had sent hundreds of WE TRY HARDER buttons in dozens of languages. On that opening day of school I was prepared to pass out the buttons so that all the boys and girls would know that Room 22 was something special.

But Maria Hoffman had other fish to fry. Instead of teaching the little children to love one another, she taught them how to ascend a fire escape and how to get from their desks to the coatroom without traffic jams. All very disillusioning—but also rather impressive. It was a bright, sunny September morning, and before school most of Elkin's nine hundred pupils seemed to be running helter-skelter through its yard, shouting, pounding backs, playing hopscotch, roughhousing, and renewing acquaintances after summer vacation. A few teary-eyed younger children clung to their mothers who, in housecoats and pin curlers, stood outside the fence watching and gossiping.

With the clanging of the school bell, play stopped. The children had all been assigned room numbers. Now they lined up in front of the numbers that were painted on the pavement. Mrs. Hoffman's class assembled in two lines, for boys and girls, in front of "22." She quickly named one boy and one girl as leaders of the lines. They would serve in that capacity for the entire semester. She told them to await her signal before moving up the fire escape to the third-floor room. Not until the lines were straight and the children quiet did she give the signal. Even then the children were not free simply to saunter up the fire escape. Mrs. Hoffman ordered the line leaders to stop at each landing while she walked from front to back, like an Army platoon leader inspecting the troops. Only when she had again given her O.K. was the class permitted to advance to the next landing. In this way her children entered the school at the third-floor level and walked down the corridor to Room 22. There they stopped. Before allowing them to enter the room, she required absolute silence and motionlessness. The girls first, then the boys, took seats at desks on the front of which cards bearing their names had been taped.

In this way the fourth-graders got from the yard to their seats in Room 22. Few teachers exercised such tight control, however. The result, in some classes, was chaos. Within a day or two I saw Elkin kids running wildly up and down stairways and fire escapes, endangering life and limb. Without discipline, Whitetown boys, I found, can become little demons in school corridors. And many of those in other classes did. Unprofessional cries of *"Shut up!"* and *"Stop!"* soon became commonplace.

But not from Maria Hoffman. That very first day she laid down the law, firmly but fairly. There would be, she announced, no gum-chewing, whistling, stamping of feet, or chattering in Room 22. Yet she was not a martinet. In midmorning, a tall, pale-faced boy rose from his seat and, without a word, ran from the room covering his mouth with his hand. A girl explained, "He's gonna throw up. He did it in third grade." Mrs. Hoffman said nothing. In a minute, the boy returned. He looked even paler. "You all right?" the teacher asked. He nodded. The class went on. An hour later I noted the boy slumped over his desk. He was asleep or pretending to be asleep. Mrs. Hoffman ignored him. Finally, searching for someone to do a chore, she looked in his direction. "Robert? No, he's asleep." And she passed on to someone else. Robert shaped up after that.

In other respects it was a typical opening day in Room 22. Patterns were established for getting to and from the coatroom, for passing out books, paper, rulers, and other materials. The children told what they had done over the summer. They sang "The Grand Old Duke of York." They played Simon Says, studied a world map, and read a little. Clearly, Mrs. Hoffman's was not the "singing, swinging" classroom that Jacqueline Grennan had called for at orientation but there wasn't the noise and stripped gears that Miss Grennan spoke of, either. Then and later I got the impression that Whitetown teachers and parents probably preferred Maria Hoffman's approach to Jacqueline Grennan's.

While Mrs. Hoffman was getting her class off to such a disciplined start, other teachers ran into problems. One new third-grade teacher was reduced to tears within an hour by an emotionally disturbed boy who was mistakenly assigned to her room. During the morning recess, this teacher went to the office and told Mr. Witman that if the boy were not removed from her classroom she would leave. The boy was removed—for later placement in a special class for emotionally disturbed children in another building—but the teacher continued to find it most difficult to keep order. She went home and cried herself to sleep. For the following two months, life for this young teacher was hell. Each night she went to bed thinking she couldn't face another day. Each morning she awoke hoping her ordeal would end. Gradually, she learned the technique of survival.

Another third-grade teacher established fine rapport with her class at the outset. She was one of those "natural" teachers full of confidence and ability from the very beginning. But she had another problem. In her all-white class of thirty-four boys and girls, fifteen tested out at the preprimer level and three others at reading readiness. For these children, the teacher needed first-year readers. She couldn't get any. The only books supplied to her room were third-year readers, which proved far beyond the capabilities of her eighteen slowest children.

As a result, this teacher stayed up many nights until twelve-thirty or one A.M. preparing her own reading materials. Try as she did to tailor her homemade materials to individual needs, she still could not reach all of the children.

Some trailed hopelessly behind. Visiting her class one day, I examined the record of ten-year-old James B. He had come to Elkin from a near-by parochial school. The Philadelphia Catholic schools don't forward their pupils' academic records to other schools. In James's case there wasn't a scrap of information concerning his past performance or problems. He had simply walked into Elkin in September, and, on the basis of his age and a once-over-lightly session with the school's reading-adjustment teacher, had been thrown into the slowest third-grade class. His teacher soon discovered how lost he was. Asked to spell "look" he wrote "pim," for "sand" he made "mni," and for "takes" "aip." He didn't belong in third grade, but the school didn't know where else to put him. Such children take their toll on teachers. "I'm already worn out," said James's teacher when the fall term was only a few weeks old. "I come in here exhausted in the morning and blame it on the kids."

Even teachers adequately supplied with readers aimed at the level of their pupils ran into trouble. Elkin that fall was shifting from various reading series to the *Bank Street Readers,* which were developed by the Bank Street College of Education in New York and the Macmillan Company as a response to criticism of the all-white, middle-class, suburban-oriented Dick, Jane, and Sally books. "For the urban child," wrote John H. Niemeyer, president of Bank Street College, "the readers come to life with a continuous series of shocks of recognition: people, places and things he knows and cares about. In the pages of the *Bank Street Readers,* perhaps for the first time, the urban child will meet himself. Hopefully, this will strengthen his self concept. For to represent in textbook story and pictures is to accept, and to accept is to dignify."

This sounded fine. And I suppose one could argue that the city child, stuck in a steamy classroom on a sultry day in June, does "meet himself" in his *Bank Street* primer: "It is hot. The sun is high in the sky. It is hot. The street is hot. The boys and girls sit down. They sit on the steps. It is a hot, hot day." But does this really make kids itch to read? My own view is that the *Bank Street* books, for all their pretensions, fail dismally to picture life as it is really lived by small children in big cities. They don't begin to convey the sights, sounds, smells, and savagery of Blacktown or Whitetown. They don't picture the squalor, brutishness, and inhumanity that city kids encounter nor the fun they have raising unshirted hell. In short, the *Bank Street* books, while no doubt well-intended, are static, dull, and condescending. Books about Dick and Jane frolicking with Spot on the grass in the all-white suburbs at least offer poor city children a kind of fairy-tale glimpse of life outside the city limits. And there's nothing wrong with fairy tales as long as they are recognized as such. What is wrong, of course, is that black children who are increasingly conscious and proud of their blackness should be forced to view life through the antics and capers solely of white children.

In any event, I wonder whether reading books make all that much difference. While Elkin's changeover to *Bank Street* set teachers' tongues to wagging, I got the distinct impression that the kids couldn't have cared less. Then and later I rarely heard Whitetown children either complain about their readers or praise them. They seemed indifferent if not utterly bored by the books and by the reading instruction in general, except for a few bright children in an upper elementary grade whom I subsequently encountered in another school using programmed-reading materials that permitted them to push ahead at their own speed. I'm not sure that the competition these children set up to see who could read the most stories in the shortest time was altogether healthy, but they clearly enjoyed the individualized approach and felt liberated by it. For most children, though, the routine of meeting in a small circle every day to display their virtuosity or, more likely, to expose a lack of it, by pronouncing a few sentences aloud to teacher seemed to destroy whatever interest in books and reading they might have had.

What came home to me after observing Maria Hoffman and other Elkin teachers at work was that conditions were really worse than the Iowa Test scores had indicated. In fourth-grade reading, the results were:

$$\begin{array}{ll} \text{National Norms} & : \ 4.1 \\ \text{City Average} & : \ 3.2 \\ \text{District 5 Average} & : \ 2.9 \\ \text{Elkin Average} & : \ 3.1 \end{array}$$

But these were only averages. They didn't begin to tell the whole shocking story. Getting down to individual cases, I found many children pathetically mired. And once behind in reading, it seemed, they rarely caught up. I obtained the records for twenty-nine pupils—twenty-four whites and five Negroes. In first grade these children should have read preprimers, primer and Book 1. In second grade they should have gotten through the two second-year readers, Books 2^1 and 2^2. In third grade they were to read Books 3^1 and 3^2. Yet here is where this class stood at the start of fourth grade:

Name (All names changed)	Reading Level (Should have completed 9 levels by end of third grade under C.P.P.)	Book (Should have completed the second of two third-year readers–3^2)	Other Problems
Kim	6	2^2	Defective hearing
Lucy	6	2^2	
Jenny	5	2^1	
Barbara	7	3^1	Missed 39 days 1966–1967

Janice	7	3^1	Underweight, caries
Mary Lou	5	2^1	Defective hearing
Irene	7	3^1	
Kate	5	2^1	
Carol	7	3^1	Overweight
Colleen	6	2^2	Overweight defective hearing
Sandra	7	3^1	
Bernadette	6	2^2	Defective vision
Vincent	3	Primer	Repeating fourth grade
Albert	6	2^2	Missed 30 days 1966–1967
Gilbert	4	I	Repeating fourth grade
Henry	4	I	Repeating fourth grade
Bill	5	2^1	
Joseph	5	2^1	
Timothy	4	I	
John	4	I	
Leonard	5	2^1	
Harold	5	2^1	Defective vision
Sam	6	2^2	
Chris	5	2^1	
Walt	5	2^1	Defective vision
George	5	2^1	
Frank	6	2^2	
Mike	6	2^2	
Nat	4	I	Repeating fourth grade

Not one of these children was reading at grade level and twenty-five per cent were more than two years back. What could be done about Vincent, a big, gangling wiseacre who after four full school years was still stuck in the primer? Or the five other boys in Book 1?

What was the matter? Why weren't the children learning? I soon became convinced of two factors. The Continuous Progress Primary guaranteed failures by organizing for progress when there was none. And the daily lesson schedule guaranteed failures by skimping on reading instruction. Although reading was clearly the crucial subject in elementary school, downtown administrators had allotted only forty-five minutes to it in a five-and-one-half-hour school day. The reason given was that small children have short attention spans. Teachers were expected to stick faithfully to the lesson plan, which meant that a teacher who divided her class into three reading groups would spend only fifteen minutes with each group. Mrs. Hoffman insisted that American schools she was familiar with in El Paso and overseas devoted twice as much time to reading and got markedly better results.

But surely the deeper dilemma was far more complex. I suspect that it was somehow tied in with the whole drift of our society and how schools are adapting to it. Late in the 1940s the Philadelphia schools began making adjustments —and allowances—for increasingly large numbers of Negro pupils. In the first decades of this century, the schools' standards had been relatively high. If children couldn't meet those standards they were kept back. The ones who continued to fail were simply tipped out of school at the earliest possible age, which was fourteen. But in the 1930s the compulsory attendance age was raised to sixteen for those with job certificates and seventeen for everybody else. Suddenly the schools were forced to deal with thousands of older children whom it never had to worry about before.

Then in the 1940s, with well-paying jobs for unskilled workers available in Northern shipyards and defense industries, the vast in-migration of Southern Negroes reached flood tide in Philadelphia. The black children of ignorant

Southern sharecroppers were lost in the big, predominantly white city and in its schools. The schools found that they couldn't educate these children by conventional methods. They had to do something with them. They lacked the expertise to devise new, innovative teaching techniques. Surely they didn't want hulking teen-age black boys raising hell in fourth, fifth, and sixth grades. So Superintendent Alexander Stoddard, a widely respected educator who later headed the Los Angeles school system, enunciated a new promotion policy. Schools were advised to give borderline children the benefit of the doubt in every case, to push them through whenever possible, to hold back only the slowest of the slow, and then only for one or, at the absolute maximum, two years. Dr. Stoddard's plan came to be labeled the "mass promotion" or "automatic promotion" policy. It was sharply assailed by middle-class white parents, who feared a watering down of curriculum and quality. So heavy and persistent was the criticism that the school administration drew back, protesting that its policy had been misconstrued. It officially opposed "mass promotions." The furor died down after Stoddard left the system, but the policy was never really rescinded. Although officials wouldn't admit it, the procedures outlined by Stoddard remained in effect through the 1950s and 1960s. They are still in effect today.

This calamitous policy has been most damaging, of course, to the Negro children because they were adversely affected by it in greater proportion. But I think it undermined the Whitetown schools as well. There, too, slow children were advanced automatically. Gradually, the idea took hold among principals and teachers that this was the way it had to be, that there were certain white and black children, many more blacks than whites but an awful lot of each, who couldn't or wouldn't learn. Those with the grossest mental or pathological deficiencies might be shunted into special classes, there to vegetate. The rest just had to be put up with for a year until you could shove them into the next higher grade.

As the schools went about wrecking their standards, something funny was happening at the secondary level. Philadelphia's most prestigious high schools began moving to the suburbs, or rather to the outer reaches of the city, where they could continue to serve middle-class and upper-middle-class children, almost all of them white. First to go, in 1939, was Central High, oldest public high school in Pennsylvania and the city's most distinguished academic boys' school. It abandoned a mid-city section which was becoming black in favor of a white neighborhood near LaSalle College. The move was obviously engineered by influential white alumni of Central, of whom Philadelphia is full. Whitetowners weren't much affected one way or the other, since few had children at Central. The school accepts boys with good records regardless of place of residence, but not many Whitetowners ever applied.

However, Whitetowners were directly affected by another shift. In the 1950s, the neighborhood around Northeast High, the comprehensive school for boys in Whitetown's District 5, began to turn black. Northeast also had influential alumni. They persuaded the Board of Education to build a new Northeast in an all-white, middle-class, mostly Jewish section six miles from the old school. From the original Northeast the new school stole not only the name but also the school colors, school song, athletic trophies, alumni fund—and two-thirds of the faculty. The school board renamed the old building Thomas Edison High and ignored a brief student strike over the name change. Stripped of its traditions, its teachers, and whatever school spirit it may once have had, Edison has steadily sunk lower and is now a shell of its old self.

The savage blow dealt Edison was blatantly racist, and yet Whitetowners were badly hurt by it, too. It was their comprehensive high school. Although most of them were by inclination vocational-school oriented, over the years thousands of Whitetown children have attended Edison. They comprise about twenty per cent of the enrollment there now. Whitetown gained nothing from Northeast High's shift in 1957 but it lost much. Again it was a case of the white middle class serving its own interests to the detriment of the black and white working classes. Meanwhile, at Whitetown's Mastbaum Vocational-Technical School, conditions were changing, too. Mastbaum has always been over ninety per cent white and allegedly more than half its students are the children of alumni. It is a "family school" and Whitetown's favorite. Yet more than twenty-five per cent of its entering tenth-graders in the fall of 1967 were found to be reading at or below the fifth-grade level. So Mastbaum was hardly immune from problems.

A significant curricular change had taken place there in 1964, when its textile shops were closed and courses in cosmetology were offered for the first time. Cosmetology quickly became Mastbaum's most popular subject. Boys joined hundreds of girls for 1,250 hours of course work in finger-waving, marcel-waving, manicuring, permanent-waving, scalp treatment, facials, and hair-dyeing. That cosmetology holds such an attraction for high-school students may offer the schools an excuse for their lack of interest in educating them. Why try to maintain standards when all the kids want to do is make finger waves? Yet successful graduates of cosmetology courses can find instant employment at reasonable wages. Anyone who criticizes students for flocking to such courses must aim his attack at the larger society which has made beauty treatment into such a big business.

In this larger society other happenings may have bearing

on the failures of Whitetown students and schools. I refer to
the politics of dissent and demonstration, the new freedoms
in the arts, the cultural revolution, and the shattering of
shibboleths. A generation ago the movies, the plays, books,
and radio were almost wholly supportive of the American
Dream. Andy Hardy and Shirley Temple, *Gone With the
Wind* and *Oklahoma!,* Kay Keyser's "College of Musical
Knowledge"—none of these posed threats to our established
institutions. But in recent years threats have been mounted
by students, by artists and writers, by blacks, by war protesters, even by dissenting politicians. Never before in a time
of affluence has American capitalism come under such savage attack. Never before have the old, conservative ways of
living that Whitetowners cherish been so thoroughly rejected by so many people.

Whitetown is insular; it is inward-looking, but these cata-
clysmic events must have had their impact. One effect may
have been to make Whitetown kids less willing than their
parents to accept the same old nonsense in the schools. The
older generation feared and respected such authority figures
as priests and principals; the younger generation doesn't, at
least not to the same extent. As a group, Whitetowners even
today would probably be more likely than other Americans
to put up with absurdities in school and out. But the culture
shock is being felt in Whitetown, too. And this may be a
factor in the failure of Whitetown kids to perform with conventional curriculum.

As for teachers and administrators in Whitetown schools,
something strange has happened to them as well. Few of
those I talked to at Elkin and later at other schools appeared
to be surprised by their pupils' appallingly bad records. They
agreed that, technically, fourth-grade children should be
reading fourth-grade books. But they seemed to think these
levels were established for middle-class and upper-middle-

class children in the better sections of the city and in the suburbs. They didn't expect Whitetown children to measure up to them. If a Whitetown second-grader was reading the primer and a fourth-grader stumbled on Book 2, well, that was fair enough . . . considering the homes these children came from.

When such attitudes are found among white educators in black schools, they are cited as proof of white racism. But here I found white educators—not all of them but too many —writing off white children. In this case, the cause was not racism but something almost as pernicious educationally. In teaching children to read, Whitetown schools—again, not all of them but too many—are losers. They've been losing for so long that they've become inured to defeat. They've become so inured to it that they no longer realize that they're losing. Research has shown that schoolchildren generally do what is expected of them. If teachers' expectations are low, pupil achievement is low. That is what has happened in Whitetown. And the result has been almost as tragic and damaging to the children of Whitetown as racial prejudice and discrimination have been to the children of Blacktown.

I mulled over these matters as I watched Maria Hoffman work with her children in Room 22. Within the limits of the rigid lesson plan—forty-five minutes each for reading, arithmetic, and social studies each day—her performance was consistently impressive. I sensed that she wasn't going to pull any miracles because miracles just don't happen in city schools. But for children who were willing to learn she established and maintained a classroom atmosphere that made learning possible.

She spoke softly but firmly. She was warm but completely unsentimental. When children did well, she told them so gracefully, not condescendingly. She treated her black and white pupils exactly alike. She seemed apolitical. She had no great urge to improve the lot of ghetto masses or to right the urban wrongs; she simply wanted to teach as well as she could.

Maria Hoffman was temperamentally unable to function effectively in one of those "creative" classrooms where kids chatter happily and do their own thing. For other teachers such a permissive atmosphere might be fine, but not for Room 22's boss. Despite Philadelphia's absolute ban on physical punishment of pupils except by principals with permission of parents, some Philadelphia teachers often slap and whack recalcitrants. Maria Hoffman's method was not to strike or shout but to admonish and warn children against slouching, snoozing, scuffling feet, moving chairs, drumming pencils. So that the peaceful majority could work, she kept after the noisy minority. In the space of two hours one morning, I recorded twenty-five separate admonitions that she gave her class. No two of them were the same:

"I hear someone talking."

"Don't start talking."

"Who's chewing gum?"

"Put your crayons away."

"If you people are talking, you're not going to hear me back there."

"Boys and girls, that doesn't mean you have a chance to talk at this moment."

"Henry Reynolds [name changed], I have asked you three times. That's enough." [Mild hyperbole: she'd only asked him twice.]

"Sit up, Bill. Come on."

"Sit up straight, boys and girls."

"I've only been here fifteen minutes and look at you. I'm not going to put up with any nonsense from you."

"I asked you to clear your desks back there."

"Sit up in your chairs. You're not *that* restless."

"Wait a minute. We've only been in school a short time. You shouldn't be that restless."

"Chris, you don't have to supply everybody with pencils, do you?"

"As long as you keep playing with it, Walt, I'm not going to pass the papers."

"Colleen, are you trying to make sure we have to wait for you every time?"

"Sandra, I don't believe you're listening."

"Put the toys away. You're not a baby."

"Let's get the feet still."

"Don't do that to your desk."

"George, every time we come in, I have to tell you to put your things away."

"Boys and girls, I don't know who's doing all this talking, but it better stop."

"I have a little competition. Somebody is talking at the same time I am. Is it you, Jenny?"

"Don't sing—fifteen times I've said it since recess."

"Carol, are you going to stay and color for us for lunch. I think everybody'd rather eat than stay here and color."

When lifted out of classroom context and placed one after another in cold print, these may read like the scoldings of a harridan. They weren't. Maria Hoffman delivered them quietly, matter-of-factly. Rather than disrupting the learning process, they made it possible for work to proceed.

One morning less than two weeks after the start of school, Maria Hoffman was summoned to substitute for a fifth-grade teacher at Elkin who had called in sick at the last minute. Such sudden "illnesses" were not uncommon. Under their union contract, all Philadelphia teachers can take ten days off for sickness each year without losing any pay. A large number seem to view these "sick" days as paid vacation time and they miss ten days of school each year regardless of the state of their health.

When Mrs. Hoffman left Room 22 that morning, I was in

charge. My moment of truth had arrived. Two years before, in England, I had visited the Cambridge boarding school where the master after whom James Hilton modeled his Mr. Chips taught for many years. I had talked to the headmaster. He had told me how Hilton's master had won the hearts of generations of English schoolboys while filling their minds with knowledge. Now was my chance to show that I, too, was a Chips-like teacher, knowledgeable, warm, human, spurring good students on to greater heights, spotting and assisting the late bloomers, patiently setting the slow kids onto the path of learning.

Maria Hoffman's lesson plan called for arithmetic and reading before recess. I set to work. Using an abacus, I showed the class that nine disks in the ones column and one disk in the tens column made nineteen. They took turns making two-digit and three-digit abacus numbers. Interest was high. During reading, I made the children come up in small groups and read aloud from the *Bank Street* reader. Each child took a different part. Again, I was pleased. They seemed to be responding and working hard.

There was a brief interruption when a school doctor entered our classroom. He was taking part in the school system's annual search for bugs in pupils' heads. Those children with nits or lice, he explained in a whisper, were "excludable." The infestation is termed "pediculosis," and there always seems to be more of it in Kensington than anywhere else in the city. Kensington's public schools in 1966–1967 recorded 222 cases of pediculosis and its parochial schools counted 155 cases. Together, these schools accounted for more than half of the 715 cases found in the annual "head survey" in all Philadelphia public and parochial schools. Yet Kensington could claim only ten per cent of all the children examined. For years it has been the "lousiest" district in the city—nits are a Whitetown problem: they don't fasten themselves to Negro heads.* Among District 5's schools, all cases of nits and lice were concentrated in half a dozen white schools. Proportionately, the infestation was slightly higher among parochial-school pupils. And there were no cases in Room 22, which I found gratifying.

I took the class out for recess. Standing in the play yard while exuberant youngsters ran and shouted all around me, I thought, These are good kids. They do what they're told. I also knew that, despite their reading problems, they weren't stupid. Not one was truly mentally retarded and several of the worst readers were alert and observant. I'd had evidence of this a few days before, when Mrs. Hoffman played a game. She had all the children close their eyes and then sent one silently out of the room. The class had to figure out who was missing and describe what he (or she) was wearing. I was hopeless at this little game, but the kids nailed down a good police-relay description every time. One boy who had been identified as a candidate for a special class for retarded educable children recalled that the girl sitting directly behind him before she left the room was wearing a red sweater, brown skirt, and yellow socks. Watching the class at recess, I thought that maybe I could achieve some kind of breakthrough.

But it was the children who achieved the breakthrough. They broke through me. In no time at all after we returned to our classroom, things got out of hand. I was trying to teach a social-studies lesson. But I wasn't prepared, and they soon sensed my unpreparedness. They began probing for weaknesses in my defenses. They found them. And soon the floodgates opened. They started talking among them-

---

* This was bad news for one mother I talked to in Fishtown. She thought that nits and lice had been transported to her school by the black children being bussed in from North Philadelphia. She was shattered to learn that only white children are buggy.

selves. They got up and walked around the room. A few of the older boys scuffled playfully. They threw punches and shadowboxed. Others chewed gum and sailed paper airplanes.

I was furious. I was mortified. This was an outrage. Here I was, a well-traveled education expert who had visited schools on four continents. Why wouldn't these bloody Whitetown kids listen quietly? I had a lot to tell them, if they would only pay attention. Well, they wouldn't pay attention. Not to me anyway. I shouted, "Boys and girls, stop that! Don't do that! *Stop!*"

It was all to no avail. The paper airplanes continued to soar wildly across the room. For an instant I thought of *Scientific American* magazine's paper-airplane construction contest. I wondered frantically if there were some way to turn paper-airplane throwing into what educators call a "learning experience." I concluded that there was not. Gradually, some order was restored. I plodded on with the lesson, trying to get the class to locate Broad and Market streets, the site of Philadelphia's City Hall, on maps that had been passed out. Some of the children, maybe even a majority, joined me in pleading for quiet, but the vocal minority raised hell. Some of the pupils found City Hall on their maps. Others insisted that the point representing City Hall was actually "the Poconos" or the "Atlantic Ocean." I got the distinct impression that the little monsters were pulling my leg—just about pulling it off.

And so lunch. Ashen-faced and shaken, I joined the other teachers in the second-floor lunchroom. They told me to keep trying. Each had a horror story about pupil misbehavior. The conversation was hardly reassuring. And the afternoon session was worse. A phonics lesson was supposed to deal with the consonant blends *sh* and *ch*. I had met these consonant combinations at the teacher orientation. Using cards and pictures that Mrs. Hoffman had prepared, I tried to get across the idea that ship, sheep, shirt, and shoes all start with *sh,* while chalk, China, cherry, and change start with *ch.* Again, turmoil. A sea of hands appealed for permission to get drinks or visit the basement toilets. When I rejected all of these pleas, there were noisy protests. Bells clanged. A note was brought in from another teacher: "Can you lend me a dime? I took 10¢ from a girl for safekeeping and it's been stolen out of my desk." By coincidence, a girl in my own class was just then complaining that *her* dime had become wedged in a crack in her desk. Could I help her get it out? No, I couldn't. And I didn't have a dime for the other teacher.

Another note from another teacher: "Will you please keep your class quiet? We can't hear ourselves think." Very funny. Well, I couldn't think, either. The kids simply ran roughshod over me. I felt like Plimpton dropping to his knees in the Lions' scrimmage. Paper Teacher. Somehow it became two o'clock. Time for physical education in the basement. The gym instructor awaited my little band of hardened criminals. The class lined up raggedly and, on my signal, raced down the stairwell as though shot from a cannon. Hardly the kind of disciplined descent that Maria Hoffman would have required. Where the hell was Maria Hoffman? I needed help. Well, she was busy with the "sick" teacher's class but unexpected assistance suddenly appeared in the person of a mathematics "coordinator" assigned to work with elementary-school teachers in District 5. He was in Elkin for the day. Passing Room 22, he saw me slumped at my desk and came in to find out what awful event had occurred. Before I could complete my tale of woe, the class came trooping back. The physical-education instructor had refused to accept such a disorganized, uncontrolled horde. I really couldn't blame him. The math teacher, an old hand, got the class back to something approaching normal. He lectured quietly, persuasively. And he got results. The kids quieted down and behaved themselves. From *Lord of the Flies* to *Little Lord Fauntleroy* in twenty-five minutes. When the dismissal bell sounded they left in reasonable order.

The experience had left me bloodied but not yet ready to quit. It was Friday afternoon and I had the weekend to prepare for my next encounter. I read the teachers' edition of the math book we were using and I studied the teachers' guide to Bank Street's 2^2 reader, which was written for children in the second half of second grade. I got ready to prove that six tens and seventeen ones equal seven tens and seven ones. I reviewed the short *a* (as in cat, not gate), the short *e* (pet, not weed), the short *i* (sit, not nine), the short *o* (hot, not road).

At the kitchen table in our house, I wrote sentences with color pens on big three-foot-by-two-foot writing tablets. The tablets were to be hung from hooks above the blackboard in Room 22. I readied arithmetic problems for dittoing on Elkin's ditto machine. To fetch more books, I returned to Elkin on Saturday afternoon. Using a key that the principal had lent me, I entered the locked building and went up to my room. After the turmoil of the day before, all was peaceful and serene.

I hoped that this tranquillity would carry over to Monday. Before eight A.M. Monday I was in the building. Early portents were ominous. Saturday night two windowpanes had been smashed in Room 22. I found bits of shattered glass strewn on the floor. In the teachers' room, the ditto machine was on the fritz. When somebody repaired it, I ran my arithmetic problems through. All came out backward. Great. I had written the problems on the wrong side of the master sheet. Hasty corrections made. Back in Room 22, I wrote the preschool (eight-forty-five to nine A.M.) arithmetic drill on the blackboard, fetched books from another classroom, collected reading workbooks, and went outside to get the children.

In the schoolyard they were quiet. They usually are on Monday mornings; it takes them a little while to work up a head of steam each week. They mounted the fire escape to our room without incident. They tackled the blackboard drill. It was very easy. The idea was to get them off on the right foot. There was just simple addition: 18 and 7 and 25 and 6 and similar sums. Of thirty-six pupils on roll that day, however, only seven completed the work correctly. The children did so poorly—fourth-graders, remember—that I had them repeat the drill. Even the second time around they performed abysmally. We went on to the flag salute.

For purposes of "character education," as promised in the week's lesson plan that I had prepared on Sunday, I quizzed the class. How many stars in the American flag? Several thought fifty-two. After some other wrong guesses, a boy supplied the correct answer and explained that each star represents a state. How many stripes? "Six," said a boy. "Six," echoed the class. I went to the flag in the corner of the room and held it so that all could count the stripes. They counted thirteen red and white stripes but nobody knew why that number had been selected. I explained that each stripe represented one of the original thirteen states.

It was now time for arithmetic. There's an axiom in teaching that one way to motivate children is to move them from a "known interest" to a "new knowledge." To start the arithmetic lesson, I drew from my pocket a John F. Kennedy half dollar. That was the known interest. These kids were nuts about money—who isn't? And during my visits to schools in Rhodesia, Israel, and West Germany in 1966, I found that children invariably were thrilled at the sight of fifty-cent pieces bearing the likeness of the assassinated President. I thought Elkin kids would react the same way. I was wrong. They showed no particular interest in the Kennedy half dollar. "Oh, yeah," said one boy tonelessly. "We've got one at our house," said another who seemed equally bored. Undaunted, I took a penny from my pocket. It was my plan to show the class how many different ways you could make fifty-one. I had a supply of nickels, dimes, and quarters, too.

But it was no good. By this time the class had recovered from its Monday-morning lethargy. Once again, it became a juggernaut running over its hapless teacher. Boys talked and girls giggled. Small fights broke out. A girl complained that a boy struck her. Paper airplanes sailed every which way. My frenzied shouts for order were ignored. I yelled louder. Bedlam. Another near-by teacher complained of the racket. I suppose I could have made an object lesson of the most obstreperous boys by sending them to the office. It would have been almost impossible to single them out, however, because the whole class was exploding. I remembered reading of the experience of Robert Sebastian, a lawyer, writer, and Philadelphia Board of Education member, who, to get a taste of teaching, had served briefly as a substitute in a number of city schools. He, too, had run into stormy weather. At one point he described himself as being "transfixed by the bedlam." He felt, he said, as though he were "in the eye of a hurricane."

I felt the same way that morning. So I did the only thing that seemed to make sense—for me and for the kids in Room 22. I walked out of the hurricane and down to the office and I asked that somebody else take over the class. And so, good-by, Mr. Chips. I filled in on occasion after that and gave talks to many classes, but my career as a Whitetown teacher really ended that awful morning.

One lesson that I drew from this was probably the same one that Sebastian had learned. It was that in the schools of both Blacktown and Whitetown, teaching is a tough, demanding, frustrating, often nerve-frazzling job. As the schools are organized, it's no job for amateurs. If you can't stand the heat, you've got to get out of the classroom. And that's what I did.

But why had I failed? Was it because the kids sensed that I was trying to fake it? Was it my lack of experience, my lack of presence, and my thin skin? Or was there something wrong with the classroom situation itself that made teaching impossible? In a sense, I think the answer to all these questions is yes. My failure was my fault. I tried to trick these kids and they caught on soon enough. They did sense that I was faking it. I lacked the control mechanisms that grade-school teachers use to keep order. All new teachers face a tremendous challenge. In city public schools, teachers and pupils are essentially in an adversary relationship. The kids will, if they can, drive a teacher up the wall. If they can exploit a teacher's weakness, they'll do it every time. I don't mean that all children become disruptive. Most of them don't. I think that most of the kids in Room 22 were on my side. They wanted me to run the class and teach them something. But in this game the minority rules. It takes only a couple of kids to make a teacher's life utterly miserable. And of course new teachers are most vulnerable. Most of the teachers I've talked to agree that the first year is the worst and the first weeks of the first year are the worst of all. As they get to know the children and the ways of handling them, teachers learn the art of survival. Even for a veteran, though, a new class poses new problems. Later I saw Maria Hoffman reduced almost to tears when she took over Elkin's slowest and most unruly sixth-grade class during the regular teacher's absence.

My own problems were compounded by my not really believing in the courses I was trying to teach. Teachers are trained to take a course of study and teach it. Theirs not to reason why. Some of them, of course, develop their own units and show a lot of ingenuity, but truly creative teachers are rare just because truly creative people in any profession are rare. Most of them have to play it by the book. And if the book calls for the making of salt maps of Pennsylvania or the teaching of Pennsylvania history with an unbelievably dull, badly written textbook that makes the Indians seem as remote and unreal as, well, wooden Indians, in that case, teachers will follow the book and do the best they can. And somehow most of them get by.

I didn't get by. Perhaps because the courses of study were uninteresting to me, I made them uninteresting to the class. And perhaps the children responded appropriately. Their reaction was understandable and maybe even proper. If they had put up with me placidly and uncomplainingly, there might have been something to worry about. In another school several weeks later I substituted one day in a special class for newly arrived Spanish-speaking children. Their regular teacher was a Puerto Rican woman who put up with no nonsense. She was the children's first contact with United States schools, and they were clearly in awe of her. The fact that their room was directly across the hall from the principal's office may have affected their behavior, too. At any rate, with these children I spent a very pleasant—for me—day. I didn't teach them much because I can't speak Spanish and they couldn't speak English. But we groped our way through very simple lessons and they behaved beautifully. I was the same inept amateur in the classroom that I'd been at Elkin, but these Spanish-speaking children didn't take advantage of me because they were scared to. Give them a little longer in the U.S., a little more confidence in themselves and they would have wiped me out. I wouldn't say they were inherently better children than those in Room 22 at Elkin or necessarily more eager to learn. They just weren't school-wise enough to spot a fake in the classroom and get him out of there.

Although I was a fake and a failure as a fourth-grade teacher in Whitetown, I think I might have certain qualities and abilities which, used properly under different circumstances, might help children learn. Paul Goodman, the social critic, poet, and philosopher, has said that "any literate and well-intentioned grownup knows enough to teach a small child a lot." In his view, the chief criterion for selection of a teacher is "liking to be attentive to children." And George Dennison, in his remarkable account* of the First Street School on New York's Lower East Side, told how "amateurs" made genuine progress with poor children there by stripping away all the costly trappings of formal education and dealing with individual children as individuals, on their own terms. What Goodman, Dennison, and such others as Elliott Shapiro advocate for big cities are small schools, minischools, schools that tap community resources both for space and teachers, true neighborhood schools of, by, and for the people. Dennison envisions a wholly new educational environment:

All through the city, but especially in the poorer neighborhoods, where the need is greatest, there are little one-, two-, and three-room schools for young children in storefronts and ground-floor apartments, several to a block. The teachers live in the neighborhood and the schools belong intimately to

* *The Lives of Children.* Copyright © 1969 by George Dennison. Reprinted by permission of Random House, Inc.

the life of the block. Adults, adolescents, and the young all have a role and a stake in the schools; all are joined in a natural continuum. The adolescents are part-time aides, tutors, leaders in games and expeditions. Some are salaried, others are volunteers. All know the young, for they are neighbors' children, and brothers and sisters. Parents come and go as they like. Some cook lunches, help on trips, supervise cleanup and special work details. Some are salaried, some are volunteers. They are not working with younger members of "the public," but with their own children's playmates. The children in the schools feel secure and cared for. They have formed dependable relationships with adults who are important to them, and whom they see in the streets. They have made friends and working alliances with other children on the block. They know who they belong to, and who belongs to them. The gigantic public schools, in the meantime, have been transformed into centers of specialized activities. Some are devoted to the arts, others to physical sciences, others to social studies conducted as community action. . . . Nor are these larger centers known any longer simply as schools. They have become community centers and belong absolutely to the people of the neighborhood. . . . And there is no one present, not a soul, who believes that the buildings, or any other functions, belong to the State. They belong to those who use them. The uses are so intimately a part of life that the idea of compulsion has come to seem grotesque. The educational bureaucracy has dwindled to almost nothing, and responsibility now rests where it should: on the shoulders of those who are closest to the children, and those who, for reasons of their own, care most.

Goodman similarly has proposed a "radically decentralized" system of tiny schools for children six to eleven years old. By tiny school he means twenty-eight children and four teachers, one of them fully licensed and salaried. The other three would include a graduate student, a literate housewife, and a literate high-school graduate. His tiny schools might occupy church basements, settlement houses, space in housing projects, storefronts, or a couple of rooms in existing school buildings. As Goodman sees it, each small school would be largely administered by its own staff and parents, with a considerable voice for children, too. He would almost totally eliminate top-down administration. There would no longer be a need for principals, vice-principals, or their retinue of secretaries. City-wide courses of study and city-wide tests would be out. These materials would be developed as needed locally. Record keeping would be at a minimum and truant officers would lose their jobs.

Shapiro, who has won wide acclaim as principal and administrator in Harlem, also favors spotting small schools in existing vacant structures. Some years ago he said there were the equivalent of forty to fifty potential classrooms—vacant storefronts—in New York in the thirty-five blocks from 110th to 145th streets between Seventh and Eighth avenues. Such use of empty buildings, he said, would ease the classroom shortage and represent real decentralization. "It would be the stimulus," said Shapiro, "toward the creation of a new society."

According to Philadelphia's Division of Public Information there were 28,044 vacant buildings and 15,604 vacant lots in the city as of July 31, 1969. The number of vacant buildings had more than doubled in three years. Clearly, in Philadelphia and no doubt in all other big, old United States cities there are enough empty buildings available for conversion into tiny schools that could accommodate the entire school population to the age of eleven.

Of course all of these schemes are revolutionary. They strike at the heart of the American system of public education as it has developed over a hundred and fifty years. The notion that public schooling is a responsibility of the states, which delegate powers to duly appointed or elected officials at the district level, would be swept away. Instead, there would be "people's schools." Teachers' groups and administrators' lobbies would lose most of their power and influence. Gone, too, would be teacher-certification requirements and "hot air" professional education courses at teachers' colleges, standardized curricula, and standardized tests. Most important, the basic underlying philosophy of U.S. public schools, the one dating back to nineteenth-century immigrant days, that schools should be vehicles of social control rather than social change, would be ripped out.

Some will consider these changes impossible to effect, even if they are desirable, and they will consider the entire concept hopelessly utopian. Goodman himself says that most experienced teachers would reject the kind of free, inventive teaching that is embodied in his tiny-school plan. And poor parents, he says, tend to regard education that is not rigidly structured as "downgrading, not taking the children seriously, and also as vaguely immoral." Shapiro, too, speaks of the suspicions of the poor toward free activities in school. Dennison writes that some of the parents at his First Street School objected to its noise, lack of punishment, and apparent disorder. "They thought we were horsing around," he notes. Before the year was out, however, the doubting parents had observed changes in their own children, according to Dennison, and had reversed their opinions.

Dennison's school occupied one-third of an old YMCA on East Sixth Street in Manhattan. There it had classrooms, art and shop rooms, and a gymnasium. Its enrollment consisted of twenty-three children five to thirteen years old, black, white, and Puerto Rican in roughly equal numbers. All were from low-income families and half were on welfare. For the twenty-three children there were three full-time teachers, one part-time (Dennison), and others who came at scheduled periods for singing, dancing, and instrumental music. Yet because administrative and operating costs were cut to the bone and capital investment caused no drain on finances, the per-pupil cost, says Dennison, was "a good bit lower than that of the public system."

Teaching at the First Street School wasn't easy, and Dennison says one of the reasons it closed was the teachers' lack of drive. ("We ourselves were not strongly enough motivated to make the sacrifices that would have been necessary to sustain it.") And this is the problem that all school reformers and school revolutionaries face. Say what you will about the public schools, they have staying power. Year after year, they do their business, whatever it may be, for good or evil. The system was built to last. Teachers and administrators—not to mention children—come and go, but the system stays. It seems to have the ability to survive, even without dedicated, competent teachers (not that there aren't many of them). But the experimental schools, lacking tax support and wide public acceptance, depend wholly on people and not at all on structure. When the people tire or become discouraged or frustrated or must raise babies of their own, then the experimental school is in trouble. That is why such schools are so difficult to sustain over long periods.

Whether or not one is ready to scuttle the existing public-school setup for the kind of small schools advocated by Goodman, Shapiro, Dennison, and others, some of their points are, I think, unquestionably right and some of their ideas are already being adopted by public schools, even in hidebound conservative sections. For example, in some Kensington schools (Elkin for one) junior-high pupils are now serving as teacher aides for fourth-graders.* In a great

---

* After I left Elkin it instituted a number of new programs, including tutoring by Philco-Ford Corp. employees, neighborhood involvement in

many Kensington schools you find mothers coming and going as assistants to teachers, too. And with the introduction of black-history and black-culture courses there are signs of a loosening up of the curriculum. Moreover, I think—although I have no proof and am by no means certain—that poor people and working people, white and black, in many cities, are beginning to grasp the notion that the public schools are *their* schools, that they should and will have a voice in how they are run, and that as they become involved their schools become better.

Yet the pace of change in education is glacially slow. It is slow everywhere but probably slowest of all in the schools of Whitetown.

---

planning curriculum changes, and sponsorship by its Home and School Association of after-school classes in art, literature, writing, dancing, and other subjects. A cadre of concerned parents is thus trying hard to improve the school.

Whitetown vs. Blacktown

In 1967–1968 there were 35 public schools with 29,615 pupils in Philadelphia's District 5. It was the best integrated—and lowest rated—school district in the city. Negroes made up 50 per cent of its enrollment, Puerto Ricans and other children with Spanish surnames 12 per cent, and Kensington whites 38 per cent. District 5 families ranged from poverty level to working class, with a middle-class scattering in both black and white sections and with the poorest people living in the "DMZ" between. In this city within a city there were no "first families," no large landowners, no power elite. Modest affluence was rare and genuine wealth unknown. Although the whites were slightly better off than the blacks, the economic gap was far narrower in District 5 than was the yawning chasm separating the struggling Kensington whites from their suburban cousins on Philadelphia's lush, moneyed Main Line. Fishtown, after all, still had its soup kitchen.

After my classroom debacle at Elkin, I visited every school in District 5. I spent periods ranging from a day to several weeks in its twenty-four other elementary schools, its four junior highs, its one "middle magnet" (drawing children from a wide area for grades five through eight), its two comprehensive high schools, its one vocational-technical school, its two special schools for children deemed "retarded educable." As regards physical facilities, I found little to choose between the schools of Blacktown and Whitetown. Both of the high schools were over fifty years old and desperately needed renovation. Of the four junior highs the newest and best equipped (and, as it happened, best administered) was ninety-eight per cent black. By contrast, at one of the Whitetown junior highs teachers competed for the pupils' attention with pneumatic-drill operators and other construction workers. Classes continued as virtually the entire building was ripped apart. Noise, dirt, and confusion created chaotic conditions, yet the Whitetown parents frantically opposed temporary pupil transfers to other schools. They feared race mixing.

Fourteen of District 5's elementary schools were over half a century old. Of these, six were in Kensington, four in North Philadelphia, and four in the DMZ. The two oldest schools, built in 1890, both served white sections but the neighborhood of one was "changing." In the DMZ, where the schools were well integrated racially, everything was a little poorer and more neglected. Its newest elementary school was built in 1909. The others dated from 1891, 1894, and 1901. Class sizes varied from school to school and there appeared to be no pattern. Among half a dozen elementary schools with the largest classes, three were more than ninety per cent white (Elkin being one) and three were predominantly Negro. Of the six with smallest classes, two were white and four were black. However, I could detect no correlation between class sizes and pupil achievement on standardized tests. Rather, the key factors appeared to be social class and ethnicity. Working-class white pupils scored slightly better on these exams* than poor whites and both narrowly outperformed Negro and Puerto Rican children, who, besides being poorer as a group, had special difficulties with "standard English." To many of the Negro children and virtually all of the Puerto Ricans it was a foreign language.

In the matter of students and staff, District 5 claimed a whole series of unwanted distinctions. Not only were its white pupils the "buggiest" in town but its blacks were among the most mobile. In many schools pupil turnover was such as to make any sustained instructional effort agonizingly difficult if not impossible. Of 220 sixth-graders at one predominantly black and Puerto Rican grade school, all but twelve had transferred in from other schools. Some had attended half a dozen different schools in as many years. The principal had long since thrown up his hands. "I call this place a carwash," he said, mockingly. "You know, you run them through." District 5's comprehensive high school for boys recorded a higher dropout rate than any other high school in Philadelphia. Its girls' high posted the second highest dropout rate and the lowest college-going rate. Throughout the district teacher turnover was a persistent problem. In a small, predominantly white elementary school eight of the sixteen teachers were fresh out of college and the senior faculty member had spent only four years there. Of twenty-three teachers at a well-integrated school thirteen had had less than two years of experience. Of thirty-seven teachers at a large, predominantly Negro school seventeen were new.

District 5 had more "high-vacancy" schools—that is, schools with abnormally large numbers of uncertified teach-

* My frequent references to standardized-test results are not offered to suggest that such tests measure quality education. Schools and society put great stress on them, however, and it would be silly to minimize their importance as determinants of progress in our system of education, as structured at present, and in our economic system.

ers—than any other district. Scores of its teachers had "provisional" certificates that were granted only on condition that they quickly pick up the required professional-education course credits. Many of these were young men of draft age whose enthusiasm for teaching was not likely to extend much beyond their twenty-sixth birthdays, at which time their draft boards would lose interest in them. Many of the women, too, would quit teaching long before gaining their permanent certification. "We take them straight out of college," complained one embittered principal, "get them over the rough spots, and then they leave us." But District 5's principals were nothing to write home about, either. In fact, a confidential survey found a greater proportion of low-rated principals in District 5 than anywhere else in the city.

None of this should have surprised me. Within the Philadelphia school system, District 5 had long been regarded as a kind of old folks' rest home. It was the district to which you were sent if you proved incompetent somewhere else or if you just wanted to hang on for a few more years before retirement. It was a comfortable retreat for Golden Age educators. One could safely assume that Kensington would not squawk about the glaring inadequacies of its schools so long as the school people there didn't monkey with integration. And North Philadelphia didn't have the political muscle to make a complaint stick. District 5 made no waves downtown. So it was regularly shortchanged on supplies and supportive personnel by central administration, and its white, black, and brown schools were almost equally impoverished.

In August 1967, one month before I entered District 5, a new district superintendent was appointed there. His name was Richard D. Hanusey and he was its fourth D.S. in three years. Dick Hanusey broke the string of second-rate ap-

pointments to District 5. He soon proved himself, in my opinion, the best D.S. in the entire city. In a profession with
more than its share of temporizers, phonies, and incompetents, Hanusey stood out—all six feet six of him—as a solidly
grounded educator who leveled with everybody and worked
incredibly hard, and with considerable skill, to make some
kind of sense out of door-mat District 5. Long before he
ever took the job, Hanusey knew all about this turbulent
part of town and its woeful schools. He was a Whitetowner
by birth (in 1920) if not by temperament. He grew up
there, the son of Ukrainian immigrants. His father ran a
candy store until the Depression wiped him out. The family
moved to the country outside Philadelphia for a few years,
living on a farm with an apple orchard. Then the parents
and two sons moved back, and eked out a precarious existence in their old neighborhood, thirteen-year-old Dick taking odd jobs to help pay bills. In 1937 Dick finished high
school and joined what proved to be the last class at Philadelphia's old Normal School for teacher trainees. Facing
near bankruptcy, the Normal School was closed by the
Board of Education in June 1938. Hanusey then transferred
to Temple on scholarship. He was four credits from his
bachelor's degree in 1942, when he entered the Army.

During his years as a college student, Hanusey supported
himself as a professional athlete. (In those days, of course,
sports weren't the slick, televised ventures of today and ath-
letes then bore little resemblance to the shrewd, hard capitalists playing games for money now.) Under an assumed
name which he still declines to disclose, Hanusey pitched
and played shortstop for Columbus and Kansas City in the
Triple-A American Association from 1937 to 1942. In these
same years, Hanusey also played semipro football and basketball. In the fall, he was a rangy end for the Wilmington
Clippers, Philadelphia Eagles' farm team. He played Sun-

days and holidays, making fifteen dollars for an away game
and twenty-five at home. And twenty-five dollars equaled
his father's weekly income. In the winter Hanusey could
be found on the basketball court. He may have been
the only Ukrainian to play for the Philadelphia Sphas
(South Philadelphia Hebrew Association) and the only future teacher to join the House of David. For this colorful
bunch of clowns, Hanusey not only used an assumed name
but a disguise. He and all the House of David performers
wore beards made of hair imported, Hanusey recalls, from
Czechoslovakia. Basketball was really Hanusey's game and
he kept playing after his four-year stint in the Army. He
gave up the game in 1947 after playing the better part of a
season with the New York Knickerbockers.

By that time Hanusey had definitely settled on teaching as
a career. He quickly got his bachelor's degree at Temple
after the war and, in 1947, picked up his master's. He
taught for four years in a working-class section, served as
a social-studies "collaborator" for two and then was pro-
moted to principal. Over a period of a dozen years, he advanced from a small elementary school to a medium-sized
one and then to the largest one in the city (2,300 pupils).
He had come to be recognized as a prodigious worker,
a man of warmth, compassion, savvy, and tact and a skilled
educational politician in the best sense—soft-spoken but direct, trusted by whites and blacks, by his professional supe-
riors as well as by teachers, a fellow who understood the
problems of the poor because he had been poor himself and
still wasn't rich. He had long since discarded all the petty
prejudices of Whitetown—if, in fact, he had ever had any—
but unlike others who have risen from Whitetown roots to
detest the place and everybody in it, he understood and he
cared. He didn't condone its excesses but he knew that little
could be achieved by cursing the darkness. So he worked

with these people. (Long after the war he still tended bar in his spare time at his father-in-law's taproom deep in White-town. And in this job, too, he listened and he learned about human nature.)

It was to Hanusey that the Philadelphia school board turned in 1965 when it was looking for a legislative repre-sentative in Harrisburg, the state capital. Hanusey spent eighteen months in this political thicket, where partisan in-fighting and witless rancor is almost a way of life. His job was not really to lobby in the State Legislature but to serve as a kind of back-up man and information specialist for Philadelphia representatives faced with the impossible task of convincing rural-oriented politicians that the city schools were being strangled to death by the state. Most newcomers to the Harrisburg scene are appalled at what goes on there. Hanusey loved it. He looks back on this period as one of professional growth and political education. "I began to realize," he says, "how politically naïve people in education really were. And how insensitive we were to the political powers. And how the purest attitude—don't soil or muss your hands in politics—is foolish. An indefensible position. Because you can't come hat in hand asking for money and then refuse to talk to the politicians after the money is given."

Hanusey returned to Philadelphia as director of elemen-tary-school administration. He was responsible for a city-wide bussing program which, for the first time, sent Negro pupils into previously all-white Kensington schools such as Elkin. Announcement of the plans sent shock waves through white areas. Vigilante protest groups were formed and a lawsuit was filed. (It was dismissed.) To parent lead-ers at white schools receiving Negro children, a group call-ing itself the Philadelphia Committee for Racial Separation sent a vicious diatribe:

Why should good WHITE working people be forced to sacrifice their dear children in this most disgusting, degrading program to appease the lowdown Negro race? Please bend every effort to persuade your friends to oppose every effort to CORRUPT your precious children through this shaby political scheme to bus a horde of uncivilized Negro brats and force their presence on YOUR kids. It would be better to have NO EDUCATION THAN TO BE EXPOSED to this filthy tribe.

The letter was clearly intended as an incitement to riot. To combat it Hanusey and others worked closely with black and white groups, giving assurances that the bussing would be conducted with utmost care and consideration for all. Largely because of his leadership there was no trouble. Despite their apprehension, parents in Whitetown and Blacktown accepted the bussing as necessary (because of overcrowding in black schools), even if not particularly desirable. (A *Philadelphia Bulletin* survey in which I participated found parents in both sections opposed to bussing on principle and favoring neighborhood schools.)

By disposition, family background, and professional experience, then, Richard D. Hanusey seemed well equipped to deal with District 5's problems after he was named D.S. there. But what could he really do? His title was impressive but his powers were limited. There were nearly thirty thousand pupils in his district. But Hanusey had just one assistant, seven secretaries, most of whose time seemed to be taken up answering early-morning calls from teachers phoning in sick, and a staff of curriculum supervisors and coordinators who were shunted from school to school to beef up instructional programs. He had no real control over budgets or buildings. He couldn't hire teachers or fire principals. Nor could he prevent central administration from snatching whatever talent existed in District 5 for chores elsewhere. Technically, he couldn't even close a school in an emergency without first getting permission from his bosses down-town. (Hanusey overlooked this rule on a December day and shut down two schools whose coal furnaces couldn't push the heat above forty-eight degrees. But schools that were just as cold stayed open in a neighboring district while the hapless superintendent awaited word from the Administration Building.)

Of course Hanusey could and did work closely with his principals, teachers, and parents. He was everywhere—coaxing, cajoling, encouraging, suggesting. He could and did press for replacement of old, outmoded buildings and old, outmoded principals. He got white and black parents talking about their common problems together. And his personality succeeded in raising morale in District 5. But he couldn't really reform the system that so desperately needed reform because his office simply wasn't that powerful. As the drive for school decentralization takes hold, district superintendents seem certain to gain power and influence in Philadelphia and elsewhere. But in the late 1960s this hadn't happened.

Hanusey inherited a staff of principals who did not, on the whole, measure up to him. Principals make or break schools and school systems. Kids can survive one or two bad teachers but not one or two bad principals. On the other hand, a really great principal can have far more impact on more children than a really great teacher or a really great superintendent of schools. Of District 5's thirty-two principals* at the time of Hanusey's arrival, five were, by my subjective reckoning, first-rate, seven were failures, and the others ranged from subpar to good, most of them being mediocre. Within a few months, one of the quintet of fine principals transferred to another district; he was replaced

---

* There were fewer principals than schools because three had responsibility for two buildings each.

by an incompetent whose coming Hanusey could do nothing to prevent.

District 5's principals came from modest homes. Among them were the sons of a chef, a sweatshop tailor, a carpenter, a furniture-store owner, a grade-school teacher, a butcher, a postman, and a wagon maker. Three had earned doctorates and knew how to run schools by the old rules and standards. One of these was District 5's most striking principal—a ramrod-straight Whitetown conservative, wholly admirable in her devotion to her school and her dedication to the Puritan ethic, beloved by old teachers and old residents, but unable to cope with changing times, the second highest dropout rate, and lowest college-going rate among city high schools.

Two of the best principals were the children of Italian immigrants. Another whom I rated in the top five was a Negro whose own early schooling had been much like that of his pupils—he had attended five grade schools in six years. Within a year this principal, too, had left District 5 for greener pastures and a larger school. Possibly the friendliest principal was himself a principal's son, a courtly gentleman with an independent income who supplied his school with such items as a snow blower and expensive office carpeting out of his own pocket and was the soul of courtesy to everyone, but proved incapable of dealing with conditions in a large slum school.

The principals were a truly mixed bag. One, the son of Rumanian immigrants, was a vocational-school dropout who had planned to become an electrician but got interested in education while running a regimental dispensary for the First Cavalry Division in the Philippines. Another principal got into trouble as a boy and was threatened with transfer to disciplinary school. He talked his principal out of it, shaped up, continued through high school and college and finally won his doctorate. A third principal was a high-school dropout who completed his high-school and college work on the GI bill after Navy service. A white principal in a Whitetown school who retired during the year spent his last months on the phone with his stockbroker and then took off on a world tour. In the district also were two owners of camps who reportedly made more money at this summertime pursuit than they did as eighteen-thousand-dollar-a-year principals. Others skimped along with old cars and poor-paying summer jobs.

Among the white principals there was an even distribution along religious lines—ten Protestants, ten Catholics, eight Jews. The Protestants and Catholics seemed to be scattered patternlessly throughout the district, but seven of the eight Jews were assigned to schools in Blacktown or the DMZ. This was in line with past practices of assigning Jewish principals to ghetto schools. For a hundred and fifty years the Philadelphia system had been Protestant-dominated and the Protestants not surprisingly took care of their own. There were "Jewish seats" on the school board—there had even been Jewish board presidents—but never a Jewish superintendent of schools in Philadelphia and never more than one Jewish associate superintendent at a time. Jews had probably entered the system in greatest numbers in the Depression-ridden thirties. Philadelphia's Catholics, on the other hand, hadn't shown much interest in public-school teaching or administration until after World War II. Then the college-educated sons and daughters of undereducated Irish workers in Kensington, Frankford, Richmond, and other sections entered teaching as a means to upward mobility. Graduates of LaSalle College, in particular, poured into the public system and worked their way into principalships. As a result, District 5's Catholic principals, as a group, were substantially younger than the Protestants or Jews. Intellectually, there seemed little difference. But the Catholics brought a healthy pragmatism to the job. When a salty Irishman with a reputation for paddling bad actors in his Whitetown school transferred to a chaotic Blacktown school, discipline improved noticeably. The kids might not have learned more, but at least a semblance of order replaced the previous bedlam.

All four black principals in District 5 were assigned to black schools. There had never been a black principal in a Whitetown school and even black teachers there were few. Two of the four black principals were superb. Another was good. The fourth was a tyrant who ruled by terror.

Although most represented the same (lower-middle) social class, the principals differed a lot in personality and life style. Some were teetotalers while others enjoyed drinking and playing cards with the boys. No tippling during the school day, though. Not as much as a short beer at lunch because Americans in general insist that their school people behave like Boy Scouts. (However, I did get the distinct impression that a few of District 5's janitors were sneaking drinks in school basements, but nobody cared about them.) In the group of principals were a few recluses who rarely stirred from their offices and other would-be Don Juans who addressed their teachers as "honey" and "sweetheart," patted them in the right places, and played the role of sugar daddies with admiring casts of queens. Some principals were casual about their schools to the point of apparently just not giving a damn. Others were worry warts and one fuss-budget, who kept referring to his twelve-year-olds as "kiddies" and "kiddos," came to be known as "the-principal-as-Jewish-mother." Three of the nine women principals were spinsters, and a fourth, though younger, appeared headed for that status.

By far the brightest principal was a woman who ran one of the elementary schools in the no-man's land between white Kensington and black North Philadelphia. She could talk knowledgeably and at top speed about epistemology, semanticism, logical positivism, "non-intact" ghetto families, and "umbrella" phrases like "he messed with me" that slum youngsters use to describe anything from a harmless bump to rape. She complained of discrimination in the school establishment—"They still think it's a men's club." But of one woman administrator who rose to high rank, this principal snapped, "She was incredible. She didn't have two brains to rub together." Tough talk from a District 5 principal, but Rita Altman was different from the rest. At twenty-two, before beginning her teaching career, she had commanded a company of Woman Marines. She was the youngest Marine commander, male or female, in the United States. Years later she retired as a lieutenant colonel, highest permanent rank offered by the Woman Marines, and she proudly hung the Marine Corps' silver-and-gold insignia on her school office wall. But her school was not a paramilitary establishment. It was a friendly, innovative place, kids seemed happy and teachers enthusiastic. Visitors beat a steady path to Rita Altman's office and she had a well-earned reputation as a principal with pizazz. Yet with all of her brilliance—and she must have been brilliant or the hostility and jealousy of her fellow principals wouldn't have been quite so open—Rita Altman ran a school that could not win for losing. On the Iowa Tests which were given the year after I left District 5 her school ranked dead last among all elementary schools in Philadelphia.

A neighboring DMZ school was run by another fascinating character with the same frustrating results. At forty-one (when I met him), Dante J. Lombardi was a seasoned principal who talked with brutal candor of his problems. His small school was a firetrap and the only one in Philadelphia with outside toilets. His office was so small that a bigger principal, physically, could barely have fitted into it. But then pint-sized Lombardi—five-feet-five and one hundred thirty-eight pounds—was no armchair administrator. Often I'd see him, impeccable in his buckled trenchcoat and Russian fur hat, stopping a fight in the grubby play yard or interrogating boys in the hall outside his office. A volatile man, a loner, and a boat rocker, Lombardi was not popular at central administration. The bureaucrats didn't trust him. He wasn't an organization man. But he was thoughtful and articulate and had a healthy respect for scholarship. Analyzing the urban-education crisis at a District 5 staff meeting one day, Lombardi began his paper with a bit of doggerel from the Old West:

> *"Jesse rode through a sleepin' town;*
> *Looked the moonlit street both up and down;*
> *Crack-crack-crack, the street ran flames*
> *An' a great voice cried, 'I'm Jesse James!'"* *

What followed was a carefully researched delineation of Frederick Jackson Turner's hypothesis that the American intellect owes its striking characteristics to the frontier. Lombardi went on to say that the new frontier, which is urban American, is shaping our national intellect today. And in this paper, given five months before the Kerner Commission's widely publicized warning, Lombardi declared that America was developing "two permanent, separate and distinct communities and two separate and distinct mentalities. If the polarization of the poor and the prosperous communities continues," he wrote, "the quality of de-

* William Rose Benét, *"Jesse James:* A Design in Red and Yellow for a Nickel Library." From *A Treasury of Great Poems, English and American,* Simon & Schuster, 1942.

mocracy (unlike frontier democracy) can only deteriorate."

I know of no other District 5 principal who could examine his own school's shortcomings as dispassionately and honestly as Dante Lombardi did. In 1967 his school finished last among Philadelphia's 194 elementary schools in fourth-grade reading. It tied with one other school for lowest composite score in fourth-grade reading and arithmetic. Lombardi's school was then estimated to be twenty per cent Negro, twenty-five per cent Puerto Rican, and fifty-five per cent poor ethnic white. Asking for help to deal with "the most nagging and crucial problem" facing urban schools, Lombardi said:

> It is, stated flatly, an admission of failure on my part to teach seventy to ninety per cent of our boys and girls at Moffet to read effectively. Having made that admission, I am not at all willing to admit that Moffet teachers and I are doing an inferior job in comparison with other schools with similar problems and conditions. Comparisons, however, are odious and solve nothing. The fact remains that in spite of our many efforts the majority of our children are severely retarded in reading and mathematics.

An avid skier and mountain climber, Lombardi was the only principal in District 5—maybe the only one in the entire city—who belonged to the Sierra Club, the Wilderness Society, and the Audubon Society. During Christmas vacation, he would bushwhack on skis in the deep snows of New Hampshire, seeking solace from his ghetto-school defeats. In the summer he would often go west to climb. One year he underwent mountaineering training by Alpine experts in Switzerland. Unlike many—perhaps most—of his colleagues, Lombardi also read a lot, not only professional material but good literature. He was, in my view, a well-rounded human being, intelligent, hard-working, a true professional in many respects, and yet, like so many others in District 5—all of them really—a loser.

Why? Why couldn't even the best principals succeed? Why was failure so widespread? Who was to blame? The obvious answer was that the system, the bureaucracy, blocked progress. I've already suggested that the top-heavy, overcentralized structure made it difficult if not impossible for even a skilled administrator like Dick Hanusey to halt District 5's skid. There were ways to get around the system on little things but not in really important ways. And hence even the best people were beaten down. To some extent, this was true of principals just as it was of district superintendents. The principals, too, often seemed powerless. They were responsible for quality education in their schools but they couldn't go out and recruit their own teachers. They had nothing to say about salaries and very little control over working conditions. It generally took six weeks to two months to get a broken classroom window repaired, for example, and there didn't seem to be anything principals could do to speed the process. The lowest-achieving elementary schools were supposed to have smaller classes and extra help, including full-time art, music, and physical-education teachers. But while some schools got this support, others didn't—and again I could not detect a pattern on the basis of race or even on "pull" of principals.

"I have no control over my teachers," complained one young principal. "I have no control over their flagrant abuses of sick leave. They [downtown administrators] assign them to me as they see fit. I have no control over curriculum. I have no control over high pupil turnover. And I spend my time in drudgery. Why, I'm in this office at eight o'clock in the morning unloading boxes. It's not fair to say to a principal, 'Get turned on,' but not supply him with money to get turned on with. Schools like mine that sit on back streets and in districts like this are forgotten."

Of course, the fact that his teachers abused sick-leave rules may have reflected more on this principal's weak leadership than on their lack of dedication. Still, he had a point. Principals are inundated with paperwork. They mediate meaningless spats and waste hours on trivia. And the truth is, running a building full of women teachers, many of them prima donnas with personal problems and fits of temperament, is hard work for any man. Beyond that, in the poorest sections of big cities, neighborhoods are so fractious and school conditions so chaotic that principals spend much of their time trying to solve problems that are never mentioned at the teachers colleges and schools of education.

The morning of my first visit to District 5's virtually all-black Wanamaker Junior High School, the doors were closed and hundreds of students were milling in the yard. Inside I found the black principal, Charles Leftwich (one of the five principals whom I rated top-notch) coolly dealing with yet another bomb scare. Three days that week classes started late at Wanamaker while police searched for bombs that telephone callers insisted had been placed in the building and were about to explode.

The day I visited another junior high in District 5 a white pupil went to the principal with a family problem. Her mother was forcing her to marry a foreigner who needed an American wife to stay in this country and was willing to pay a thousand dollars to get one. The marriage license had been obtained and the wedding was set for that night. It was a case of white slavery in Whitetown. With some hasty phone calls, the principal and a counselor managed to get the girl committed to a church home later that day, and the last I heard the wedding was off. But the school alone had stood between this poor-white girl and a life of forced servitude.

To get a taste of a principal's life in District 5's DMZ, I dogged the steps of Dante Lombardi at the crumbling, seventy-six-year-old John Moffet Elementary School. Moffet had no auditorium, gymnasium, or lunchroom. Its creaky furnace threw up heat so unevenly that teachers and students regularly fell victim to "Moffet croup." Its wood-and-brick construction was non-fire-resistant, causing Lombardi recurrent nightmares of a holocaust. While I was there his school day went like this:

8:40 A.M.   Girl with cast on her leg knitting slowly after a break falls in schoolyard. Boy bursts into Lombardi's twelve-by-fifteen-foot office with news. Lombardi races outside, finds girl lying on cold pavement by wall of school. She's crying. Temperature is thirty. Lombardi removes his trenchcoat and drapes it around girl's shoulder. Other coats are produced and girl is made as comfortable as possible. Lombardi doesn't want her moved. He sends word to have his secretary call police and the girl's parents. Fifteen-minute vigil in frigid yard. Girl's mother arrives—a large, blowsy woman with purple veins protruding from forehead. Soon the father, a roughly dressed workingman, drives up in old-model sedan. Lombardi briefs both parents. Still no police wagon. Second call to stationhouse. Desk sergeant says wagon should be there. Father finally decides to drive girl to doctor's office. Lombardi helps her into car, and they drive off.

9:15 A.M.   Police wagon arrives. Officers are miffed to find girl is gone. They leave in huff.

9:20 A.M.   Lombardi phones district office seeking substitutes for three of his new teachers who are attending special workshop. He's told he'll get none. Instead, Temple students practice-teaching at Moffet will "cover" * the absent teachers' classes.

9:45 A.M.   Third-grade girl with toothache and big tears comes to see Lombardi. A nurse is assigned to Moffet three half-days a week but this isn't one of them. Lombardi is the resident doctor, dentist, eye-and-ear specialist, and psychologist. He examines the aching tooth, then notifies the girl's mother that he's sending her home.

10:00 A.M.   Enter a cute little seven-year-old boy with brown hair, big brown eyes, and a clip-on bowtie. He seems bright and cheerful. Recently, he tried to burn down his house. He is hostile, defiant, destructive, a real hellion at home and school. He is driving his mother crazy and her furious beatings only make him worse. Because the boy is safer in school than out, Lombardi has offered not to suspend him for misbehavior but rather to remove him from his class when necessary and place him somewhere else in the school. This is what he does now. He estimates that at least fifty children at Moffet—ten per cent of its enrollment— need psychiatric help or special counseling attention. They aren't getting it. And they probably won't get help unless they commit a crime or get into some other serious trouble. Counselor tells me half seriously that she is sometimes tempted to give troubled boys knives—just so they'll qualify for treatment.

10:15 A.M.   Two boys report to office. They'd been fighting. One is seven and in second grade—small, freckled,

---

* "Cover" is the term used by school people to describe the placing of an adult body in a classroom when the regular teacher is out for some reason. Those covering classes aren't expected to teach children anything; their job is to see that all hell doesn't break loose.

with gray eyes and wide ears. Norman Rockwellish. The other is eleven, tall, dark, handsome, with a proud, composed look. Lombardi can't get a straight story from the two so he sends them to the principal's bench in the hall to talk it over and agree on what happened. In a few minutes, they return and give the principal a coherent account: The smaller boy, Eddie, was playing hopscotch on the sidewalk when the other, Anthony, kicked a chain Eddie was using as a boundary marker. Eddie yelled at Anthony, "You black bitch." Anthony kicked Eddie. Both then were sent to see Lombardi, who lectures both boys sternly. He directs both to spend half an hour after school on each of the next two days.

10:30 A.M.   The president of Moffet's Home and School Association comes in seeking ten dollars in cookie-sale receipts to make some purchases. The counselor who keeps the money is out. In her absence, Lombardi lends ten dollars to the parent.

10:45 A.M.   The mother of the girl who fell in the yard reports that X rays show no further break but her daughter must keep off the leg for a week. Lombardi sends a note to the girl's teacher suggesting she provide books and homework while the pupil is out.

11:15 A.M.   Fourth-grader complains of feeling ill. Guidance counselor takes her temperature. Child breaks off the tube in her mouth. At Lombardi's suggestion, counselor calls city's Poison Information Center to find out if it's dangerous to swallow mercury. Center says the only danger would lie in swallowing glass from broken thermometer. Search for bits of glass is started. Glass found. Child is told to stay home after lunch.

11:30 A.M.   Fourth-grade boy who just transferred to Moffet from neighboring school tests at 2^2 in reading. He's almost two years behind national norms but on a par with

many Moffet pupils. He's another statistic in Moffet's transiency rate—about fifty per cent of the enrollment comes
and goes during the school year.

11:45 A.M. A second-grader carries a note from his
teacher to the office:

> Mr. Lombardi: Benjamin is a bit of a problem. He refuses to
> do a thing I tell him. When I told him to sit still and fold his
> hands he stuck his tongue out at me.

Lombardi knows the teacher is struggling in her second year
with a slow class. Benjamin has cut up before. His older
brother, a sixth-grader, has been suspended for striking a
teacher. The boys' parents are volatile. Lombardi sends
Benjamin home with a note saying he's not to return until
one of his parents appears for a talk with the principal.

Noon. Lombardi goes out to lunch.

12:45 A.M. While Lombardi is still out, Benjamin's
father shows up. He demands to see Benjamin's teacher. In
her presence he removes a heavy leather belt from his waist,
turns his son around and whips him fiercely. The child's
screams fill the hall. His father smiles broadly and encour-
ages onlookers to hit Benjamin any time he's bad. Lombardi
arrives after the father leaves. He is told what happened.
"As far as I'm concerned," he says, "that ends Benjamin's
suspension."

1:30 P.M. Moffet safety patrol member reports being
pricked by boy with hatpin. Says six other Moffet children
also were pricked. Names the hatpin wielder. Lombardi
summons the assailant, gets the names of all the victims. He
presses the boy for details. Almost casually the youth admits
that after picking up the hatpin in the street he had observed
a dead rat in the gutter. Says he stuck the pin in the rat's
corpse before pricking the other children. Lombardi flies

into action. He calls police and asks for a wagon. He buzzes the victims' classrooms and has them come to his office. Their parents are notified. Lombardi calls city health department, is advised to wash the wounds with green soap. He calls school board's health department, is advised to send children to hospital. Lombardi follows latter advice. Six boys go in police van to hospital. Police pick up the dead rat for tests. Boy with hatpin is suspended.

3:30 P.M. School's out.

7:30 P.M. Lombardi, at home, suddenly realizes that in all the excitement only six boys had gone to the hospital, while seven had been pricked. One had been overlooked. Lombardi knows who it was. He phones the boy's parents and they take their son to the hospital. Lombardi has trouble getting to sleep.

The case of the hatpin stickings ended happily. None of the victims was sickened and tests on the rat proved negative. The point is, though, that Dante Lombardi's day was largely taken up with noninstructional matters. During my three weeks at Moffet he had hardly any time for staff development, curriculum improvement, thoughtful supervision and direction of the school program. As a principal, Lombardi may not have been perfect. He may have been too autocratic. At faculty meetings, for example, he talked and his teachers listened. And perhaps he overstressed discipline. His pedagogical style was more European than progressive American, but it was his own and he was being honest to himself in adhering to it. He lost his temper sometimes but he had class all the time, in dress, in speech, in dealing with people. And when he was transferred at the end of the 1968–1969 school year, his teachers threw a party that any principal would cherish—complete with songs in his honor, tears, and a mock bawling out of Hanusey for making Lombardi leave Moffet.

I don't mean to suggest that Lombardi was typical of District 5's principals. He wasn't. In my opinion, he was one of the very best. Most of the others were mediocre, and this mediocrity seemed to be fairly equally distributed over the entire district. I couldn't detect important differences in the quality of principals in Whitetown vis-à-vis Blacktown. All had been selected in the same way. They were ex-teachers (almost all of them having risen in the city system). Once passing the required tests and winning appointments as principals, they were secure in their jobs. In Philadelphia, all principals are rated twice a year by their district superintendents, but it is virtually impossible to get rid of even the most hopeless incompetents. They are never fired outright but are simply shunted into paper-pushing jobs downtown.

Yet as a group, Philadelphia's principals must have felt terribly insecure. How else to explain their threat, made while I was observing in District 5, to join the Teamsters' Union? In any other modern industrial country, a unionized merger of truck drivers and school principals would have been unthinkable. It was, perhaps, a mark of Philadelphia's nagging anti-intellectualism that published reports concerning the curious amalgamation caused hardly a murmur. Philadelphians apparently didn't expect principals to behave like professionals because in so few respects were they treated like professionals.

And this brings me to another related point: If principals are, as a group, untalented, perhaps it is because the United States, as a nation, and Philadelphia, as a city, have not, until comparatively recently, paid much heed to the quality of public education. The business of America was business, and if you couldn't do anything else you went into teaching and, in many cases, from teaching into school administration. Of all graduate students, those in graduate schools of education have customarily ranked at the bottom intellectually. And prior to the school-board reforms of the 1960s, janitors in Philadelphia high schools were paid more than principals in small elementary schools. Nor was this unusual. In New York City some school janitors made more money than all but the highest-paid administrators.

But if the district superintendent and the principals could not be blamed—at least not wholly—for the failures of District 5's schools, what about the teachers? Awhile back I said that great principals affect more children more deeply than great teachers. I think this is so. But it would be wrong to underestimate the importance of teachers. Just as the cop on the beat enjoys greater discretionary power over the lives of citizens than does the police commissioner, so the classroom teacher has more to say about what children learn than does the superintendent of schools. No matter what the school or central administration does, it's what goes on in the classroom that counts. And what went on in District 5's classrooms, in a period of liberal reforms downtown, was extreme conservatism. Race was irrelevant. In Blacktown and Whitetown classrooms alike I found tough, demanding, old-line battle-axes, sticklers for discipline, foes of all behavior that differed from the conventional.

In a Blacktown school I talked to a Negro fifth-grade teacher. This man had known racism. He came home from the Korean War to discover that a restaurant on a major highway in Maryland wouldn't serve him. He'd known housing discrimination in Philadelphia. Yet he felt nothing but contempt for the school reformers. "When I went to their institute," he said, speaking of the teacher orientation that I, too, had attended, "and saw some of those beatniks . . . Let me clue you, if one of them was teaching my kids, forget it." His distaste for miniskirts equaled that of the most orthodox, up-tight Whitetowner. "I'm not old-fashioned, by no means," he said. "But this kind of dress, action, look is not going to get respect. There's a time and place for everything. Old sweaters, saggy pants, dirty shoes —that's what sixty-one hundred dollars* of the taxpayers' money goes for?" Henry H. Nichols, the black clergyman who was vice-president of Philadelphia's Board of Education, once advocated the whipping post for school miscreants, and this black teacher took the same hard line. "We should be able to kick kids out of school," he told me. "If the city doesn't have a place to put them, then build one. We've all got kids who should not be in regular school. You can't teach 'em. You can't suspend 'em. I'm different. I'm not going to take their foolishness. I mean, 'There's the door. If you don't want to learn, get out.' Life is too short to put up with foolishness in class."

On the other side of the district in a typical Whitetown school, I met a typical Whitetown teacher. A spinster of about sixty, short and dumpy, with a perpetual scowl, a Churchillian jut to her jaw, a turned-down nose, and glasses. She glowered ferociously at her third-graders. She had been teaching the same way for over thirty years and never would change. She was an old-style patriot and in her room were ten American flags. She was a gung-ho Christian —I don't know whether Protestant or Catholic—and two weeks before December twenty-fifth she started getting her class ready for the big day. There were carols to sing, records to listen to, presents to make, poems to memorize. ("What is Christmas? What is Christmas? That is what we want to know/What is Christmas? What is Christmas? What makes people's faces glow?")

Like so many Whitetowners, this teacher opposed "per-

* Starting pay for Philadelphia teachers in 1967–1968. By 1970 it had risen to $7,100.

missiveness." She was an old-style disciplinarian. "If one of my children misbehaves," she said, "he knows he's going to get whacked—right now." Lecturing to her class, she was ever the starchy schoolmarm: "We want to do what is right because our parents expect us to. Our girls are going to be little ladies. We will think it a disgrace to raise our hands in fighting. The same goes for the boys. There is no need for boys to be roughnecks. We can share what we have."

The day I watched this teacher an observer from the Board of Education popped in briefly. A liberal-arts graduate with a master's from Berkeley, she was one of the bright young people recruited by the reform administration. She was appalled. "There's no joy. These children have so much potential—and look at them." It was true. The kids were sitting like zombies. They were listening under duress, but they were hardly enthralled. The teacher was unconcerned. The kids weren't going to tune her out. They wouldn't dare.

In a Blacktown school one day a Negro teacher who practiced this same kind of iron-fisted discipline invited me to speak to her sixth-graders about my travels as an education reporter in Africa. I tried everything to loosen up this class. I told jokes. I displayed African carvings. I compared the Philadelphia school with classes I visited in African mud-hut villages. Nothing worked. I spoke for forty minutes to pin-drop silence. Any questions? None. Finally, a girl rose, apparently on signal, and thanked me on behalf of the class. Beautiful. And horrible. But who was I to complain about too much discipline? E. E. Cummings said that before you can do without punctuation you must learn to use it perfectly. The same goes for discipline.*

* A Peace Corps teacher told me about school discipline in Turkey. He'd been having trouble controlling his class. His principal gave him a tip. When the teacher entered class next day, he was to make sure that every child rose. If one did not stand the teacher was to go to his desk and, wordlessly, slap him across the face, once forehand and then backhand.

In most of District 5's schools I found generally cold, formal relations between teachers and children. There were individual classroom exceptions, of course, but the rigid pattern crossed race lines. The one really relaxed operation was the special "middle magnet" school, where all kinds of innovative approaches were being tried, one being much more freedom for pupils in class scheduling and in their relations with teachers. In the other schools, however, classes ran pretty much as they must have done thirty or even sixty years ago.

It was clear to me that among teachers the racial gap was not as wide as the age gap. The older teachers stuck together. They ate together; often I would find half a dozen of the old-timers sitting in a classroom at lunchtime, munching sandwiches and watching soap operas on the class TV. These groups would be mixed racially, but rarely would I see a young teacher lunching with the veterans, or vice versa. Especially in Whitetown, I noted that one or two old teachers sometimes seemed to have more power than their principal. In a Kensington elementary school, the principal had set up a standard reading cycle for fourth, fifth, and sixth grades. For reading instruction, these grades were split up so that the children could be grouped by ability. The two senior teachers threw a monkey wrench into the cycle by refusing to participate. The principal didn't make an issue of it because the two were his most strong-willed teachers—and possibly his best. Nor did he demur when these two teachers commandeered corner classrooms on the second floor though they belonged on the third. Teachers, I found, prefer corner rooms. The older teachers usually get them and often they won't give them up without a fight.

As it happened, one boy did fail to stand when the Peace Corps teacher entered his class the following morning. The teacher struck him as per directions. He had no more trouble with the class for the balance of the year.

"Teacher power" is often impressive. One morning I was in a Whitetown principal's office when his star teacher—an old-timer—walked in. "Did you see my note?" she asked. She had asked for a new desk. By coincidence, the principal had ordered two new desks—one for himself and one for his administrative assistant. He knew that if he gave this teacher the desk intended for his assistant, her cohort, equally determined and also fifteen years older than the principal, would demand a new desk, too. That would mean giving up his desk to her. The principal maneuvered. "It's a metal desk," he said demeaningly. But the teacher wouldn't be put off. She was adamant and the principal finally surrendered gracefully. "Marty and I don't really need new desks, anyway," he said with a smile. And so the two old curmudgeons got them.

Sometimes, though, teacher power is more destructive. At a Fishtown school, I found three fifth-grade classes divided up for reading. One group consisted of more than forty slow readers. The other two groups included the better readers and each had fewer than thirty children. These groups were set up by two old-timers who taught the faster and smaller classes, leaving the large, slow group for a first-year teacher. It turned out that the principal delegated authority to the teachers for all grouping and was not even aware of the conspiracy against the new fifth-grade teacher. Needless to say, the older teachers' decision virtually guaranteed that the slowest readers would fall even farther behind.

It was not unusual for tough old teachers to call signals that way. Teacher conservatism was most deeply rooted in a Lower Kensington school serving possibly the poorest white neighborhood in the entire city. Before its replacement in 1969, this school was in even worse condition than Elkin and Moffet. And its pupils were so dirty that the principal finally asked for and got a special inspection of all children by the school board's medical division. Following examination of heads and scalps, more than one hundred of the six hundred pupils in the school were excluded for nits and lice. The neighborhood was outraged, but the principal stuck to her guns and issued instructions on how to get rid of nits—a steel brush and strong disinfectant were recommended.

In dealing with her faculty, this principal was less successful. She was new, but some of her teachers had been in the building for decades. They were stuck in their ways and would not change. They hoarded books and wouldn't share them with new teachers. One old girl refused to yield the keys to the schoolbook closet. The old teachers rigged the duty schedule, giving themselves light loads for recesses and lunch. Only after much pleading did the principal persuade a couple of them to break their children up into reading groups—never mind the interclass and intergrade reading cycle.

In both Whitetown and Blacktown schools, I heard older teachers complaining about the dress, manners, and attitudes of the newcomers. Certainly, there was—and is—a striking difference in the outlook of old and new teachers. I suppose it's all part of the generation gap and the economics gap. Jobs simply don't mean as much to people in an age of affluence as they do in hard times. Most new teachers today take their appointments as a matter of course. Being hired by a big-city school system, in particular, is hardly a cause for major celebration in 1970. Thirty years ago, though, it most certainly was. Teacher openings then were few and the big cities attracted top talent. Often even the most qualified candidates—those at the top of the teacher-examination list—had to wait years for appointments.

Take the case of Anna Mae Wilhelm. As long as she lives she'll remember June 25, 1940. Anna Mae, though fully

qualified, had been subbing for eight years, waiting patiently
for a permanent appointment. On that June day she received her permanent appointment to the Thomas J. Powers
School in Kensington. She can still recall the joy she felt as
she drew the letter from her mailbox.

> I took that thing and jumped three feet. Out the door, down
> the street, waving it in the air. I have my appointment. I'll
> never forget it. My family—I couldn't wait to tell them.

Anna Mae Wilhelm was still teaching at Powers when I
paid my visit in 1968. She was far and away the best teacher
in the building—and possibly the best in District 5.

But of all the teachers I observed, the one who made the
strongest impression on me was teaching a very slow third-
grade class in a Fishtown school. Most of her pupils that
year were black and Puerto Rican children who were bussed
from North Philadelphia until their own new school opened.
The teacher had grown up in Fishtown. Her father was Jewish and her mother an Irish-German Baptist. Anti-Semitism
had been strong in Fishtown and both families opposed her
parents' marriage. But the young couple stayed there, raised
the daughter who later became a teacher, and enjoyed life.
"I was lucky because I wasn't told to hate," the teacher,
Judy Sheidell, said. "I never heard the word 'nigger' in my
mother's house." She went through Kensington schools and
Temple, got married, moved to Scarsdale, taught there for
five years and, following a divorce, moved back to Fishtown
with her three-year-old son. She was comfortable teaching
in Fishtown and living there. She had three first cousins and
one hundred second cousins, and many of them were her
neighbors.

In the classroom Judy Sheidell was warm, perceptive,
understanding—just an all-around first-class teacher. When

I visited her school the teachers were making out report cards. For many this was a humdrum job to be disposed of in an hour or so. For Judy Sheidell it was a labor of love taking a great many hours. She viewed the report card as her single best chance of communicating with the parents of her pupils. In the "Comments" section of the cards she poured out her hopes, fears, and evaluations of each child. "I implore you to reconsider your decision concerning Roy's class placement," she wrote the parents of a (white) boy who had insisted that their son be advanced into fourth grade despite his miserable third-grade record.* "Unable to cope with class assignment, he is floundering in a sea of failure. Please rescue him. Give him the special training he so desperately needs. I will be available for conference at any time. Please make an appointment to see me in the very near future." In another case, Judy Sheidell's excitement at signs of true progress burst through: "What a joy to watch John's metamorphosis—his development from a shy child lacking in many basic skills to a more self-assured student. We must help him keep up both the direction and pace of this growth if he is to be ready for the fourth level next fall. I trust that you will continue to work with him each evening. Numbers need particular attention." Or, again: "A warm, sweet child, Nicky is a classroom delight. He tries, truly tries to complete each task. His attempts are thwarted because of his lack of basic academic skills. His reading, writing, and number proficiency are far below grade level. Let's work with him at school and at home to develop them. He has the will. We can find the way."

Far more common, of course, were the cold comments about under achievement that could be dashed off in less

* Under the Continuous Progress Primary, the slowest children take four years to complete the first three grades. However, they cannot be held back in grades one or two and parents can block a decision to have children repeat third grade.

than a minute. "Evelyn needs to work harder in reading and arithmetic," wrote a typical teacher who was just putting in her time. "Her work shows careless mistakes and a lack of paying attention." And a first-grade teacher, following the rule of saying something nice before lowering the boom: "Frederick is courteous. He does not seem too interested in school. He must concentrate on his work. Please help him count at home." A report on this teacher might note that she, too, like Frederick, was courteous but not too interested in school. One principal was close to the mark when he told me, "It's amazing the way children reflect the teachers' attitudes. They give back what they get. There are teachers who teach thirty years and retire. And there are teachers who teach one year thirty times and retire."

It is clear that no real teaching takes place unless it is accompanied by learning. Yet very often what passes for learning is merely an exercise for the teacher. But I should be the last person to underrate the trials of big-city teaching. Many teachers I talked to felt that their principals were not backing them. Often I was told of principals who winked at wild behavior because they didn't want outsiders to discover how awful the classroom conditions actually were. "Principals accept very deviant behavior from kids when they should be much tougher," said one new teacher. "They want to keep the problem in the school."

For many of the Peace Corps teachers the transition proved too much. One young man had been born in Russia but grew up in Philadelphia and, as a Peace Corps Volunteer, taught school in Bolivia. He was assigned to an elementary school in District 5's Blacktown. When I encountered him he was at the end of his rope.

In Bolivia the kids had respect for learning. They didn't know what it was but they had respect for it. Here there is a com-

plete absence of motivation for learning. I see no realization
that education is, in fact, good. Here the people are from too
many backgrounds. Most are drifters, coming in in September,
leaving in December, and they don't really care. There are
so many kids in some families nobody seems to know how
many. No family organization. No community organization.
A drifting society. A society that has no roots. Compounding
the problem is the permissive society.

This young man's idealism—he had, after all, joined the
Peace Corps—had vanished in District 5.

More typical, perhaps, was another teacher, the daughter
of a common laborer who had worked her way up from
poverty and just couldn't stand seeing poverty again every
day in the eyes and bodies, clothes and behavior of her
black pupils. "They come off the bus," she said of youngsters who were attending a school in a white section outside
District 5 while their neighborhood school in North Philadelphia was being rebuilt.

They look so sour. Some haven't had any breakfast. They're
exposed to problems we have no awareness of. Most are very
dirty. Their clothing is unchanged for days. No matter how
poor you are, even if you are too poor to buy soap, there is
always water. Teaching is hard enough without fighting these
problems. Your heart must really be in it and I know that
mine is not.

A third teacher really did have his heart in teaching the
poor. A veteran of the Peace Corps and the Job Corps, he
was a dedicated civil-rights marcher and antiwar demon-
strator. His teaching assignment in District 5 was to the
Blacktown school whose principal was the black martinet I
mentioned earlier. For his class of virtually nonreading fifth-
graders, he developed some fresh, innovative approaches.

He wanted to discard the conventional readers and let the class, in effect, write its own simple books. After one week, when the principal got wind of what he was doing, she ordered him to cease and desist and to resume using the regular readers, or else. Even at that, she gave him a D rating, just one notch above unsatisfactory. After one year, this teacher gave up his job in Philadelphia and took a teaching assignment in Maryland. He was terribly depressed and ready to believe that he could never succeed in a black school. "There really is a difference between black and white," said this discouraged integrationist. "A difference in personalities. I see it in me. I see I have more in common with white people, even conservatives." Thus had the system —the economic and social system as well as the education system—beaten him down.

I came to respect the ingenuity of some teachers. The best ones are great collectors. Almost anything is grist for their mill. An Elkin teacher who had prepared a skit about Franklin D. Roosevelt's visit to George Washington Carver at Tuskegee Institute was on her way to school the day of the play when she suddenly told her husband to stop the car. It was trash day and the sidewalks were piled high. In the junk she had spotted a pair of crutches. She grabbed them for the boy who played FDR—just the needed touch, and out of a trash heap.

There were some wonderful moments. Like the time the third-grader in the Whitetown school, asked to name some of the animals her class had seen at the zoo, spoke of lions, elephants, bears, and a "cantaloupe."

More often than not, though, the prevailing mood was grim and forbidding. It seemed to me that the public schools of Whitetown were more starchly, prissily, evangelically re-

ligious in their orientation than the parochial schools themselves. It was not only the vastly overdone pre-Christmas
preparations but a kind of holier-than-thou atmosphere that
permeated so many classrooms. In one school this piety was
given verbal expression at the base of a plaque honoring the
man for whom the building was named. HE WAS THE REPRE-
SENTATIVE OF CHRISTIANITY IN ITS PURITY, said the inscrip-
tion, dated February 12, 1909, and presented by a Protestant church. Yet in this school and others in Whitetown
racial prejudice was just as pronounced among the white
faculty members, I suspect, as it was in the community generally. It was not the blatant, vicious bigotry of the hell-of-a-
fellow Whitetowner but the old-fashioned, these-people-are-
different, a-little-dirtier, a-little-less-intelligent-than-we-are
mentality of strait-laced, churchgoing, middle-aged white
women, many of them unmarried.

Yet in all of this the Whitetown schools were a pretty fair
reflection of the community they served. And in both Whitetown and Blacktown the parents generally were noncom-
mittal about their schools or overtly supportive of them.
I heard very little criticism of the schools. One principal
who had been vainly seeking to update teaching techniques
in her school observed that she was virtually alone in opposing the staid old ways. "Rarely do you get a complaint from
parents about the quality of teaching," she said. I came
away convinced that Whitetowners and Blacktowners alike
were basically conservative in their views toward education.
They favored a curriculum that was more attuned to the
nineteenth century than the twentieth. They were unim-
pressed by abstractions. They wanted meat-and-potatoes
basic education. They wanted drill in reading, writing, and
arithmetic. They wanted homework. They wanted prayers
and Bible reading. They wanted physical punishment. They
wanted all these things because they had never been exposed

to any workable alternatives. And they didn't trust change.

Perhaps they would have reacted as did New York's Lower East Side lower-class white and black parents whose children attended the experimental First Street School. George Dennison wrote* that, with two exceptions, the parents of the twenty-three children weren't libertarians to begin with.

> They thought that they believed in compulsion, and rewards and punishments, and formal discipline, and report cards, and homework, and elaborate school facilities. They looked rather askance at our noisy classrooms and informal relations. If they persisted in sending us their children, it was not because they agreed with us but because they were desperate. As the months went by, however, and the children who had been truants now attended eagerly, and those who had been failing now began to learn, the parents drew their own conclusions. By the end of the first year there was a high morale among them and great devotion to the school.

But the District 5 parents didn't have the option of sending their children to a First Street type of school. The nearest thing to it was the Conwell Middle Magnet. While its innovations proved popular with many parents, most of the other principals badmouthed it. And, in any event, Conwell could accommodate only a tiny fraction of the children in the district. So white and black parents alike stood foursquare behind the three R's. Said a Fishtown father in an interview, "I told my daughters to come home and tell me the same day whatever's being taught to them. It better be education. It better be education that I know of. Not something new that they want to get away with." Wrote a Blacktown mother in a letter to the editor, "I would not march merely to seek the addition of black history but I would be

* *The Lives of Children.*

very grateful if the teachers would try teaching my children just good, old-fashioned reading, writing and arithmetic."

During my stay in District 5, I prepared questionnaires on parents' attitudes toward their schools and teachers and their neighborhoods. With permission of principals at two elementary schools, one in Fishtown and one in North Philadelphia, I passed out these questionnaires to the children, who took them home for their parents to fill out. At these two schools, more than a thousand questionnaires were distributed and the response was better than thirty per cent.

OPINION SAMPLING

	WHITETOWN SCHOOL PARENTS	BLACKTOWN SCHOOL PARENTS
Do you favor Bible reading in school?		
Yes	88%	80%
No	6%	6%
No opinion	6%	14%
Do you believe in physical punishment of pupils?		
Yes, by all means	8%	9%
Yes, with safeguards	49%	58%
No	36%	23%
Uncertain	7%	9%
Impressions of neighborhood school		
Wonderful	38%	19%
O.K.	60%	37%
Like the school but not the building	2%	24%
Don't like the school		8%
Want kids bussed out		12%

	WHITETOWN SCHOOL PARENTS	BLACKTOWN SCHOOL PARENTS
Impressions of teachers		
Excellent	33%	19%
Good	49%	53%
Fair	14%	26%
Poor	4%	2%
Is your neighborhood being neglected by the city?		
Yes	57%	57%
No	21%	12%
No opinion	22%	31%

The parents who took the time to fill out and mail back the questionnaires were probably those most interested in education and in their children's futures. To this extent, my survey may have been skewed to reflect the views of the most responsible people. The Fishtowners who responded were virtually all working class. A third of the fathers had had fewer than nine years of schooling and less than one in ten had been to college. Eighty-one per cent reported family incomes under $8,000 a year and only four per cent said they earned over $10,000. Two-thirds of the Fishtown men and three-quarters of the women were native Philadelphians.

The all-black North Philadelphia school served a population that, economically at least, was more diverse. About half the families lived in a public housing project, a quarter in slum housing and a quarter in a middle-class private housing development—the first to be built for Philadelphia Negroes. More than a third of the fathers quit school before finishing ninth grade, but fifteen per cent said they had gone to college and seven per cent were college graduates. Two-thirds had family incomes under $8,000 a year and seventeen per cent earned $10,000 or more. In contrast to the

Fishtowners, two-thirds of the North Philadelphia fathers and fifty-nine per cent of the mothers were from out of state.

I spent more than a week in each of the two schools and rated them a tossup. The Fishtown building was newer and better but the North Philadelphia faculty may have had a slight edge. A few of the teachers there showed real originality, and their principal, a well regarded Negro, encouraged them to do so. In the Fishtown school, teaching was more hidebound and traditional. Yet Judy Sheidell taught there and she would be an ornament for any school.

What was most striking about the survey answers was the similarity of views of the Whitetowners and Blacktowners. The poor and working-class parents at these two schools, less than a mile and a half apart by road but separated by the huge racial gulf, agreed on almost everything. In both neighborhoods educational conservatism won handily. As the table shows, four-fifths of the respondents at both schools favored Bible reading and a majority of each favored physical beatings for ill-behaved pupils.

In both neighborhoods, too, the schools and teachers won overwhelming endorsements. The North Philadelphians did evidence some dissatisfaction with the condition of their forty-year-old building, which lacked a gymnasium and was overcrowded. But neither they nor the Fishtowners raised any serious questions about the quality of the teaching; indeed, both groups of parents seemed well pleased with their respective faculties, even though pupils at both schools ranked below District 5 averages, city averages, and national norms in fourth-grade reading and arithmetic.

On the other hand, the two groups had a bone to pick with City Hall. An identical proportion—fifty-seven per cent in each case—felt that their neighborhood was being neglected by the city. In their comments, whites and blacks expressed similar points of view. Whitetowner:

Kensington is a fine neighborhood and could be a nice place to live in if our area was given the same consideration as other areas. Our swimming pool was closed four years because it had a crack in it. If this was West, North, or South Philadelphia it would have been repaired right away. We had to wait four years. Why?

Blacktowner:

This neighborhood could be an ideal place for anyone to raise children if we would be supported by the agencies of the city whom we support by our taxes. The police ignore you when you place a complaint short of rape or murder. When we ask the city to replace trees that died this request was ignored. When the street workers collect our trash they spread it around instead of cleaning it up. Storekeepers put their trash out on the streets for it to be blown around and children to carry it off. Rats have infested the place and every year I complain to the health center.

If anything, though, there seemed to be more hope and optimism in North Philadelphia than in Fishtown. Fifty-nine per cent of the Fishtown parents thought their community was going downhill. Sixty-six per cent of the North Philadelphians thought their community was getting better. While North Philadelphia was clearly beset with woes, many of the parents were optimistic about its future:

I think the Harrison School is a great school for my children to attend. The neighborhood is wonderful to raise any children. The neighborhood has improved tremendously. We have new homes, play areas and soon we'll have a new shopping center.

Harrison neighborhood has its good and bad points like any other community. I think our biggest problem is the gangs who fight and make the neighborhood look bad. Other than that I think it's beginning to look nice and most families take pride in their home and yards.

The Harrison neighborhood is changing for the best for those who need it the least. This is the inevitable result of urban renewal. The poor, uneducated and untrained former residents of this neighborhood have been replaced by the more affluent blacks. These people can afford the mortgages and high rent, but I wonder what has happened to the people who really need this better housing.

This last comment, reflecting the generous, compassionate concern for the less fortunate on the part of a Blacktowner earning more than $10,000, contrasted sharply with the attitudes of some Whitetowners toward the new people moving into their neighborhood:

The [Kensington] neighborhood is changing because of a different class of people, people on welfare who don't have no respect for others. We had to do without, why can't they? —and be a little cleaner. We like the original people that lived in Kensington that are nice.

I am ashamed to tell folks where I live. Property owners rent homes to many undesirables with no regards as to what will happen. Teenagers constantly destroy homes, businesses and automobiles. Adults are afraid to prosecute. The poor police get blamed for not protecting us, but how can they? My heart aches to see such a fine neighborhood going downhill.

It's going down, not real fast, but it's going—in fact it's gone. You have nice trees planted by the city in front of your house so it will look nice, and then the next day you look out and they are cut down by smart children that are probably out past curfew and don't have nothing better to do.

Of course, Kensington's obsession cropped up time and again: "Kensington has a wonderful future as long as it stays all white." . . . "My opinion of Kensington is, if you keep the Negroes out, it will continue to be a good place to live in." . . . "Forced integration and open housing will be the ruination of Kensington—as well as the whole of Pennsylvania and the country." It's true that some North Philadelphians expressed a wish to live in integrated neighborhoods as a means of gaining better police protection and improved municipal services. But many others were clearly willing and eager to let Kensington stew in its own juice. "I don't want to live next door to the white man. I just want my equal rights." . . . "Relative to integrated neighborhoods, that's a lot of noise. Who is concerned as to the color of their neighborhoods as long as they are decent?" . . . "I like people; I could care less about skin color." . . . "I would not like to live in a racially mixed neighborhood. I did all my life. The relationship between our neighborhoods was alien and phony." . . . "I'm not particular about living in an integrated neighborhood. I just want to live where I please and if it happens to be integrated, all well and good. I like our neighborhood." . . . "I think the worst thing any black would desire is to move into a racially integrated neighborhood. The desire should be to improve one's own neighborhood with one's own ideas and with one's own *chosen* leaders."

Dick Hanusey, on taking office as District 5's superintendent, put a premium on getting people involved in their schools. He urged principals and teachers to go into their neighborhoods and find out what the people were saying and thinking and how they thought the schools could be improved. Not all schoolmen saw merit in community involvement. "When you talk of community involvement," one veteran elementary-school principal told me, "you're talking of one or two loudmouths. And those who shout loudest get what they want. The rest can be swayed. I can sway these people." Another principal thought soundings of the community were a waste of time. He knew what the people wanted. "You know how I can please parents in this community?" he asked. "Give a lot of homework. Write 'cat' one hundred times. If a kid is bad, bring him in the office and smack him hard. Parents want rigidity." And this, of course, is what many of the parents at least *thought* they wanted.

Probably the best job of getting into the community was done by Charles Marshall, one of the top-rated principals, who later left District 5. After being named principal in January 1967, Marshall, a Negro, set up a series of ten block meetings with parents in his racially mixed DMZ neighborhood. (His school's enrollment was twenty-nine per cent Negro, forty-eight per cent Spanish-speaking, and twenty-three per cent poor white.) The block meetings were generally segregated at the choosing of the parents. Following the meetings, teams of Marshall's teachers started visiting homes. The plan was to visit the homes of all children in the school before the year was out. At the time of my stop, seventy-five homes had been visited. It was clear that most of the parents wanted the school to bear down on their kids. Of a Negro mother, a teacher-visitor had written: "She says all the children will try to get away with things. Teachers will have to be hard on them." Of a Puerto Rican mother: "Mrs. Torres likes Luis's new teacher. She says he is strict with Luis and that is good." Of a white mother: "Mrs. H. doesn't let children go to the library any more because they would never return books on time and she would have to pay."

An attempt to get parents involved in planning for new schools was officially encouraged by the Board of Educa-

tion, and put into effect in Kensington—with predictable results. A group of parents led by the Reverend John Shenk
and his wife, Ruth, had convinced the board of the necessity
of replacing Elkin School. The question was where to put the
new one. School board officials had their fingers crossed the
night a neighborhood meeting was held to discuss locations.
It was just about the first time in history that the Board of
Education had ever consulted Elkin people on anything. The
Whitetowners, suspicious of these Greeks bearing a gift of a
new school, thought they were being jobbed. Details were
vague but rumors swept the community that the old school
was to be razed to make way for "public housing for niggers." Two hundred angry men and women jammed Elkin's
makeshift auditorium—formed by rolling back partitions
separating three classrooms—and awaited the worst.

Herman Witman, Elkin's principal, opened the meeting:
". . . and I'm confident our [school-board] guest will
leave this meeting knowing we can discuss our problems
with dignity and respect."

Voice from audience: "Shit."

The school-planning expert arose to explain that while
five possible sites for the new school were under consideration, no decision had been made.

Voice: "I'll be dead by the time they build it."

The official described Sites A, B, C, D, and E, all in the
same general locality but with different shapes, sizes, and
costs of acquisition. He seemed to favor Site D. Now the
people were sure the fix was in.

"I don't know why you have a meeting when it's all settled."

"That's right. It's all set up."

"Funny how he fights for that site."

"Yeah, he owns some of it."

"Why don't you say you got the site picked already?"

For no very clear reason, several in the audience supported Site B, in the extreme corner of Elkin's attendance zone. The official pointed out that construction there would leave some pupils with a six-to-nine-block walk.

"Bus 'em," shouted a red-faced man. "You bus the niggers. Why not bus the whites."

Somebody else noted that the existing Elkin School was built on one acre in 1908. Why in the world, he wanted to know, did its replacement require three acres?

Again a distrustful soul was sure he knew the answer: "More niggers are comin'."

"Let's be ladies and gentlemen," lectured the principal, grabbing the microphone. He cautioned the crowd against making so much noise.

Voice: "Stop condensing to us."

Wildly the meeting careened on for a couple of hours more of confused questions and answers. In a show of hands, the site tentatively favored by the school-board official was overwhelmingly opposed. On that inconclusive note the stormy session ended. After more meetings and many months, a site was chosen. It was neither D nor B but C, an extension of the existing school grounds. There were seventy small row houses and four stores on the site. All would have to be purchased and demolished to make way for the new construction. When everybody at last became convinced that the board was acting in good faith and that a new Elkin School, and not an integrated housing project, was to arise on the site, the decision was accepted without protest.

But construction money for Elkin and many other new schools was to come from a ninety-million-dollar bond issue that was submitted to the Philadelphia electorate in the spring of 1969. The bond issue was rejected by the voters. All of white Kensington, including the ward of which Elkin

School's neighborhood is a part, helped produce the heavy "no" votes that defeated the bond issue. Meanwhile, black North Philadelphia supported the bond issue. In November, 1969, a scaled-down sixty-five-million-dollar school bond issue finally passed but again Kensingtonians opposed it.

What it all goes to show, I guess, is that wishing that community involvement will lead to community support doesn't always make it so. Not in Whitetown.

The Catlicks
and the Publicks

They come early, at five or six o'clock in the afternoon, to claim their "lucky" seats. They sit waiting in big, drafty church basement rooms with pillars and fluorescent lights. They are mostly women in their fifties, sixties, and seventies. They are tired women in cheap dresses. They are white people of the city. In the lines on their faces, the stoop of their shoulders, and the dullness of their eyes are written the defeats, tragedies, and frustrations of working-class urban life. Yet there's a camaraderie in the big room, too, a murmuring of friends and acquaintances. These are proud people who ask no favors. All they want is a little luck.

And that's why they're here: to get lucky. They sit on folding chairs at long utility tables. Some bring cushions for comfort. Their tools are Scotch tape, Magic Markers, aprons, and money. With the money they buy sheets of numbered squares, which they tape to the tables in front of them. And when the game begins promptly at seven-thirty they hunch over their sheets, marking the squares when numbers are called.

The number caller stands at the front of the hall holding a

microphone. Beside him is a tank of bouncing ping-pong balls. He appears to be making popcorn for a race of giants. The balls fly around inside the tank, buffeted by air pressure; each bears a number. One at a time, the balls are sucked out of the tank and onto a small stand. The caller takes each ball as it appears and, loudly and distinctly, calls its number.

One hundred thirty-two players listen intently, then scan their sheets hoping to find the number called. Some have as many as thirty sheets to check. Wherever they find the number that has just been called they mark it. And they wait for the next call. On and on goes the game. There is no confusion, no merriment, just businesslike concentration. When a player speaks to her neighbor, she doesn't look up. She keeps studying her sheets. And as the numbers are called all players are silent. Few got through high school and there's not a college-educated person in the big room—except for a priest who comes and goes—but these women know their way around numbers.

The payoff in this game is instantaneous. As soon as a player finds that five numbers in a straight line—up and down, across, or diagonal—on one of her sheets have all been called, she utters the magic word. She cries it loud, so that all can hear, and with a ring of triumph in her voice. A male member of the parish, acting as a game official, comes to her table. He checks her numbers. If he finds that all the numbers marked on her line were in fact called by the caller, she wins. He draws a fat roll of bills from his pocket. The caller decides at that moment what the payoff will be. "Ten points," he intones. The official gives the winner ten dollars. Or if the caller decrees "five points," the winner gets five dollars. Or fifteen dollars. Or sometimes two or three. It all seems to depend on the length of the particular game, whether it was a "special" game of some kind or just an ordinary garden-variety one, and whether two or more women cried out at the same time. Very often there are multiple winners. As soon as the winner or winners have been paid, another game starts. And another and another.

Play continues for two and a half hours. The sole distraction is the movement of a few teen-age girls of the parish who come from a kitchen off the big hall selling hamburgers, French fries, and soft drinks to the players. Wisely, the girls head for winners' tables. And among the one hundred thirty-two players there are many winners. Of the fifteen hundred or so dollars taken in through sale of the numbered sheets this late spring night, about a thousand goes out in prizes. The remainder stays with the church for support of its school. And the following week, same day, same time, most of the same players will be back in the same place playing the same game.

The game, of course, is bingo. Next to the numbers racket, bingo is probably Philadelphia's most popular game of chance. But the numbers racket, which preys on the poor, enriches the Mafia; bingo's profits accrue to the greater glory of Christendom. Winter and summer, in fair weather and foul, the voice of the bingo caller is heard in Roman Catholic church halls all over the city. Kensingtonians who are really hooked on bingo can play six nights a week. Tuesday nights there's always a game at St. Adalbert's, a Polish national parish which restricts its membership—but not its bingo players—to those of Polish descent. Wednesdays the game's at Ascension of Our Lord, Thursdays at Nativity B.V.M., Fridays at Our Lady Help of Christians (German), Saturdays at Holy Name of Jesus, and Sundays at St. Laurentius (another Polish parish) and Our Mother of Divine

Grace (Italian). Mondays are off nights allowing winners time to count their earnings and losers to scrape up a few dollars for the next week's round of games.

Like the numbers racket, bingo is illegal. But Pennsylvania police show much more diligence in ferreting out pot-smoking long-haired college radicals than in prosecuting numbers writers or bingo impressarios. Periodically police in some of the small towns with large Protestant constituencies shut down bingo parlors. In 1967 a Roman Catholic priest in Allentown was fined three hundred dollars for running a game. Governor Raymond P. Shafer, himself a small-town Protestant who won election in 1967 with the votes of Pennsylvania's Protestant farmers, announced his opposition to bingo during his campaign. However, he has not pushed for enforcement of the antibingo statute and has said he wouldn't veto a bill legalizing the game. But such a bill hasn't been enacted.

In Philadelphia several bingo games were shut down in 1960 at the behest of Protestant militants. Since then the police have winked at the games. Indeed, wives and mothers of policemen are among the most enthusiastic players. The city's unofficial policy is to permit bingo in churches. A full-scale attack on bingo playing would start a religious war, and would be unthinkable, in 1970 anyway, because Philadelphia's mayor, the president of its city council, and its police commissioner belonged to the bingo-playing Church. Furthermore, a campaign that succeeded in stamping out bingo would cripple if not actually destroy Catholic education in the archdiocese of Philadelphia.

Although Pennsylvania in 1969 became the first state in the nation to provide cash grants to Catholic and other non-public schools, bingo remains the parochial-school lifeline. Without the small but steady weekly revenue that it brings in, the most hard-pressed parish schools would go under. Indeed, the Philadelphia archdiocese sometimes seems like a large body of schools entirely surrounded by bingo players. Most of the suburban parishes can survive without bingo— and, in fact, few of them ever play the game, although they do run raffles, car giveaways, and other chance-selling games.

But the poorer the parish the greater the reliance on bingo. And the poorest ones rely on it absolutely. This is true in both poor-white and poor-black sections. Unlike so many Protestant denominations, the Catholic Church has stood firm in Philadelphia, keeping its inner-city parishes open even after the flight of their white membership; for these increasingly black Catholic parishes especially, as bingo goes so go the parish elementary schools. (Asked how he managed not only to keep his church operating in a Negro section of South Philadelphia but actually to expand its facilities, a Belgian-born priest smiled and said, "We do it with mirrors—and bingo.") In working-class white sections, too, in Roxborough and Richmond, in Fishtown, Manayunk, and Southwark it's a rare priest who can make ends meet without resorting to bingo. In some parishes there are games twice weekly. In one Kensington parish the mother superior told me her teachers often run off quick bingo games in their classrooms on Friday afternoons to raise money for books. In parish after parish bingo pays the bills. It's hardly an exaggeration to say that the entire structure of Catholic education in Philadelphia—the nation's fourth largest diocese and the one most fervently committed to the proposition that every Catholic child should attend a Catholic school—rests on such shaky underpinnings.

Even more important in the development of this astonishing school system, however, has been the devotion and support it has enlisted from generations of Catholic faithful. Largely uneducated themselves and of modest means, they have supplied the funds needed to provide minimal facilities for nearly eighty per cent of the Catholic children of school age in Philadelphia and four suburban counties. They have put up the money year after year with remarkably little complaining or even questioning. Very often what the Kensington factory worker drops into his parish collection plate on Sunday would shame the fat-cat Episcopalian on the Main Line. And while contributing the dollars to build and operate elementary and secondary schools for 270,000 children without a tuition charge until a financial crisis in the late 1960s, Philadelphia Catholics have, of course, been paying taxes that support the parallel public system.

Separatism has thus become an educational way of life in Philadelphia. If there are now to be separate schools run for and by black Americans, the precedent for such apartness exists in the Philadelphia Catholic schools. The difference is that most current proposals are for public subsidies to separate nonpublic schools and systems. Until very recently, the Catholic schools went it absolutely alone. Even now, they get only token aid. The burden on individual Catholic families has obviously been very high. In Philadelphia nobody knows the cost in dollars and there is no firm basis for estimates.

Despite its size, the Catholic system has no central control over school finances. The administrative staff responsible for curriculum development, textbook selection, teacher pay scales, and myriad other chores consists of a superintendent, three assistants, a library-services director, two directors of lay personnel, a director of elementary curriculum and a director of human relations education. That's it. Nine people running a city-suburban system that actually enrolls more white children than do the Philadelphia public schools, while the public school administrative staff has long since filled its nine-story building and spilled into other facilities around the city.

As may be imagined, Philadelphia's parish schools are remarkable institutions. Their buildings are old, their classes huge, their lay teachers often very young and inexperienced, their materials and supplies virtually nonexistent. Yet most Catholics are fiercely proud of these schools. Among non-Catholics there is a strong suspicion that the parochial schools' primary reason for being, in cities at least, is as an escape valve for whites fleeing blacks. No doubt some Catholic families patronize the parochial schools for precisely this reason. But there's more to the parochial schools' phenomenal popularity than that. And there's more to it than blind faith or compulsion, although these, too, are factors, especially in Philadelphia, one of the nation's most conservative archdioceses. More important, I think, is that Catholic schools give many Catholic parents what they want for their children: discipline.

In the Catholic schools of Philadelphia there is very little real education in the sense of free inquiry, the clash of ideas no matter how heretical, and the search for truth no matter how dangerous. There is, instead, indoctrination by all-powerful Authority. Ideas are accepted, not questioned. Teachers pass out information which pupils write down and memorize. Between teachers and taught there is rarely free-and-easy conversation, much less "meaningful dialogue." Children are treated as children, just as their parents were before them. As a result, there is an order, a tidiness, a discipline in the Catholic schools that contrasts sharply with the hurly-burly confusion, disruptions, and abrasions of urban life outside. As a result, too, there is something very reassuring about a parochial school. Unexciting, unstimulating, anti-intellectual—but reassuring. And this, I think, is what many parents are looking for.

Christopher Jencks, explaining why young radicals of the so-called New Left were ready to attack all established institutions in this country, has written:*

---

* *The New Republic,* Oct. 21, 1967.

These are children of the 1940's, raised in relatively permissive middle-class homes where authority was supposed to be rational rather than arbitrary. Unlike earlier generations of Americans, their parents were reluctant to take advantage of their monopoly on physical, economic and legal power. Their youngsters were free to challenge the legitimacy of parental authority from an early age, arguing that their parents were not using their power reasonably or wisely. . . . The emphasis on consensus and rationality in these young people's upbringing was accompanied by reliance on new forms of discipline. The distinctive feature of a "permissive" home is not that "anything goes." It is that the limits are supposed to be set by the child's internalized sense of what is reasonable and unreasonable.

The children Jencks is describing attended public, not parochial, school. It was their parents' permissiveness, their reluctance to crack down on children and willingness to let them challenge authority that so many Catholic parents and Catholic schools rejected and continue to reject. Because Catholics view public schools as permissive they reject them, too. Public-school supporters in their turn dismiss parochial schools as hopelessly archaic and autocratic.

Little love is lost between the "Catlicks" and the "Publicks." From generation to generation in Philadelphia word has been passed in the parishes that "our" (Catholic) schools are better than "theirs" (public). Elsewhere Catholic school systems have been retrenching heavily, but the Philadelphia parochial schools have managed to keep open with only comparatively minor tinkering and cutbacks. It's another instance in which Philadelphia is in a class by itself.

Philadelphia Catholics may have felt a greater need to maintain their own schools because of the virulent strain of bigotry they encountered. We have seen how anti-Catholic prejudice had its roots in Kensington with bitterness against the "bloody Irish transports." We have seen, too, that in the 1830s and 1840s Philadelphia seethed with hostilities—whites against blacks, Protestants against Catholics.

The anti-Catholic riots of 1844, besides guaranteeing the growth of parochial schools in Philadelphia and throughout the country, must also have contributed to the hardening of attitudes among Catholics that whatever they were going to get in Philadelphia would have to be gotten on their own. This "siege mentality" persists to the present day. And so, it might be added, does much of the discrimination. Nathaniel Burt, in *The Perennial Philadelphians,* describes Philadelphia Catholics as traditionally Irish and "socially outcast." Even distinguished, upper-class Catholics have steered clear of the Old Philadelphia Protestant establishment. The McCloskeys and McShains have made no effort to mingle in Philadelphia Society. Despite her international renown, Princess Grace *née* Kelly isn't listed in Philadelphia's Social Register nor are any members of her family, even though they are among the most widely known Philadelphians since Benjamin Franklin.

In business and commerce, too, Catholics have remained largely outside the Philadelphia mainstream. Gradually, barriers are breaking down, but for decades virtually no Catholics were to be found in the higher echelons of the city's "best" banks.

In politics, as well, there has been a long history of exclusionism. Although Catholics have lived in the city since William Penn first sailed up the Delaware in 1682, not for two hundred eighty years did a Catholic occupy the mayor's office. And the first to do so, James Hugh Joseph Tate, got the job only because a good Episcopalian, Richardson Dilworth, resigned as mayor in 1962 to run for governor. Tate,

then president of City Council, automatically succeeded
Dilworth. He subsequently managed to win the mayoralty
twice on his own, first defeating a coreligionist and then a
Jew. In 1952 Thomas J. Gibbons became the first Irish
Catholic to head the city's police force. Catholics now hold
firm control over most branches of the city government, and
they will probably retain it until Negroes take over. But it
was a long hard fight and the period of Catholic hegemony in
municipal politics may be comparatively short.

Sometimes, of course, it is difficult to tell when Catholics
have been excluded and when they have chosen to exclude
themselves. For more than half a century the Philadelphia
archdiocese has been run by tough, tightfisted, ultracon-
servative cardinals thoroughly distrustful of the modern
world and particularly of non-Catholic individuals and institutions. It is no accident that, although the United Fund of
Philadelphia and Vicinity collects contributions from workers regardless of race, creed or color, the two hundred fifty
agencies that share its proceeds include just one Roman
Catholic agency, a hospital. Of more than $18 million raised
in 1968 the Catholic hospital received $4,000. Meanwhile,
Jewish and Protestant agencies receive U.F. support ranging
into the hundreds of thousands of dollars. United Fund officials would be much happier if Catholic agencies applied
for U.F. support, but the agencies are under instructions
from the presiding archbishop not to do so. This rule of non-
participation was laid down by Dennis Cardinal Dougherty
in 1923 and has been upheld by his successors. The archdiocese apparently believes that participation in United Fund
drives would dilute its own highly successful annual drives
for Catholic charities and hospitals.

In education, however, the Philadelphia Catholic penchant for going it alone is most marked. Pope Pius XI said,
"There can be no ideally perfect education which is not

Christian education." And the late Jesuit editor Paul L. Blakely, "The first duty of every Catholic father to the public school is to keep his children out of it." More than in an any other United States diocese, Philadelphia Catholics have heeded these admonitions. Canon Law 1374 of the Roman Catholic Church, adopted a century ago, prohibits attendance by Catholic children at "mixed" or "neutral" schools without special permission. Nationally, this canon has proved unworkable. Fewer than half the Catholic children in this country attend Catholic schools and the proportion is steadily decreasing. Liberal Catholics have called for repeal of Canon Law 1374. In Philadelphia, though, the canon has been enforced virtually as an article of faith.

For more than thirty years, starting with Cardinal Dougherty and continuing with John Cardinal O'Hara and John Cardinal Krol, the incumbent, the archdiocese has put most of its time, money, and energy into school construction. In a fourteen-year period it built fourteen big high schools costing $40 million and financed on a pay-as-you-go basis through collections from the 312 parishes. Whereas other dioceses clamped limits on class sizes to control expanding enrollments, Philadelphia never did. In its elementary schools classes of eighty or ninety children were commonplace and those with more than one hundred pupils were not unknown. Whereas other dioceses began charging tuition to meet skyrocketing costs, Philadelphia held out. Instead of billing the parents of children attending its secondary schools, the archdiocese assessed each parish a fixed amount for each one of its children enrolled. This policy had the effect of broadening the base of support for secondary education and of encouraging parents to send their children to the "tuition-free" Catholic high schools.

Not only did Philadelphia Catholics send their children to Catholic schools in record numbers but these schools made sure that their college-bound graduates attended only Catholic colleges. Students who wanted to attend non-Catholic colleges were easily thwarted: their high schools simply neglected to send transcripts to those colleges. Since it is impossible to get into college without submitting a secondary-school transcript, the Catholic students either went to Catholic colleges or didn't go to college at all. Cardinal O'Hara, who was president of Notre Dame University before his Philadelphia appointment, absolutely forbade Catholic secondary schools to help their students enter other than Catholic colleges. The form letter that a private Catholic school in Philadelphia sent to parents of students accepted for admission in the 1940s and 1950s spelled out its aims:

> We are trying to train boys for CATHOLIC colleges. . . .
> We believe that the present day teachings in the majority of secular institutions, based on chaotic philosophies, defeats the purpose of our existence. . . . To place [a boy] at the mercy of atheistic or agnostic professors at a time when his mental habits and spiritual values are just forming is unfair to him and unnecessary when one realizes the excellence of the Catholic colleges in the vicinity, and, indeed, throughout the country.

Of course that was the rub. The Catholic colleges in the vicinity of Philadelphia and in the United States generally were in lamentable shape. Years ago Denis W. Brogan, Cambridge University historian, observed of the American Catholic Church that "in no western society is the intellectual prestige of Catholicism lower than in the country where, in such respects as wealth, numbers, and strength of organization, it is so powerful." Agreeing, Monsignor John Tracy Ellis wrote in *American Catholicism,* "The failure of American Catholics to achieve distinction in the world of scholarship and learning still remains the most striking weakness of what is otherwise, perhaps, the strongest branch of the universal Church."

Such scholars as Thomas F. O'Dea have also cited the American Catholics' failure to evolve a vital intellectual tradition or to develop national leaders in numbers proportionate to their share of the total population. Ellis saw three roadblocks: Anti-Catholic discrimination fostered "an over-eagerness in Catholic circles for apologetics rather than pure scholarship"; Catholics, being an immigrant group predominantly of peasant origins, were preoccupied with making material gains rather than exploring the intellectual life; and the native American anti-intellectualism soon infected those immigrants who didn't land with it as part of their psychological baggage.

Also operative perhaps was what George Orwell termed the "healthy instinct" of working people to reject education. Orwell, in *The Road to Wigan Pier,* was talking about British workers, but his observation seems equally valid here.

The time was when I used to lament over quite imaginary pictures of lads of fourteen dragged protesting from their lessons and set to work at dismal jobs. It seemed to me dreadful that the doom of a "job" should descend upon any-one at fourteen. Of course, I know now that there is not one working class boy in a thousand who does not pine for the day when he will leave school. He wants to be doing real work, not wasting his time on ridiculous rubbish like history and geography. To the working class, the notion of staying at school till you are nearly grown-up seems merely contemptible and unmanly.

Yet those same Catholic immigrants who may have questioned the value of liberal education for those old enough to work unstintingly supported their parochial schools. This makes their feat in sustaining a vast private school system all the more remarkable. And it may help to explain why the Catholic schools are so persistently pragmatic, so devoid of the education-for-education's-sake ideal. In Kensington I found Catholic- and public-school enrollments to be about equal—roughly twelve thousand pupils each in the public and parochial schools of that section. By all standard measures—school facilities, class sizes, teachers' training, equipment, supplies—the Catholic schools were no match for the public ones. For example, I rarely saw a parochial school with any kind of gymnasium or auditorium and none had libraries before the onset of Federal aid. Similarly, the only art and music teachers I saw in parochial schools were public-school instructors working there part-time under a Federally financed program.

James Coleman's study of public education found, however, that physical facilities were less important determinants of public-school quality than had previously been thought. The finding may apply equally to the woefully undermanned and undersupplied Catholic schools. Beyond that, the Catholic schools have a key advantage in that they rarely concern themselves with "problem" pupils. Children who can not or will not conform to their strict rules of conduct are thrown out. Few Catholic schools take emotionally disturbed children, physically handicapped children, mentally retarded children, those with learning disabilities of any kind. The public schools are the dumping ground for most of these "ugly ducklings."

In 1969 the Philadelphia archdiocese pointed with pride to its pupils' performance on nationally standardized tests. It released results showing that over the entire five-county area Catholic pupils exceeded national norms. But it declined to give school-by-school results and would only say that suburban Catholic pupils generally outscored city Catholic pupils.

The same could be said of public-school children. If one were to average the scores of all public-school pupils in Philadelphia, Bucks, Chester, Delaware, and Montgomery counties, one would probably find that overall, despite the city's poor showing, the pupils ranked above national norms, just as the archdiocesan children were said to do. There was no way of knowing whether Kensington's Catholic pupils, like their public-school counterparts, fell below par. I would have been surprised, however, if they didn't. I would have thought that pupils at St. Michael's Parochial School, for example, faced difficulties similar to those confronting youngsters down the street at the John Moffet Public School.

St. Michael's was one of the churches destroyed in the Know-Nothing holocaust of 1844. Its school opened a few years after the church was rebuilt. Just as it was then in the storm center of Protestant-Catholic turmoil, it now finds itself deep in the heart of the black-white DMZ. To the east is white Kensington, to the west black North Philadelphia. The immediate neighborhood is thus one of extreme volatility, tension, mobility, and poverty. Thirty-five years ago, St. Michael's counted thirty-five hundred parish families, mostly Irish. It ran not only a church and school but also a "literary institute" in a separate building near by. Now it is down to an estimated eleven hundred families, many of them living on public assistance. The parish continues to be predominantly Irish, but it has a leavening of Polish, German, and Hungarian families, as well as a small but apparently growing number of Negroes and Puerto Ricans.

The pastor, gray-haired, blunt-spoken, sick, and aging, was sent to St. Michael's a year before my visit, after serving in half a dozen Philadelphia parishes. He appears in a red sweat shirt, a scarlet basketball jacket, and trousers that need mending. He says St. Michael's is "holding its own." By running weekly bingo games, he can keep the parish out of debt and its school operating. He professes to be unaware of racial tumult in the neighborhood. He doesn't discuss racial issues from the pulpit and never hears his parishioners talking about them. "I've heard no slurs on the Puerto Ricans," he says, "or slurs on the colored." Like so many priests, he is scornful of public education and is convinced that parochial schools are far superior in every way. Of Dante Lombardi's trouble-beset Moffet School, just one block distant, he says, "I would say Moffet has for the most part what we don't want. At least that's my impression."

St. Michael's school is housed in an ungainly gray building of stone-and-wood construction. It sits back from a busy street. Behind it is a lovely old churchyard. And behind the cemetery eight pre-Revolutionary houses are being renovated. I find the school a dingy place, gloomy, heavy with age. In physical appearance, though, it is typical of the parochial schools in Kensington. Most are architectural monstrosities whose only virtue—sturdiness of construction—precludes their being replaced.

Like all Philadelphia parochial schools, St. Michael's starts at grade one (no kindergarten) and runs through grade eight. Like most of the others, its principal and all of its teachers are women. For its enrollment of about five hundred there are eleven teaching nuns from the Order of the Sisters of St. Joseph and two lay teachers. The average of just over thirty-eight pupils per class, very small by Philadelphia Catholic-school standards, results from the extreme transiency in the neighborhood and the out-migration of so many white families. I noted the same pattern throughout Kensington: the parochial schools are losing enrollment while the public schools are gaining. In both cases, families are poorer, less stable and secure than had been the case a generation earlier.

St. Michael's mother superior, Mother Concelia Marie, has spent a long lifetime in parochial schools and now will finish her career at St. Michael's, where she was assigned a year ago. A gentle nun, she succeeded a firm disciplinarian. She is seeking to shift the school's emphasis. "You can't get anywhere without discipline," she tells an interviewer in her office. It is as small as Dante Lombardi's, but her desk is clear and there are few interruptions. "But this harsh discipline—you do it or else—" Mother Concelia continues, "is no good. They act out after school. You have to win them. You have to make them feel you like them. You have almost as many dispositions as there are children."

Visiting St. Michael's classrooms, I am reminded of elementary schools I saw in Moscow and Leningrad some years before. While Communism and Catholicism are poles apart doctrinally, there are superficial similarities in how their schools function. In both the Communist and Catholic school systems, children wear uniforms. They sit primly at wooden desks neatly lined up in rows. In class at least, they are clean, courteous, and respectful of authority. When their principal or a visitor enters their classroom, they rise together and recite a greeting. Their teachers are women who take no nonsense. Their classrooms are generally bare of modern educational gadgetry. Above the blackboard in every classroom in both systems is a symbol of their respective faiths. In the parochial schools it is a crucifix, in the Soviet schools a portrait of the Communist "saint," N. V. Lenin. In classrooms in both school systems there is a certain hard-to-define feeling, not of warmth and compassion but of old-fashioned order and firmness, a kind of maternalistic caring, a feeling that we know what is best for children and this is it.

But generalizations are dangerous, and there may be almost as many dispositions among the teaching nuns at St. Michael's as Mother Concelia finds among the children. Some nuns run relatively relaxed classrooms. One, a perky sister from New York who came to Philadelphia from years of teaching in Virginia, criticizes the regimentation. "It's ridiculous," she says. Another functions as a kind of cheerleader, constantly exhorting her charges to speed up their phonics drill. "Quick, c'mon, c'mon, c'mon. Fast, fast, fast." She addresses her fifth-graders as "cuties" and "pets." "You have to study those blends tonight, dolls," she says. "Gregory, come here, dear. You would bother Our Lord Himself."

But most of the teaching is by the book. For the largest class, sixty first-graders, the blackboard is sectioned off. Vertical yellow lines run from top to bottom every few feet. On signal, children advance to the blackboard and stand facing the class. Teacher claps once. The children turn with military precision and start doing preassigned blackboard work, taking pains to stay within their prescribed yellow boundaries.

For fifth-graders, English instruction consists of memorizing rules concerning formation of plurals. There seem to be almost as many rules as words:

> *Tree—plural trees*—most nouns form the plural by adding s to the singular.
>
> *Leaf—leaves*—any word ending in v or ve, you make the plural by adding ves. Noun ending in f or fe change to ves for plural.
>
> *Splash—splashes*—words ending in ch, sh, add es to make plural.
>
> *Mouse*—some nouns form their plural by change in singular. Mouse thus differs from house.
>
> *Echo*—nouns ending in o preceded by consonant add es.

The teacher notes that some words have the same singular and plural. She lists sheep, salmon, trout, molasses, swine, deer, and cod. A pupil volunteers one of his own: "Gold." Teacher cuts him off. "I don't think so. That's not on our list."

Another fifth-grade class is having a geography lesson. The subject is Eastern Europe. The nun has passed out mimeographed fact sheets. Now the children are reciting the facts on the sheet. As the teacher asks questions the class recites the answers in unison:

NUN: What three countries are connected by the Danube?
CLASS (*chanting*): Sister, the three countries that are connected by the Danube are Austria, Hungary, and Romania.
NUN: What is the population of Poland?
CLASS: Sister, the population of Poland is twenty-eight million.
NUN: How much of Poland is forest land?
CLASS: Sister, one-fifth of Poland is forest land.
NUN: What is the capital of Poland?
CLASS: Sister, Warsaw is the capital of Poland.

In this fashion, the children chant that Poland is about the size of New Mexico, that northern Poland is sandy and swampy, that most of its rivers flow north to the Baltic, that its principal crops are rye, barley, beets, and flax, and that its principal minerals are iron, petroleum, and coal.

When a visitor enters the room, the nun halts the mass recitation. "Do not call out together," she says. "Raise your hand." After all the questions on the fact sheet have been answered, the nun tells the class a little about postwar Austria. She says the United States gave Austria ten billion dollars "to get back on its feet," and Austria is now "free." She elicits from her class the fact that Austria's capital is Vienna and that people interested in music and medicine often are drawn there.

On the desk of a girl in the second row nearest to the windows are a clock, a bell, and a class schedule. This girl is the timekeeper. There is no clock on the classroom wall and the nun doesn't wear a watch. It is the girl's job to see that the class sticks to its schedule. At 11:05 A.M., the girl dings the bell. It is time to quit geography, after twenty-five minutes, and take up handwriting.

Philadelphia parochial schools pride themselves on their handwriting instruction. Their pupils learn to write very neatly, their letters well rounded and carefully formed. It is said that you can distinguish a parochial-school child from a public-school pupil by comparing their writing. The former is likely to have a smaller, more precise and legible hand. At the dinging of the bell, the children know what to do. Into their desks go the geography fact sheets. Out come handwriting workbooks. To warm up, they make ovals in their workbooks. They make ten ovals, one on top of another, and as they make each they count: "One, two, three, four, five, six, seven, eight, nine, ten." Then, counting aloud again, they make ten more ovals, and ten more after that. Then they practice the letters A and C until the timekeeper dings the bell.

Next comes vocabulary. Again, the routine is rigid. Asked to complete a simile begun by the nun, "I'm as hungry as a . . .", one of the children answers, "Sister, bear." I smile at the possibilities this opens up. If the priest were teaching, the answer would be, "Father, bear." And if the principal, "Mother, bear." But all is serious and nobody else sees the touch of humor.

Down the hall a young lay teacher is struggling with her second-grade class. The teacher is one year out of high school. The diocese paid her tuition for a year at a Catholic college in the area on condition that she then teach in parochial school for at least two years. That is what she is doing. She is also continuing her college work at night, with fees being paid by the diocese. Her teaching salary is forty-five dollars a week. She's concerned about her reading instruction. Many of the children read aloud beautifully without comprehending anything. They know how to pronounce all the words but they don't know what they mean. She thinks this may be the result of too much rote instruction, stuff memorized but not really learned.

Up two flights in another section of the building is the other lay teacher, a young, recently married twenty-year-old. I never do find out what class she is teaching because the children have gone home for lunch and the teacher is too angry to discuss class work. She hates the school and the system. A top student herself, she won a four-year full-tuition scholarship to a Catholic woman's college but quit after one semester because it was so "frivolous." Now she finds parochial-school teaching in Philadelphia almost unbearable.

"It's just so frustrating," she says. "You can't find out what's interesting to the kids. God! Their minds are in another world and they won't let you in. All the Catholic schools seem to be doing is making them docile. All they do is stick for eight years. Yet there's so much potential here.

"You just know this is a Catholic school," she continues. "Kids marching around. Discipline. If I ever got a kid to stand up and argue with me in a classroom I think I'd do handstands."

She had taught the previous year in a parochial school in Norristown, a working-class industrial town northwest of Philadelphia. It was a third-grade class, seventy-two children, that had had four teachers before her. She threw away the syllabus and taught the way she felt like teaching. "I made some obvious and intentional mistakes so the kids would correct me," she recalls. "I broke the barrier and got them talking. We had good rapport." The last two weeks of the year, she drilled the class furiously for exams. Her class, she says, finished first in the diocese. But now at St. Michael's, she finds little hope, and she gives the impression she won't be there long.

Whatever becomes of her, this lay teacher represents a certain wave of the future in Catholic education in Philadelphia and elsewhere. Because of the drop in numbers of young women entering religious teaching orders, the parochial schools are relying more and more on lay teachers. In ten years the lay teaching staff in the Philadelphia archdiocese has more than doubled—from 1,015 lay teachers in 1959 to 2,697 in 1969. In the same period, the number of religious teachers dropped by eight per cent. The result has been skyrocketing costs, attempts to unionize lay teachers, increasing pressure for higher salaries, and increasing secularization of the Catholic schools. These changes have been felt most keenly in the diocesan high schools where college-educated laymen teach. In the parish elementary schools most of the lay teachers are women, most of them high-school graduates several years away from college degrees. With few exceptions—the angry young woman at St. Michael's being one—lay teachers in the grade schools accept their inferior-salaried status uncomplainingly. And the teaching orders, working with parish priests, still dominate the parish schools completely.

For many of the nuns, teaching city children about the "real world" of poverty, racism, and war would be out of the question because they are themselves so far removed from that world. Consider the twenty-six nuns of the Sisters of St. Joseph who, with five lay teachers, staff a fourteen-hundred-pupil parochial school in the center of Kensington. They live in a convent on the church property just a few steps from the school. Except for those nuns who do the shopping, they rarely set foot in the "community" or in a house where Kensington people live and breathe.

Every morning at four-fifty A.M., a bell rings in the convent. The sisters rise and go to chapel for prayers and meditation. At five-fifty A.M. they attend Mass. Breakfast is at six-thirty and school begins at eight. They return to the convent for lunch between eleven-thirty and twelve-thirty, then back to their classrooms until three P.M. After school they are free until four-forty-five P.M., when there is meditation until five-fifteen. This is followed by fifteen minutes of prayer. Then supper. By six-twenty the dishes are washed and the sisters can watch TV (they have two sets, one color), read, or talk. Nine P.M. is bedtime. And so the days pass. The sisters need permission to eat in a restaurant and few ever seek it. Similarly, they can't go to the movies or the theater without an O.K. from the mother house in Chestnut Hill. The church pastor pays the convent's heat and light bills and gives each sister $91.62 per month for her food, clothing, hospital bills, travel expenses, and the like. On Friday afternoons the mother superior goes by station wagon to the Reading Terminal Market, a famous Philadelphia food market. There she buys a week's supply of fresh fruit and vegetables. Another nun shops for meat and staples at a supermarket. She makes out the menus. A cook comes in daily to prepare a hot meal at noon. Supper is light; the sisters get it themselves and clean up afterward. This is their life. And some nuns spend their entire lives in the same convents. At the time of my visit the convent's senior nun was completing her fifty-sixth year there. She was retired but filled in as a substitute teacher when needed. (Substitutes are virtually unknown in parochial schools. When a sister or a lay teacher falls ill, one of the other regular teachers takes the sick teacher's class as well as her own. With so much emphasis on drill and discipline, classes can be left unattended for long periods without calamitous effects.)

At this church school, as at St. Michael's, enrollment is down and Catholic families in the parish are poorer than they were a generation ago. Most of the school children are of Irish descent. A few are Italian. "We don't have any— what do you call it?—Porta Rikkans," says the mother superior. Among the fourteen hundred pupils are two Negro children. The mother superior says they are "black as the ace of spades," but there's never been any racial strife. There would be trouble, though, she says, if her pastor hired a Negro lay teacher. (Since pastors pay teachers' salaries, they, and not the nuns, do the hiring.) "I think the parents would take their kids out of the school right away," she adds. She tells of the time a white couple came to enroll their daughter at her school. The girl was dark-skinned and kinky-haired. "The day they came to register, recalls the principal, "I thought, 'Dear Lord, here comes another one.'" Somebody did call the child a nigger and there were fears of trouble for a while, but things quieted down and the school returned to the even tenor of its ways.

In the immediate neighborhood racial tensions often flare, but so long as these tensions don't spill over into the school the sisters see no point in getting involved. The mother superior recalls that when a Negro family moved into a house two blocks from the church "they were wiped out the very next day." She adds, "We didn't have any trouble here, so therefore they [the sisters] didn't bother about it at all." And at another point, discussing a fund-raising gambling game called fifty-fifty that is played at the church every Wednesday night, the mother superior says, "There are never any colored around. There's never any trouble."

The mother superior is a mild, gentle woman who means no harm to anyone. Her view on race relations apparently is that Negroes spell trouble, that white people always have regarded them as inferior and presumably always will. The fact that white people don't want to live near Negroes and will use violence to prevent Negroes from moving into their neighborhoods raises no moral or ethical questions in her mind. Hers is the view, widely held in Kensington and in all Whitetowns, that the Church's job is to minister to souls and not to get mixed up in politics or social issues. Or perhaps she feels that her one school couldn't do much to change attitudes if it wanted to and that in fact it might destroy itself over just such an issue.

On the other hand, she is concerned about such things as reading instruction. She recalls her early days as a teacher. Every Sunday morning after church, the sisters went to their classrooms and wrote the upcoming week's work on the blackboards. One column on the board was allotted for each day's work. Children weren't divided into reading groups. The teachers taught phonics to the whole class at one time. They spent forty-five minutes with everybody. But today, the mother superior observes wistfully, because of grouping (the "Blessed Mother" group for fast readers, the "St. Joseph" group for slow), individual children get only fifteen or twenty minutes of daily reading instruction. And the reading books! "Maybe I'm old-fashioned, but we're not teaching reading any more. These are picture books."

Like public-school people, most of the parochial-school teachers and principals tend to avoid controversial subjects on grounds that nothing very good could come from examining them and trouble might result. What they fail to recognize is that the children themselves are itching to discuss these issues. In recent years, the very capable superintendent of Philadelphia's Catholic schools, Monsignor Edward T. Hughes, and his mini-staff have made strong efforts to improve human-relations instruction. Some of the textbooks authorized for use in parochial schools are excellent, stressing the dignity of all races and religions and the importance of the civil-rights struggle in the United States.

The difficulty is that few of Philadelphia's hard-pressed parish schools have the money to buy the better new books. And it is very hard for the system's director of human-relations education to have much impact on the 270,000 children all by herself.

The most animated, interesting, and educational class discussion I witnessed in any Kensington parochial school was a formal debate on school integration in a Polish national parish school. The eighth-grade pupils themselves picked the subject, took sides, researched it, and then debated for forty-five minutes. The teacher, who was also the school principal, permitted me to record the session. In this debate the children of Polish-American truck drivers, longshoremen, machinists, police, and firemen, poured out all the anti-Negro venom for which their neighborhood is well known. But counterarguments were often well put. In several instances, the children seemed to be parroting their parents' racist line, while in others they perhaps uttered sentiments that they thought would please their teacher, whose pro-integration views were known. Yet it was instructive to hear these fourteen-year-olds from what is widely regarded as Philadelphia's most militant working-class white stronghold speak on such a subject in such a forum. What follows are some of the most salient points made by the debaters:

PRO-INTEGRATION: I think Negroes should not be denied their social standing. . . . After all, we were the ones who brought them here as slaves in the earliest days of our country. . . . Many people believe they are criminals. That is largely untrue. There are many wicked white people as well as Negroes. Sure, many people say Negroes are unclean but many white people are dirty also.

CON: The schools are being integrated. The Negroes go to the schools but they do damage. They go to school but they do not pay taxes. And these Negroes, when they go to school, they set bad examples for other children. They start smoking and drinking in lavatories. And Negroes should have their own schools and teachers because many teachers are quitting their jobs because teachers cannot put up with Negroes. And the schools close down and many white children get out of the schools and education is very low in the city.

PRO: There's just as much whites doing damage to the schools as the Negroes are.

CON: Negro people want the same rights as the white people but they don't want the responsibility that goes with it. They want a house with the white people but they don't want to take care of it. They wreck their houses and then move to other ones. They try to integrate white people's neighborhoods and they don't want to pay for their own children. They start riots because they want equal rights. They break windows into stores. They cheat. . . . Negro people have new cars but they don't want to pay for the rent of their houses. Their children go around half starved. They go around stealing because they don't have any food. They stay in gangs and go around jumping people because they don't have any money. They don't do anything together. The Negro people live in slums. Their men don't have jobs. If they have them they don't hold them because they have no sense of responsibility. To the Negroes, life is easy come, easy go. The Negro people are very unreliable. They once had jobs like the white man but they could never hold them. Nowadays the Negro people are asking too much. Not all the Negro people are bad but most of them are.

PRO: Housing is one of the major problems of integration, because there are many slums in which Negro and white people live. And that's where hatred is bred. Because people hate one another they can't get good jobs or anything. So I think we should support any laws or anything like that to pass low-cost housing projects and everything, so both races can afford it. And we don't have to live in poverty, disease, and dirt, or anything like that. And I believe if Negroes were given a chance to live in good houses they would take care of them. But they're—most of the time they're sent to bad neighborhoods, slums, and often ghettos. And they don't have a chance to prove it.

CON: They're building houses for 'em and everything. They go around breaking windows. They buy a new car every year and they don't have nothin' even to feed to their children.

PRO: If Negro families tried to move into a white neighborhood, what could they do? You saw what happened around our neighborhood, didn't ya? They knocked the doors down, knocked the windows out. They broke all the furniture in the house and after that they set the house on fire.

PRO (*speaking of a Negro neighborhood in another section of the city*): They keep their homes nice and dress nice.

CON: You'll find those about one in a hundred.

PRO: What about the white people? On Kensington Avenue right by Cumberland, all those houses—the block before you hit Kelly's Korner there. All those houses, the windows are broken out. Boards on the doors and everything else. They're not well-kept houses, but nobody says anything about that. I mean it's all right because the Negroes, they can't keep the houses clean, they shouldn't be over there. When they try to lift themselves and raise the standard, how are we going to let them do it?

PRO: You say, the Negroes, they don't take care of their houses and slums develop. Before the Negro migration north, there were slums before that period. And white people were mainly the inhabitants of them.

PRO: They say that Negro boys and girls get in gangs and cause riots. But white children get in gangs that come from low families. And then they have riots. Even in our own city there was riots against our own police officers.

CON: Do whites go around shooting up cops? Do they stand on the roofs? Do they have to send tanks and troops to keep them from burnin' half the city?

PRO: How about the man in Texas who shot all the people from a tower? That was one man who killed more people maybe than all the Negroes in the riot.

CON: He was crazy.

PRO: Well, that's no excuse. He was white, right? Maybe the Negroes are crazy, too, some of them. Right? Well, you don't give them a chance.

CON: Well, when I was at the fire-prevention award, I was around the house where they give out the basketballs. And so I walk around the corner and about ten of 'em, niggers—colored guys, came around and they jumped on me. And I fell to the ground. And then they all went into that house there and they ransacked the whole place. And it's not even safe to walk the streets in the afternoon around there.

PRO: All right, now, if you were a Negro and there were about fifty white kids standing on the corner and they turned around and called you "nigger." Like you just said now—you slipped. You went around and they called you "nigger." You can't say to me that you wouldn't go and get a whole bunch of more Negroes and then you'd go around and you wouldn't start fightin'? Or, wait a sec. If they called you white trash, would you take it off 'em?

CON: No.

PRO: Well, they have to stick up for their rights just as much as we have to stick up for ours.

CON: It works two ways. When you're by yourself and there's a whole bunch of 'em, you're ascared even to walk down a dark street. 'Cause they'll jump on ya. They carry knives. Even under their lockers they have knives pasted up. My Mum was walkin' down and she was on a bus and she saw three white kids comin' out of Joe's and about fifty nigger kids followin' 'em.

TEACHER: Negro.

CON: Negro.

PRO: How do you think a Negro child would feel walkin' down a mainly white neighborhood and a whole bunch of white children standin' on the corner? Don't you think he's gonna feel funny, too? Don't you think he'd feel like he was gonna get jumped? With the hatred that's goin' around with the Negro people?

PRO: I think that nothing like this would happen if we had integrated schools and the children would learn to get along together.

There was further discussion of Negro job opportunities, the pros arguing that Negroes work on trash and garbage trucks because these are the only jobs open to some of them, the cons saying Negroes take lowly jobs because they're too lazy to strive for anything better. The cons said Negroes cheat on their income taxes. The pros said whites are bigger cheaters especially when it comes to claiming phony medical bills and church contributions. There was this rebuttal:

PRO: We have come to the conclusion that most segregation is caused by prejudice. . . . Like for jobs, the Negroes have to rob because the white employers won't give them a decent enough job. And schooling, if it would be integrated, it would be better. This would teach us to live with the Negro like Pope John says in his encyclical, *Pax Mittetis*. We should live with him like a brother, as God wanted us to be. And also that the Negroes today embezzle the government less than the white men do. And that the Negroes aren't the only cause of the slums.

CON: The Negro people are asking too much from white people but I think that the white people are gonna give in to them. They start the riots and everything. And that their children are uneducated. Now they're realizing that they're gonna have to get an education and everything. But it's too late. And how would you like it if there was a couple of Negro persons in your classroom? Would you feel prejudiced about them?

The last question went unanswered. To a chorus of gasps, the student judges decided the debate in favor of the pros. Most of the arguments were obviously simplistic, but they were honestly stated. This was rare talk in a parochial school, as it would have been in a public school. (For public schools in a biracial city such issues as integration are not debatable. The public schools at least pay lip service to fellowship, justice, open housing, and such causes. You never hear public-school students arguing the "bad" side as the Polish parochial school students were so willing to do.) In allowing such a debate, the sister superior was taking a gamble—or believed that she was. She was convinced that many of the parents of her pupils would resent the discussion. "Our people are very much against the colored," she told me. "I've been trying for years to inculcate brotherhood. But you have to be careful not to arouse animosity. Right away they'll say I'm a nigger lover."

By this time some of the differences between Catholic schools and public schools should be evident. Yet in Whitetown particularly the similarites are marked. Some of Kensington's stern old dowager public-school teachers enforce discipline and drill in a way that the most conservative teaching nuns would envy. And at some Kensington public schools, as I've indicated, preparations for Christmas and other religious festivals are more elaborate than in any parochial school. In fact, the parochial schools' religious training seemed to me to be perfunctory, and Catholic educators themselves point to religious education as the weakest link in the parochial school curriculum.

Another point: despite their many shortcomings in race relations, both in precept and practice, parochial schools in Philadelphia, and, I suspect, in other areas, have a strong appeal for striving Negro parents. Some 15,000 Negro children attend Philadelphia's Catholic schools. And I keep meeting middle-class, college-educated blacks who prefer Catholic to public education. They prefer it, I think, not so much because of their religious faith. Most of those I'm thinking of are liberal Catholics, who believe in ecumenism and also believe in the ideals of public education. They pick their Catholic schools carefully and would avoid the most conservative ones epitomized by the Kensington classroom with the girl timekeeper. But choose Catholic education many of them do. And I think they choose it because they believe that a pretty stiff dose of discipline, order, and direction is good for children.

Donald K. Cheek, a Harlem-born Negro who is vice-president of Lincoln University in southeastern Pennsylvania, is a third-generation Catholic. He picketed the Philadelphia chancellery in 1967 to protest Cardinal Krol's decision transferring out of his archdiocese a liberal Jesuit teacher in a private Catholic boys' school. Cheek thinks the Philadelphia archdiocese "has missed the implications of the post Vatican Council period." He thinks Catholic-school graduates are often narrow-minded. At the same time, though, he finds much to admire in Catholic education. "People still want to get their kids into old buildings and overcrowded classrooms," notes Cheek. "That says something about the teaching. Discipline is stressed and this is good. Creativity comes through discipline. You're not necessarily squashing the creative child in a disciplined setting; you may be liberating him."

I would go further and venture a prediction that when and if black and white community groups gain control of their schools in big cities they will stress discipline, drill, perhaps even the uniforms of parochial schools. I say this because, as Paul Goodman and others have observed, poor people generally prove to be educational conservatives. They favor basic instruction with no fancy rigmarole. And all things considered, this is what Catholic schools provide.

Of course, many Catholics themselves are dissatisfied. I remember attending a National Catholic Educational Convention in New York, where for three days Catholic educators screamed about how bad Catholic education was. Said Dr. Paul Mundy, chairman of the sociology department at Loyola University in Chicago:

> I suspect that the dead hand of our rural past haunts us in our continued confusion at every level of our educational system. We are plagued by the sure but unsophisticated opinions of the past that prompted us to put most of our eggs in the elementary basket, creating our bottom-heavy educational system.

Said the Reverend Louis J. Twomey, director of the human relations institute at Loyola University in New Orleans:

If we were to total the racists and the inactive nonracists in the [Catholic] Church, we would probably come to a figure that would cover the large majority of clergy and laity in the United States.

Since then there has been much, much more criticism of Catholic education by Catholics and non-Catholics alike. The fact is, though, that despite all kinds of problems, it has thrived. In no other country in the world has a church or religious group developed a huge school system completely on its own, with no government support. In the Catholic countries, of course, the Catholic schools are state supported, but in England, Scotland, and Australia they are, too. Only in the United States has such a tremendous network of schools been sustained by the people themselves unaided by government. (And with an assist from bingo.)

And despite justified criticism, the parochial schools, by all accounts, have done what they set out to do. The most comprehensive study of Catholic education's social effects was made in the 1960s by the Reverend Andrew M. Greeley, Peter H. Rossi, and Leonard J. Pinto, of the University of Chicago's National Opinion Research Center. Their three-year survey was supported by a grant from the Carnegie Corporation of New York. They found that those Catholics who were educated exclusively in Catholic schools enjoyed "notably higher social status" than Catholics who attended Catholic schools only for certain years or not at all. Even under a control for parental educational and income level, those who attended Catholic grammar schools were more likely to graduate from high school than those whose grammar-school education was mixed or exclusively public. And those Catholics who went to Catholic high schools were more likely to go to college than were those who attended public high schools.

Father Greeley, Rossi, and Pinto found "rather dramatic correlation between Catholic education and upward mobility." * They found strong evidence that at lower age levels "the Catholic population is catching up socially and economically with Protestants from comparable regions." And they expressed the belief that Catholic schools "have made a unique contribution to the acculturation of the immigrant groups." They did not credit the parochial schools with giving American Catholicism its vitality; indeed, they almost argued the opposite, that the schools were a result of the vitality. But they did indicate that those who attended Catholic schools exclusively "do even better those things done reasonably well by most American Catholics."

Since their study the financial bind has tightened for parochial schools in many dioceses, Philadelphia included. In an interview in March 1965 Cardinal Krol, a shy, ascetic man, the son of Polish immigrants and a leader in the conservative wing of the American hierarchy, expressed confidence that the Catholic school system in Philadelphia could keep running indefinitely as it had in the past. The system's huge enrollment boom was leveling off, he said, and future expansion would be "more or less normal." An increase in young Catholics entering seminaries and religious communities promised a great supply of teachers. "The prospects for the future," he told me then, "are bright and optimistic." Yet little more than two years later he went before the Greater Philadelphia Council of Churches "as a beggar, a beggar for the parochial schools." In an open admission of error, he said, "The fact is that we have now extended ourselves beyond our resources."

The Cardinal had been betrayed by changing times. The winds of reform stirred by the Vatican Council had suddenly

* *The Social Effects of Catholic Education*, A Preliminary Report, National Opinion Research Center, University of Chicago, Sept., 1964.

made old-time Christianity unattractive to vast numbers of young people of all denominations. The emancipation of the arts, the new morality, the widely reported death of God, the world-wide challenge to established ways of thinking and acting—all played a part in the decline of religious vocations just as they did in the decline of Kensington. As a result, the orders of teaching nuns found their numbers sharply reduced. Even sprightly new modes of dress weren't enough to attract novitiates. Lay teachers making $5,000 a year in diocesan high schools replaced religious receiving $75 a month. And St. Charles Seminary, the Philadelphia priest factory, not only found its numbers reduced to record lows, but at least a handful of seminarians engaged in experimental Masses in defiance of the Cardinal, who had them thrown out.

As school costs rose, the archdiocese which for years charged parishes $50 for every one of their children in a diocesan high school increased the assessment to $100 and then to $150. These increases put extremely heavy burdens on individual parishes. One working-class West Philadelphia parish, for example, paid $159,000 for 1,060 high-school pupils while also meeting the costs of running its own parochial school, reputedly the world's largest, with more than 3,000 pupils. A member of this parish, State Representative Martin P. Mullen, mounted a drive for public aid to parochial schools in the Pennsylvania Legislature.

Mullen's campaign met with limited success in 1968, when Pennsylvania became the first state in the nation to authorize state aid to nonpublic schools. At first, however, the aid was limited to some of the receipts from harness racing. Philadelphia's Catholic schools were allocated one and one-half million dollars in 1969. This amounted to less than six dollars per pupil and would not keep the schools from going under—if in fact they were headed under, as some observers thought. The aid went to support instruction in four subjects—science, math, modern foreign languages, and gym. All nonprofit, nonpublic schools in the state were eligible. The aid was prorated on the basis of actual costs. Since such posh private schools as Germantown Academy and William Penn Charter spend several times as much per pupil in these four areas of instruction as do the parochial schools, they stood to receive several times as much per pupil enrolled, even though their needs were correspondingly much lower.

The aid program faced a certain court test. In any event, even substantially increased aid probably would not forestall further cutbacks in the Catholic schools and enrollment losses. The Catholic schools of Philadelphia and elsewhere thus faced perhaps their most serious financial squeeze just as the principle they established—that of separate, private schools in competition with public schools—came to be viewed with favor really for the first time. In the past, the separate-school concept had been attacked as divisive and undemocratic. Now New Left radicals and black leaders are seizing on the idea as a way of beating the public-school system, which they consider beyond redemption. Thus, for almost the first time in their history, the Catholic schools are no longer under assault as harmful to the democratic ideal and their right to exist is not being questioned. Yet rising costs and falling numbers have placed in jeopardy their ability to exist.

That is the supreme irony facing the Catholic schools in 1970. Because of the ethnic and religious make-up of the Whitetowns of America their futures are intricately bound up with the future of the Roman Catholic Church schools.

The Ivies
and the Alienated Whites

"It should be perfectly clear to anyone who reads the daily roster of violence, hatred, and despair which fills the newspapers," Mark R. Shedd, Philadelphia's incoming superintendent of schools, told a meeting of all his principals in May 1967, "that this country needs a social revolution—a revolution in human values and human relationships. If this does not occur, I see no reason for bothering to educate our children. And if it is to occur, the schools must be the cauldron whether we like it or consider it our traditional role or not."

Shedd was forty. A Methodist minister's son, he had grown up in New England, gone to the University of Maine —a "Maniac," his critics would call him—and gotten his doctorate at Harvard's Graduate School of Education. Over a period of fifteen years, he had moved from high-school teaching in Maine to a rural superintendency in Connecticut to a small-town superintendency in New Jersey. Now he was tackling a big-city superintendency. He was shifting from Englewood, New Jersey, with its four thousand pupils and six schools, to Philadelphia, with its two hundred eighty thousand pupils and three hundred schools. Shedd had been picked by Philadelphia's reform school board to breathe new life into a staggering system, to push it into the twentieth century before the century ran out. His reputation was of a young, vigorous, creative man of action. And in his talk to the principals he came on that way. He promised to decentralize the schools, to stir a "lively dissatisfaction," to encourage teachers and principals to take risks, rock the boat, and "try the way-out idea."

"It is this sort of person we need in the school system at all levels," Shedd said, "and it is precisely this kind of lunacy which we must reward and which we must stimulate in the system. No one can sit on his hands—or whatever else he sits on—if his responsibility is clear. And it should be clearly understood that anyone who takes risks may experience some failure. The system must develop an expectancy —even a hope—that there will be some dramatic failures. But it is part of my job, and part of the job of central office staff in general, to make sure that those who fail . . . are not punished. Faced with the uncertainties we all face in education today, there are no safe bets and we must all be gamblers."

Never before had a Philadelphia school superintendent talked as Shedd did in introducing himself to his staff. For at least thirty years the city schools had in fact waged war against change. The system was inbred, unimaginative, calcified. One bright principal who fled in disgust termed the bureaucracy an "arthritic turtle." It was filled, to mix the wildlife metaphor, with scared rabbits. And it was run not by Harvard-trained reformers but by a high-school dropout. From 1936 to 1962, the man who made all major decisions on city school budgets, city school taxes, even on assignment of key instructional personnel in Philadelphia was not the superintendent of schools but the business manager. His name was Add B. Anderson.

Under a curious system of "dual control" of administrative functions, the business manager and superintendent were separate but equal. Each reported directly to the appointed school board. When one got a raise the other did, too, though the board paid its superintendent one thousand dollars a year more than its business manager.

In practice, however, the business manager ran the show. Add Anderson outlasted three superintendents and completely dominated a fourth. He not only told the board what to do but he also helped pick the board members themselves. Technically, the choices were made by the city's Common Pleas Court judges—a system instituted at the turn of the century to take the corruption-ridden schools out of politics. In practice, the choices were dictated to the judges by the political bosses. And in telling the judges whom to appoint, the politicians always obtained the advice and consent of Add Anderson.

They trusted him. They knew he would recommend safe, conservative defenders of the *status quo* whom he could control and whose fiscal outlook matched his. Add Anderson's eye was always on the balance sheet. He gained power during the Great Depression when the schools cut costs to the bone in order to survive. He remained a penny pincher all his life. He was a ruthless man filled with contempt for "educators."

And well he might have been. Despite his lack of formal education, he consistently outmaneuvered and outfoxed those with master's and doctor's degrees. His was an American success story. He quit high school in tenth grade to take a five-dollar-a-week job as office boy at the school board. In twenty years he worked his way to the top and stayed there.

He was a demanding taskmaster. For employees reporting to him, Anderson kept a ledger. Any who didn't measure up heard from him. Nobody ever crossed Add Anderson and got away with it. He became a legendary figure, a Scrooge with rolltop desk who blocked all efforts at liberalization and made the school system dance to his tunes. It was during his long rule that the system became ever more ingrown, that janitors were paid more than principals, that per-pupil spending and teachers' salaries sank to national lows, that the teacher shortage soared, that the Board of Education creaked and groaned with senior citizens—at one point the youngest board member was fifty-one and the average age was sixty-six—that board financial policies were ultrasecret and ultracautious, that the lawyer who for years had argued the Chamber of Commerce's case against school-tax increases won appointment to the board and became its president.

It's easy to blame all these school sins on one man—Add Anderson—and in analyzing Philadelphia's lamentable school history many see Anderson as the villain. The fact is, though, that Add Anderson gave influential elements of the community exactly what they wanted. He gave the politicians what they wanted—schools that seemed to roll along placidly without making waves and without costing much. He gave the businessmen, most of whom lived in the suburbs or sent their children to private schools in the city, what they wanted—low city taxes. Indeed, Anderson's stewardship won official endorsement in the early 1950s from the city's most prestigious business group, the Greater Philadelphia Movement.

As for the people, they did very little complaining. In those days, to be sure, dissent was easily stifled because there was no real forum for debate. But the parents, through their home-and-school associations, consistently supported school-board policies. In fact their bylaws barred them from opposing the board on anything. The dominant teachers' group, an affiliate of the National Education Association, was also a creature of the system. It meekly sought salary increases every year but never raised a finger when they weren't given. Civil-rights groups were rarely heard from. When protests were mounted over Philadelphia's racially segregated schools—separate appointment lists for white and black teachers were kept until 1937—the board would listen politely and then do nothing. Usually the protests simply died out. All school-board decisions were made behind closed doors and then ratified at sterile public meetings. Board members went through their paces like trained seals before audiences that rarely numbered more than a dozen citizens. There was never any debate, any speechmaking, hardly ever any negative votes. The fifteen board members agreed unanimously on almost everything. The Supreme Soviet couldn't have functioned more smoothly.

What is most stunning about all this, however, is not that Philadelphia was out of step with urban education trends in this country, or that it was slumbering while schools in other cities were surging ahead. On the contrary. Philadelphia was asleep, all right, but so were the other city school systems. The pattern was virtually the same everywhere—vast, muddle-headed educational bureaucracies shielded from public view, making decisions affecting millions of children and tens of millions of taxpayers without consulting anybody and without being challenged or questioned. Because of Add Anderson's amazing influence, Philadelphia was perhaps a little unusual. But only a little.

Change was resisted everywhere. All city systems were ingrown, insecure, and united in their opposition to "outsiders." It was partly for this reason—although other factors were also at work—that Pittsburgh's former superintendent, Calvin Gross, was chewed up so quickly after becoming the first outsider in half a century to assume the superintendency in New York City. During most of this period city school systems managed to keep teachers and parents quiescent. As in Philadelphia, school boards generally were captives of business establishments whose chief educational goals were low taxes and uncomplicated, noncontroversial instruction. Most of the boards succeeded in avoiding meaningful citizen participation in school planning and decision making. And for a long time they escaped heavy criticism. In Philadelphia and elsewhere the white middle class and upper-middle class often got the public schools they wanted even when this meant gerrymandering boundaries and transferring old schools to new locations, as in the case of Philadelphia's Central and Northeast highs. The lower classes, black and white, were voiceless and, apparently, apathetic.

In the 1950s, pressures for change built up. City school boards began to draw fire from many quarters. Although the United States Supreme Court's historic 1954 decision attacked *de jure* segregation in Southern schools, it forced Northern school districts to examine their own blatant *de facto* segregation. Gradually, black communities awakened to the outrages that had been perpetrated against them for so long. Schools in North and South became civil-rights battlegrounds. Teachers got militant. Parents grew restive. Even students found a voice.

Then, on October 4, 1957, came Sputnik. In beating this country into space, the Soviet Union shook America's confidence in its public schools. Nikita S. Khrushchev became, in Francis Keppel's view, "the U.S. commissar of education." Certainly, the Soviet feat made Americans, especially movers and shakers in the business and financial establishment, wonder what in the world was going on in our own educational system. Why were we behind? Who was to blame? What had the schools been doing? As a direct result of Sputnik, Congress in 1958 passed the National Defense Education Act, marking the first time in history that Federal funds had been earmarked to strengthen basic instruction in public schools.

At last the spotlight was turned squarely on the schools and, since they were the biggest targets, on the city schools. In city after city schools became important news. School stories moved from the truss ads on back pages of newspapers to the heady air and big black type of page one. In Philadelphia in the sleepy 1930s, reporters used to play chess during school-board meetings. In the ferment of the 1960s, they were dashing to phones with the latest shocker from school-board headquarters.

Add Anderson died in 1962. An era died with him. Even had he lived it is questionable how much longer he could have kept his finger in the dike. Civic and community groups led by the Citizens Committee on Public Education in Philadelphia were massing for an assault. Parents and teachers were up in arms. Within the board itself a reform-minded member, Mrs. Albert M. Greenfield, pushed hard and effectively for improvements. The Greater Philadelphia Movement, with a new, perceptive executive director named William H. Wilcox, had already seen its previous error. It published a report before Anderson's death urging an end to "dual control" and many other reforms, including the scrapping of judicial appointments of school-board members. G.P.M. favored mayoral appointments from lists supplied by a citizens' nominating panel. Anderson's death set off a battle royal between reformers and standpatters.

After several years of hard fighting, the reformers won. They got a new school board—nine members to be chosen by the mayor from a panel's list and to serve no longer than twelve years. (Under the old system, board members got virtual life appointments. One woman served more than thirty years.) The reformers also got a new educational home-rule charter which authorized Philadelphia City Council to levy school taxes. Previously, Philadelphia and Pittsburgh, alone among more than twenty-two hundred school districts in Pennsylvania, were forced to go to the State Legislature every time they wanted to raise their own school taxes. (Actually, this particular reform proved to be illusory. Even though Philadelphia City Council is now empowered to set school taxes, it keeps passing the buck to the Legislature, and the same old battles ensue. In 1965, however, it appeared that genuine home rule had been won, and reformers were jubilant.)

The reformers were jubilant, too, when the first school-board selections were announced. Heading the board was Philadelphia's former reform mayor, Richardson Dilworth. The civic groups were hoping that Dilworth would be able to work wonders in the schools comparable to achievements he and Joseph S. Clark, later United States Senator, posted in the 1950s as the first Democratic mayors of the city since 1884. Although Dilworth was an obvious choice for the school board and wanted the job, there was doubt whether his successor at City Hall, James H. J. Tate, would make the appointment. Tate, too, is a Democrat, but he and Dilworth don't get along. (Dilworth is a blithe spirit and the list of fellow Democrats with whom he doesn't get along is probably longer than the list of those he does get along with.)

As it happened, Tate made the appointment. As it happened also, the much-heralded selection process was violated with that appointment—violated by Dilworth himself. Before accepting the appointment, he had, in private talks with Tate, laid down two conditions. One was that he be named board president. The other was that he be granted, in effect, a veto power over the other eight appointments. Tate couldn't name Dilworth president of the board, since the board itself elects its own president. He could, and apparently did, tell his appointees that Dilworth was his man for the presidency. He and Dilworth quarreled over a few of the appointees but agreement was reached. When word of the conditions that Dilworth had exacted leaked out there was no protest from the reformers. Dilworth, after all, was their candidate and they didn't want to risk losing him by fighting for the inviolability of the new appointment system. With this overriding of the rules, however, the new procedure which had been won with such pain and struggle lost some of its luster.

Within a few years the same reformers began to question its value altogether. A similar appointment method was similarly disavowed in New York by those who had originally supported it. In Chicago it has also lost favor although it continues to be used.

As I see it, there were two major flaws in this school-board selection machinery. One was that in forcing the mayor to make appointments from recommendations of a blue-ribbon panel, the reformers eroded the mayor's power. This, of course, was their intent. It reflected the distrust of the reformers, most of them middle-class Protestants and Jews, of big-city mayors, many of them Roman Catholics with working-class antecedents. In Philadelphia I'm not sure the nominating-panel idea would have been advanced if Dilworth had been mayor when the school-board appointment system was changed. But besides being designed for individuals rather than offices, the panel setup made it impossible to pinpoint responsibility for school board appointments, good or bad. The mayor couldn't be blamed or credited because he was hamstrung by panel recommendations.*

The other mistake lay in the make-up of the panel. It consisted largely of representatives of prestigious institutions, such as universities, or of city-wide organizations, such as the chamber of commerce or bar association. There was no place on the panel for grassroots Whitetowners or Blacktowners. As a result, these "little people" were largely overlooked by the panel in nominating school-board candidates. Mayor Tate named a board that was ethnically, religiously, and racially fairly well balanced, as he could be expected to do, but the working-class neighborhoods were ignored.

Besides Dilworth, the original school-board appointees were an aging movie-theater chain magnate, Jewish, a member of the old board who actually lived outside the city but being a heavy Democratic-campaign contributor kept his place on the board; a physician and medical-school professor, Protestant, with no previous ties to or known interest in public education; a veteran labor leader, Jewish, who also had not evidenced any prior concern for the schools; a Negro clergyman; a versatile lawyer-writer-ex-businessman, second-generation Italian foreign stock, Catholic, equally unknown to education groups; another lawyer, Irish Catholic, no previous involvement in schools; a young black businessman active in his neighborhood and in school reform groups; and the aforementioned Mrs. Greenfield, the old board's most progressive member, who also was named to the new unit. Although not Jewish herself, she was married to a Jew who was the city's most prominent real-estate man, and some viewed hers as a "Jewish" seat on the board. The Negro businessman, George Hutt, was the only true grass-

* In Philadelphia, the mayor must make each school-board appointment from a maximum of six names submitted by the nominating panel.

roots representative. Not one spoke for the city's working-class white groups, the Whitetowners. Although the Italian-American lawyer had grown up in South Philadelphia's Little Italy and could remember his immigrant mother dusting lint off living-room furniture, he had long since moved to an expensive center-city apartment. He had little in common with the vocal, volatile, uptight South Philly Italians in their neat row houses, often with well-tended fig trees out back. The Irish lawyer also lived in an upper-middle-class neighborhood. He was the first to quit the board after winning appointment as a Federal judge and was replaced by another Irish Catholic lawyer.

In 1970, with youth on the march and with communities in New York and other cities actively seeking control of their schools, the composition of Philadelphia's first school board under the new rules hardly seems impressive. It is a measure of how thinking has changed in five years that in 1965 the appointments were generally well received and high hopes were expressed for the success of the board so chosen. To its credit, the new board took several steps to gain community backing. Instead of always meeting in the afternoon at its downtown headquarters, it took its show on the road to high schools all over the city and met at night so more taxpayers could attend. It held more public meetings than any previous board and more public hearings on crucial education issues. To keep taxpayers informed it tripled its mailing list. It operated much more openly and it permitted its board meetings to be televised in their entirety by Philadelphia's educational-TV station.

In the board's first year of operation, before the arrival of Shedd, it piled up accomplishments which, by past Philadelphia school standards, were staggering. It formed task forces of private citizens with expertise in finance, manpower, capital spending, and the like. These task forces analyzed the situation and set goals for the schools, goals which

Dilworth and Company set about meeting. The board in those first twelve months increased spending by $145 per pupil; purchased more than $9 million worth of new automated teaching devices; established learning materials centers in 100 schools; added 100 kindergartens and started fourteen prekindergartens; set up seven experimental "magnet" schools designed to attract pupils from wide areas and, among other things, thus become racially integrated; began a record building program by putting $66 million worth of school construction under contract; started moving towards a K4-4-4 building plan; hired 3,000 new teachers, thus virtually ending the teacher shortage; hired 2,500 teacher aides and other assistants and signed up 600 volunteer workers; doubled spending for books and instructional supplies; bussed 9,150 pupils to underutilized facilities; hired 179 neighborhood people as links between homes and schools; set up special afternoon and Saturday classes for academically talented and potentially able pupils.

Most significantly, the new board took a realistic look at school financial needs and sought to meet them. Past practice had been to save money and cut costs whenever possible. These short-run savings were leading to long-run disaster. The new board saw vastly higher spending requirements and hunted in Washington, Harrisburg, and City Hall for the funds. Dilworth, the old pro, and later Shedd developed close ties with U.S. Office of Education officials. Thanks to them, Philadelphia outperformed all other U.S. school districts in getting Federal aid for school projects. In that first year alone, the board obtained $32 million in additional Federal funds, secured over $2 million in government-planning money and private-foundation support, gained City Council approval for tax increases raising $12 million and picked up $20 million more by shifting its fiscal year. This added up to $66 million in new money.

In 1959 Add Anderson and the old board had run the

entire school system on only about $90 million. But that was eons ago. The new board obviously was willing to search anywhere for money, even if it meant legally juggling its books, which is what the fiscal-year change added up to. And it moved fast. It prepared and adopted in four months its new operating budget calling for a forty per cent increase in spending and a new capital budget setting forth six years of school construction at a rate five times that of any previous period.

Yet there was a missing ingredient. The task force chairmen noted it in their first-year progress report. They reported that, despite all the improvements, "there is little evidence, vocal or otherwise, of a stirring of excitement or strong support from the majority of citizens. This kind of support must be mobilized," they continued, "and made emphatic. The crucial problem of increasing the responsiveness of individual parents and community groups must be solved if progress is to continue."

Within the bureaucracy itself dissatisfaction and resentments seemed to boil up rather than simmer down. The coming of Mark Shedd in 1967 merely increased tensions. Every entrenched bureaucracy fights change. The Dilworth-Shedd team posed a special threat because of its heavy reliance on outside educators and on noneducators.

In his first major appointment, even before leaving Englewood, Shedd picked as his administrative assistant and speechwriter a twenty-six-year-old former Harvard shotputter and *Philadelphia Bulletin* education reporter named Richard H. de Lone. Brash and bright, radical in his politics and sloppy in his dress (his shirttail was usually out), de Lone, while a reporter, had written a series of articles based on a week's experience as a substitute teacher. In the articles he blasted bigoted teachers, insensitive principals, and the whole faltering system. His polemic stirred an angry reaction from school people who accused him of distortions and one-sided reporting. In joining the school establishment, de Lone quickly became Shedd's *enfant terrible*. Rather than trying to smooth ruffled feathers, he seemed to go out of his way to infuriate the bureaucrats. As *Philadelphia Magazine* later put it:

> De Lone, you understand, has this . . . manner. Arrogant is the general word for it. Stories quickly spread about the way he talked of "shaking the system up" and the way he went around telling principals to "shape up or ship out." This— kid—telling men old enough to be his father . . . Well!

Actually, de Lone more than anyone else was responsible for Shedd's coming to Philadelphia. He was a close friend of Theodore R. Sizer, dean of Harvard's Graduate School of Education, key training ground for reform-minded American educators. When Dilworth was casting about for a superintendent, reporter de Lone put him in touch with Sizer, who recommended Shedd. After being offered the Philadelphia job, Shedd conferred with de Lone before accepting, then wooed the reporter away from the newspaper business.

To critics of the establishment, any establishment, and to anybody who believes in calling a spade a spade, de Lone was—and is—a delightful presence and a rare bird to be poking around inside a school bureaucracy. But he would have sent Add Anderson up the wall. Asked to suggest ways of presenting the school board's 1967 budget for maximum citizen support, de Lone wrote an interoffice memo that made headlines when one of his school-board enemies— their numbers were legion—leaked it to the papers. The memo created a sensation. Here was Dr. Shedd's trusted aide urging that the school system artificially "create a climate of crisis" so that heavy spending would be more palatable. Here he was calling for development of a "good Madison Avenue type" of budget which would be "sexy" and "convincing," the drafting of a "quick and dirty staff development program," and visits to newspaper offices "paving the way for a media attack" stressing the danger of building-program cancellations. De Lone also wrote: "If we decided to make, say, adult education the expendable item, we could play really dirty pool by giving the teachers materials to present in class explaining to the adults why their classes will be cut and who's to blame."

All this was a case of straight, honest talk in a business with more than its share of phoniness and hypocrisy. The techniques that de Lone recommended are ones that school systems habitually use in seeking to sell budgets and building programs. Of course, they never level with their constituencies as candidly as de Lone did. Hence what he wrote suddenly seemed in woeful taste if not immoral. De Lone remained on the job despite criticism, but after the 1968–1969 school year he left to become a Whitehead Fellow at Harvard.

De Lone was one of the coterie of liberal-arts swingers, the Ivy Mafia some called them, whom Dilworth and Shedd recruited to save the schools. On grounds that, as one Young Turk put it, "education is too important to be left to the educators," they ignored the teachers' colleges and instead brought in young, talented idea men from some of the nation's best universities. Besides Shedd himself and de Lone, four other administrators came with degrees from Harvard, three were Yale men, and others were drawn from Dartmouth, Princeton, Amherst, Antioch, Oberlin, and the University of California at Berkeley.

From the ranks of the board's former critics came Robert W. Blackburn, the bright, witty, and aware ex-director of the Citizens Committee on Public Education. With G.P.M.'s Wilcox, Blackburn had masterminded the old board's ouster. After a Peace Corps stint in Africa, he joined the new board as director of its integration and intergroup education office.

Some of the new board's freshest ideas came from non-educators. The most notable idea of all, that of creating a so-called Parkway School, one without its own building that would draw on the resources of the museums, libraries, newspapers, and other institutions in and near the Benjamin Franklin Parkway in Philadelphia, was brainstormed by Dilworth's former press agent at City Hall and later his assistant at the school board, another former *Bulletin* reporter named Clifford Brenner. Brenner's Parkway School became an instant hit and soon curious high-schoolers from the suburbs were riding buses into the city to enroll there.

Many other bright ideas died aborning, however. The Ivies had tough sledding. In the 1950s, Dilworth and Joe Clark had similarly recruited from all over the nation to get top talent for their cleanup of City Hall. And they pulled it off. But educational reform was something else. Brenner, who played a role in both, saw a big difference in trying to reform City Hall and trying to reform schools. "The contrast," he said, "is that City Hall had a political mandate. This gave momentum to reform. The schools don't have it. And their problems are much more complicated than simply ending corruption and throwing the rascals out. So movement in the schools is more difficult."

Just before the start of school in September 1967 I joined my fellow teachers at Philadelphia's cavernous Convention Hall to hear Shedd's sendoff. Although his appointment officially took effect that month, he had been commuting from Englewood since the first of the year and was fully in charge. To more than ten thousand teachers and administrators, Shedd spoke rousingly. He advocated a "dialogue of discontent, tough but honest," that would include critics of the schools as well as students, whom he labeled the "shrillest, silliest, most profound. We cannot meet discontent with dogmatism," Shedd said. "What we should not do is tell these alienated youngsters to cut their hair."

Two months later, on November 17, 1967, the "dialogue of discontent" erupted into a bloody battle between black students and police. From the outset Shedd had sought to establish lines of communication with black students, blacks working in the system and in the community. To advance black administrators who failed to meet qualifications for upper-echelon jobs, he took frequent advantage of a rule permitting the superintendent to promote five per cent of his administrative staff without regard for eligibility lists. Soon the word got around that Shedd was favoring blacks over whites at all levels. This added fuel to fire. Shedd also showed a willingness to meet with black students and militants, listen to their demands and, where possible, accede to them. His willingness to go at least halfway with black students led to charges of mollycoddling. On November 17 Shedd and the board scheduled a meeting at school-board headquarters with representatives of black high-school students demanding African history and culture classes, name changes of certain high schools, black clubs at the schools, and the right to wear African clothing and natural haircuts. It was agreed that black students at high schools throughout the city would be excused early that day, if they so desired, to lend moral support outside the administration building while their leaders met with school officials inside. The school board informed Philadelphia police of the rally and a detachment of nonuniformed officers from the civil-disobedience squad was assigned to keep watch.

Some twenty-five hundred to three thousand students—more than school officials expected—showed up at noon that day and stood milling around the school board's "Palace on the Parkway." As might be expected in such a crowd, there were a few pranksters. At one point a couple of students climbed onto parked cars and stood on their roofs surveying the scene. The small police detachment grew nervous. At City Hall, less than a mile away, Police Commissioner Frank L. Rizzo, a hard-nosed cop with a reputation for swinging first and asking questions later, was swearing in more than two hundred new police sergeants and lieutenants. Word reached him that the school-board situation was getting out of hand. Rizzo piled his new officers into police buses and sped to the scene.

As Rizzo's men arrived, two civil-disobedience squad members sought to arrest one of the car-hoppers for disorderly conduct. The arresting officers were surrounded by students who blocked their way. There were shouts, jostling, and great excitement as the crowd swarmed in the constricted area. Rizzo sent his men into action with clubs swinging. The black students were routed. In their flight, they overran and injured numerous innocent bystanders.

Within a few minutes the fighting was over but recriminations, charges and counter-charges rent the air for months. Dilworth angrily denounced Rizzo's action against the "children." Rizzo defended his tactics and his men and said they had prevented a major outbreak of violence. Altogether, about forty persons were hurt, none critically, and many blacks were arrested. Civil-rights groups went into Federal court seeking Rizzo's ouster. They lost their suit. On the other hand, charges against those arrested at the scene were later dismissed. And Rizzo, while continuing to defend his actions on November 17, practiced restraint for more than a year after that and made a serious—generally successful—effort to get along with white and black civil-rights activists. But the trouble on November 17 pitted the school board and the superintendent against the police chief and law-and-order. It further alienated Dilworth, Shedd, and the Ivies from much of the white community.

In numerous other ways, the Shedd-Dilworth team showed it was prepared to buck the system itself and to push for social change. De Lone worked with an experimental summer-school class examining controversial issues. He organized picketing of City Hall and marched with the class to protest all-white housing in the city's heavily Jewish, lower-middle and middle-class far northeastern section. Black militants were invited into high schools to address students at assemblies. To ventilate school problems and make clear to school principals and administrators the extent of black hostility toward the public schools, Shedd scheduled a series of "sensitivity retreats."

These were marathon weekend sessions held in private quarters where the atmosphere was conducive to free and easy conversation. Participants were urged to speak their minds. Black students and community representatives did just that. High-school principals heard themselves cursed and vilified as racists. The administration's specialist in affective development, who had played a major role in setting up the retreats, asked a girls'-high-school principal, a spinster, what students meant when they said, "Fuck the system!" Before the principal could gather her wits, a black community representative, according to a report submitted later to school-board members, interjected with, "What's the matter, white woman? Don't you understand black folks' talk? Or don't you know what 'fuck' is because you're a maiden lady?" The principal dissolved in tears.

Principals also were subjected to comments such as: "Are you an American or are you a human being?" "White man, if you're not out of your school by Friday, we're going to burn it down." "You old fool, why don't you quit before we make you." In a report on the "sensitizing workshops," Shedd later wrote:

> The process followed . . . is basically one of conflict confrontation and resolution. The effort at each [workshop] has been to get problems and emotions out on the table, directly and openly. This inevitably involves some conflict, some heat and some pain. . . . The confrontation is not seen as an end in itself, however. Rather, it is viewed as a critical first step for ventilation of feelings which inhibit true communication; identification of problems and issues and establishment of honest dialogue.

While some principals supported the workshops, others were appalled and horrified at the whole business. In a protest to the school board, a group of them termed the workshops "denigrating, humiliating, and demoralizing." They charged that only "black-power advocates" were invited as community representatives while "the great majority of Negroes who consistently strive for understanding and concerted effort is ignored."

"Never before," the principals alleged, "have professional persons been subjected to such intimidation, vilifaction [*sic*], and character assassination without the slightest chance for rebuttal. . . . Never before have those who have given their lives to the education of deprived children felt less appreciated."

The net result of the workshops, said the principals, was "extreme polarization of staff and a lessened sense of dedication." They asked the board to "come to the assistance of God-fearing, decent people who abhor Gestapo tactics."

Shedd himself, in arranging the workshops, had warned against educational programs that took place in an atmosphere of "hostility, frustration, and misunderstanding between students, communities, and schools." The workshops were supposed to get at this problem as it bore on high schools. From the principals' point of view, however, the sessions only exacerbated the hostility, frustration, and misunderstandings. The workshops were quietly dropped but the bad feelings they aroused lingered on.

Then in May 1968 Shedd did something without precedent in modern Philadelphia educational history. To get rid of administrative deadwood, of which the system was full, and to save money, he announced elimination of 381 administrative positions. Of course he couldn't fire tenured officials, but he could demote them or move them into non-administrative posts. In many instances, that is what he did. An associate superintendent was named principal of a disciplinary school, a district superintendent moved to a vocational-technical school principalship. Scores of unfilled positions were eliminated. While critics of the school bureaucracy were overjoyed, the bureaucrats themselves, even those unaffected by the cutbacks, were outraged. A lawsuit was filed to block implementation of the superintendent's directive. Shedd held his ground and won, but the price—in shattered morale and widening discontent within the system—was high. It was the mass firings that led the principals to make noises about joining the Teamsters' Union. They never carried out this threat, but many clearly saw amalgamation with the truckers as a means of guaranteeing job security and escaping from the clutches of Mark Shedd.

With the teachers, too, Shedd and the Ivies seemed to make more enemies than friends. And this was true despite vastly improved teacher pay and working conditions. Shedd fought hard for a contractual rule permitting him to transfer teachers, against their will if necessary, as a means of ending faculty segregation, of which there was and is a great deal in the Philadelphia schools. The Philadelphia Federation of Teachers, AFL-CIO, turned a deaf ear to this plea. It simply didn't trust Shedd. Like the principals' association, it felt threatened by him and resisted his moves. In the process, it appeared to take on the coloration and temperament of the *status quo* simpletons who had run the system into the ground and whom it had battled in the years before 1965, when it gained the right to represent all teachers. This flip-flop of the teachers' union, from an important force in the reform movement to one opposing Shedd-style changes, was perhaps predictable. Some would say it was clearly a case of success spoiling the teachers' federation. Or a case of a union's bucking the establishment when it represented the "outs" but then defending that establishment when it gained status and power.

This may have been part of the story but it was only part. The teachers' union and its most thoughtful, intelligent leaders really did have grave reservations about Shedd's leadership. In their view, he was truckling to black radicals and turning his back on talented whites. They saw him refusing to examine the truly abominable conditions—the teen-age rapes, the threats to teachers' lives and property—that make teaching in the worst ghettos such frightening work.

On her return, past retirement age, to one such school as a guidance counselor Celia Pincus, the *grande dame* of Philadelphia's teachers' union, a widely respected battler for better education, became convinced that Shedd was on the wrong track. And while the words of many, perhaps most, teachers'-union representatives must be weighed against their own obvious self-interest and biases, Celia Pincus deserves an audience because she has made so much sense for so long. Her conclusion was that, despite all the changes, all the increased spending and imported brainpower, Philadelphia's schools under Shedd had merely widened the gulf between blacks and whites, both inside the system and out.

While Shedd lost the backing of Celia Pincus and the teachers' union, one might have expected him to have picked up support from the returned Peace Corps volunteers and other idealistic young teachers who were flocking to Philadelphia. He didn't seem to be able to reach many of them, either. The system was too big, too remote and these teachers were wholly involved in their own classroom problems. Being newcomers they had nothing to compare conditions with. They didn't realize how much the system had changed, how much better supported it was financially. All they knew was that they had their hands full, teaching was tough, and nobody seemed to care about them. Shedd did institute a program of money grants to teachers who wanted to try new techniques or were creative in other ways. But the program was necessarily small and few teachers benefited. Feeling neglected by their own principals as well as downtown bureaucrats, many of the young teachers quit.

Among parents, too, Shedd and Dilworth encountered great difficulties. And this was strange, because under their leadership Philadelphia school reforms won national acclaim. Three New York City educators who studied half a dozen big-city systems for the United States Office of Education found Philadelphia in the midst of "the most dramatic revolution in a city school system in the postwar period." The 1967 report by Marilyn Gittell, T. Edward Hollander, and William S. Vincent cited Dilworth for special mention as a school board head who clearly perceived his role as a "change agent."

Similarly, a report by a Philadelphia citizens' group on

achievements in 1967 declared that "probably no large school system has ever moved so far so fast, in so many ways as has Philadelphia during the past twelve months." As I have indicated, the achievements did seem impressive. Teacher shortage——wiped out. Teacher pay——enormously increased. New schools——rising at a record rate and filled with all the latest innovations. Administrative brains——top quality, thanks to national talent hunt and attraction of Shedd-Dilworth team. Aid——unprecedented contributions from Washington, whose officials bet on Shedd-Dilworth and gave them millions, and from Harrisburg, whose legislators did much—not enough but a lot—to wipe out the historic state inequities against city school districts.

But while all this was going on the schools failed to gain the backing of many taxpayers. Blacks welcomed the board's new directions but their support was, at best, wavering. In today's climate of racial divisiveness and contention, it is probably asking too much to expect Negro parents to back wholeheartedly a white-dominated school board of whatever quality, especially when the school system in question had failed black people so miserably for so long. The whites were something else. Far from welcoming changes, they feared and resisted them and were outraged at what they took to be the board's pro-black policies.

Many of the most active and concerned parents belonged to home and school associations, Philadelphia's version of P.T.A.s, and to their parent group, the Philadelphia Home and School Council. Before the coming of the new board, the council was in the school system's pocket. It regularly supported all school board initiatives and in turn it was recognized as the group that spoke for parents all over the city. Shedd and Dilworth, believing the council and its member associations to be unrepresentative and ineffective, began bypassing them to deal directly with neighborhood activist groups. Often the people they dealt with were black; the Home and School Council has always been white dominated. The council got very bitter and stopped supporting the school system.

The board got into more hot water with whites when, under pressure from the state, it developed a desegregation plan that called for massive citywide bussing. Under the plan, black and white children were to be transported out of their neighborhoods one or two days a week for integrated classroom experiences in other schools. In white working-class and middle-class sections the reaction was violent. Busloads of mothers descended on the board in September 1968 to demonstrate against the plan. Actually, the scheme was not popular with any segments of the community and the board itself was far from enthusiastic. In the eyes of many people, though, the white parents who objected were viewed as bigots seeking to protect their lily-white refuge. "We didn't even go down to protest," said one mother. "We just went down to find out what was going on. But the board wanted to expose the whites as racists. And that's how it came out in the papers."

Then in the spring of 1969, the board placed a ninety-million-dollar school-bond issue on the ballot. In the past, all Philadelphia school-bond issues had passed handily. But this was the biggest one ever sought and it came at a time of taxpayer revolts. Beyond that, the whites were clearly disaffected. The black wards supported the bond issue but their turnout of voters—it was a lustreless primary election—was low. The white wards defeated the bond issue. Some of the heaviest outpourings of no votes came from white areas where schools were most overcrowded and which stood to gain new schools should the bond issue pass. An analyst who conducted a postmortem of the defeated bond issue for the Board of Education concluded:

There was a feeling that the black community was getting all the improvements at the expense of the whites. At the same time there was a feeling that Shedd and Dilworth did not listen to the [white] parents. . . . The dismay must be drastic for people to vote no, because people do not want to cripple education.

In the months following that stinging setback, the board took several steps to regain the confidence of the White-towners. It refused to rename all-black Benjamin Franklin High School after Malcolm X, the martyred black leader, despite heavy pressure from black youths. It patched up its relations with Police Commissioner Rizzo and worked with his men in seeking to curb gang warfare and drug abuse in high schools. When black students at a West Philadelphia high school sought the transfer of a white social-studies teacher on grounds of incompetence, the board obtained a court injunction to halt the protest. (The injunction also prohibited a strike which the teachers' union had called if the teacher were in fact shifted out of the school.)

In November 1969 a reduced sixty-five-million-dollar bond issue was overwhelmingly endorsed by voters despite opposition in Kensington.

Still, Dilworth, who will be seventy-three when his six-year term on the board ends in 1971, sees group conflicts growing. "There's a tremendous tendency on the part of everybody to distrust everybody else," he said in a *Philadelphia Bulletin* interview. "I think the situation is going to get cumulatively worse."

I have told the Philadelphia school story at such length because it relates, I think, to the entire problem of American Whitetowns and Blacktowns and the people living in them. White liberals, often for the best and most generous of reasons, have tried to impose their values on the disaffected

Despite the merits of the white-liberal position, the efforts have frequently failed. They have failed because they have lacked popular support. In the America of 1970 all change —even that which stands to benefit everybody—is suspect. The reason the Philadelphia Board of Education couldn't get even a simple majority for school construction which would clearly benefit the entire community was that it had lost the confidence of too many people. What has happened is that all our institutions are now distrusted, not only by disaffected blacks but also by disaffected whites.

Clearly, it is time for a much closer look at the mechanics of social change and at the forces working for and against change. We have generally failed to recognize that in a great many instances those people and groups most vocally supporting change are safely outside the battle and would be unaffected by it. In his struggle with teachers and others over New York City's schools, Mayor John V. Lindsay has drawn much of his support from those whose children, like the mayor's, attend private schools. In Philadelphia, Mark Shedd, I suspect, won his original backing and subsequent support from influential whites who had no direct stake in the city schools. To cite another example, the most publicized school-desegregation fight nationally during President Dwight D. Eisenhower's Administration occurred at Central High School in Little Rock, Arkansas. On the President's orders, Central High was integrated at bayonet point. But Central High was Little Rock's working-class school. While National Guard troops watched Negro children enter that building for the first time, Little Rock's upper-class public high school on the heights remained above the battle and lily white.

In housing and jobs, as well as in education, black gains are made in competition not with WASP liberals but with lower-class and lower-middle-class Irish, Italians, Poles, and Jews. The WASPS, being on the sidelines, can afford to cheer for the blacks because they have nothing to lose. It is the non-WASP whites whose fears are scoffed at and whose complaints are dismissed as racism. We have tended to lump all whites, regardless of social class, ethnic background, or religion, together and assumed that they equally enjoyed the fruits of unparalleled affluence. As was indicated in an earlier chapter, this is simply not so. Many of the ethnics are hurting. S. M. Miller, professor of education and sociology at New York University, has theoretically divided white families into five income groups for the decade from 1956 to 1966. Only the top and bottom ranks advanced economically in that period, he found. The second- and third-layer whites—and many of these would be the Whitetowners—were actually worse off as regards purchasing power of dollars earned in 1966 than in 1956. And as of February 1969, the average worker's purchasing power was thirteen cents less than it had been a year earlier.

We have noted, too, that the workingman's way of life has been threatened by inflation, automation, high taxes, and many manifestations of the sociological revolution which have thrown his ways of thinking and acting into question. If this is not enough, recent studies show that blue-collar workers are more tightly controlled on the job than are white-collar workers. As the Associated Press put it: "White-collar workers waste more time in their offices than their blue-collar counterparts in the shops." The AP quoted work-measurement experts to the effect that only about five per cent of office workers are subject to work-measurement standards, while eighty to eighty-five per cent of production workers are. As a result, according to James H. Duncan, president of Wofac Company, a division of Science Management Corporation, the utilization of manpower rarely exceeds fifty per cent in most offices and sometimes falls below forty per cent. Yet in plants with management controls, effectiveness hovers around the seventy per cent mark.

What is required now, I think, is a series of strategies designed to develop a healthy pluralism in this country. I would define a healthy pluralism as one in which various ethnic, religious, employee, neighborhood, or civic groups make positive demands on government, schools, business, or industry. The melting pot need not melt; at last we should recognize that fact. But groups that may be organized by race, creed, or color—because that is how we seem to organize ourselves, whether we like to admit it or not—should be fighting *for* things rather than *against* things. What we have today is an unhealthy pluralism in which many groups, notably the blue-collar workers in the Whitetowns of America, find themselves almost constantly on the defensive, in opposition to rulings of the Supreme Court, acts of Congress or state and city governments and school boards.

In seeking to develop a healthy pluralism, the beginning of wisdom is for WASP and Jewish liberals, those who set the cultural and intellectual pace in this country, to put aside their own ethnic biases. With some reason, they sharply criticize working-class whites for stereotyping all Negroes as stupid, immoral, and lazy. This is what many working-class whites do, and they should be criticized for it. Yet the liberals go ahead and stereotype the ethnics as beer-swilling, racist Neanderthals. One stereotype is as wicked, cruel, and inaccurate as the other.

There's been very little research into the nature of the ethnic groups that make up this country. There should be a lot more research. It could lead to greater understanding between ethnic groups and races. The Reverend Andrew M. Greeley, of the University of Chicago's National Opinion Research Center, is one of a handful of students of American ethnicity. He warns, in a booklet, *Why Can't They Be Like Us?*, that ethnic problems are likely to persist and that it does little good to wring hands over them. He warns against the "luxury of superior attitudes toward behavior which, if the truth be told, we dislike mostly because it's not the sort of thing 'our kind of people' might do." His plea is for understanding. Touching on conflict between Poles and blacks, Greeley says he can find nothing in the Polish cultural background to explain racism. He therefore sees the conflict almost entirely in social, economic, and psychological terms. That is, the blacks have become militant at a time when the Poles are still at an incomplete stage of their own integration into American life. They haven't made it yet themselves, but they see blacks seeking to leapfrog ahead of them. Greeley writes:

> . . . unless we recognize the validity of the Polish home-owner's attachment to his home and neighborhood and the legitimacy of his fear that both of these are threatened, we are in no position to cope with the intense animosity between Poles and blacks over this issue. If our reaction to the fears of black immigration is merely to condemn the prejudice of the Poles or, even worse, merely to describe it as a Polish prejudice, we might just as well say nothing at all, because we'll be doing more harm than good.

The essential first step, then, is to accept all groups on their own terms as legitimate competitors for a fair share of the nation's bounty. Next should come programs aimed at helping working-class Americans across the board, without regard to pigmentation, religious affiliation, or nationality background.

At a conference in Philadelphia in 1968 on "The Problems of White Ethnic America," Irving Levine, national director of urban projects for the American Jewish Committee, listed many problems which, if dealt with adequately, would help build a healthy American pluralism. Levine spoke as a longtime civil-rights leader seeking a "depolarization" strategy:

However we might wish to assert the priority of the most disadvantaged, we can no longer define the major problem of America only in terms of blacks . . . some of the brilliance which articulated Negro demands will have to be similarly developed to speak for and with lower-middle-class America. White ethnic groups must feel the security of recognition by mainstream institutions. Only when we grant this recognition and listen to their insightful spokesmen can we arm ourselves with a strategy that will lessen frustration and polarization. With new understanding, we can help lower-middle-class whites identify and solve their own problems, often along lines which parallel the self-interests of blacks.

Following is my summary of some of the problems Levine cited and the solutions he offered to meet needs of lower-class families, both white and black:

1. Crime in the streets. There is no denying that American cities are dangerous places to live in. Police brutality is a problem in many cities but violent crime is a greater problem in most. Said Dilworth, who lives in center city Philadelphia: "I've never seen people so afraid. I very frankly don't go out in the evenings now unless I have to, and if I get into a car, I lock all the doors."

During World War II a system of block wardens guarded against surprise air raids and also built "neighborhoodness." To guard against crime and restore that feeling of neighborhoodness, we should consider organizing security agents, like block wardens. They would be responsible for safety on their blocks and would be supplied with adequate communications gear to call out regular police reinforcements when necessary. To help protect merchants, storefront police stations might be organized. The idea would be to get neighbors involved in solving their own problems but without setting up Wild-West-style vigilantes who would be more dangerous than the evil they were supposed to combat.

2. Unfair and burdensome taxes. Federal, state, and local taxes discriminate against the man in the middle and below. He pays a regressive ten per cent surtax. He pays a regressive sales tax. The entire tax structure in this country needs to be reorganized to end inequities now facing poor and low-income families.

3. Inadequate and uncomfortable transportation. The United States is one of the last Western societies to keep raising the cost of mass transportation. Americans seem never to have understood the need to provide decent, clean, reasonably priced mass transport for poor or lower-middle-class people. It's time we did.

4. High credit rates. Competing credit systems are needed. There's no reason why church groups couldn't begin to operate in this field.

5. Housing. The record here is one of broken promises. The nation seems incapable of providing adequate shelter at reasonable prices for the poor and the not-so-poor. The only way to do it is through subsidies.

6. High medical costs. In the last few years Americans have settled for considerably less than national health insurance. We haven't provided adequate medical care for the poor or the aged. Less affluent nations do much better by these groups than we do.

7. High cost of entertainment. No strong effort has been made to bring High Culture down to the neighborhoods. It has been assumed that the lower classes are interested only in TV violence. Among alternatives which could be offered is authentic Ethnic Culture, which third-generation descendants of immigrants often crave.

8. Financial burden of parochial education. If local, state, and federal governments finally recognize the pluralistic nature of our society they may also accept pluralism in education. This means not just putting up with private

schools but helping to support them, while continuing to put major emphasis and most public funds into public schools.

9. Poor mental-health facilities. Lower-middle-class whites have serious mental-health problems that go unattended. As a group they have resisted mental-health techniques in vogue for upper- and middle-class families. The lower-class whites especially are a closed people moving in tunnels. They are terrified. They need help in mental health to deal with their kind of alienation.

10. High cost and lack of opportunity for higher education. This problem is widely recognized. What has not been seen clearly is that recent—and long overdue—recruitment of black students by many of the top colleges and universities has reduced the number of places for lower-middle-class whites. They need special help here, too.

The foregoing list—and it could be extended indefinitely —outlines practical ways of balancing the scales for Whitetowners and Blacktowners. The steps seem sensible. Perhaps in the decade of the 1970s the United States will move in some of the directions Levine has suggested.

There is a major stumbling block, however. Levine's list represents a white, middle-class, liberal prescription for dealing with some of the ills of society. It is not a Whitetown prescription. As we have seen, the Whitetowners are not asking for many of these reforms and might, in fact, oppose some of them.

On a number of key issues their supposed leaders are silent. Philadelphia's Mayor Tate, for example, has Whitetown roots, and a number of Philadelphia's city councilmen do, too. Yet in higher education, in urban renewal, in mass transportation, they have consistently missed opportunities to assist lower-middle-class people in Whitetown and Blacktown. If the changes that Levine favors are to come, such leaders must throw their support behind them. Up to now they haven't.

In the long run, though, what appears to be needed is a total reordering of national priorities. Dilworth, in the *Philadelphia Bulletin* interview, put it this way:

We've really managed to get everything turned upside down by permitting wealth to really go unchecked. Here we are, the wealthiest nation the world has ever seen, and yet in the essential fields we're faced with bankruptcy. Cities are virtually bankrupt, big city school systems, which will either make or break our urban civilization, are virtually bankrupt, and nobody is really doing a thing to solve either of these problems. Our values have just gotten all cockeyed.

The truth is, of course, that as America is constituted today the likelihood that help will be extended to those on the lower rungs of the economic ladder seems slim indeed. But if progress toward meeting the genuine needs of these groups is not made then the poison that is infecting our national life, the hatred of race for race, will continue to rage unabated. It's time to take chances. For, to paraphrase Mark Shedd, faced with the uncertainties in today's world, there are no safe bets and we must all be gamblers.